STRAIGHT AHEAD
The Story of
STAN KENTON

STRAIGHT AHEAD
The Story of
STAN KENTON
by Carol Easton

William Morrow & Company
New York 1973

LIBRARY OF CONGRESS CATALOG CARD NUMBER 73-9840

ISBN 0-688-00196-3

1   2   3   4   5   75   74   73

To Rosemary Lewis, Mentor and Mensch

A complete list of all the people who contributed to this book would be prohibitively long—and unreadable. Special appreciation, however, goes to Chico Alvarez, Milt Bernhart, Buddy Childers, Red Dorris, Bob Gioga, Bill Holman, Gene Howard, Shelly Manne, Jack Ordean, Art Pepper, Howard Rumsey and Dick Shearer. The most generous contribution of all came from Stan Kenton, who accepted on faith my assurance that the book would be honest, and who will see it for the first time after publication—at which time he will undoubtedly say, "None of that personal crap about me means anything. All that matters is the music."

Contents

Introduction

In the jargon of jazz musicians, the term *straight ahead* is the ultimate compliment. It applies to those dedicated individuals who unswervingly follow their private artistic visions, never veering off course in the direction of compromise or commercialism.

In the context of this book, the phrase has ironic overtones. Focusing one's sights, laserlike, with such intensity requires a kind of psychological tunnel vision that excludes extraneous scenery, people and feelings. But Stan Kenton is a man with a mission; and when you have a mission, sacrifices come with the territory.

Although every effort has been made to make this book authentic in feeling and in fact, hard-core Kenton fans who take pride in their total recall of who played each solo on any given take of every number ever recorded by their idol may find here a windfall of inexact minutiae with which they may gleefully take exception. Remarks here attributed to an anonymous trombone player may quite possibly have originated with some anonymous trumpet player, and an incident that occurred in a Philadelphia hotel room may magically turn up in a Boston restaurant. In other words, this book can be a nitpicker's picnic. But nitpickers invariably miss the point.

Stan Kenton has represented many things to many people. Hundreds of admittedly biased observers—musicians, recording-company executives, disc jockeys, vocalists, managers, entrepreneurs, relatives, ex-wives and fans—have contributed their impressions, reminiscences and in some cases confessions to this book. The views from their respective vantage points vary widely:

SHELLY MANNE, *drummer*: "He was never afraid to try something he believed in just because it wasn't commercial."

CHARLIE BARNET, *bandleader*: "He killed the dance-band business."

HOWARD RUMSEY, *bassist*: "He's the greatest influence on jazz since Gershwin!"

EDDIE CONDON, *critic*: "Music of his school ought only to be played close to elephants and listened to only by clowns."

JUNE CHRISTY, *vocalist*: "If he ran for President, it would be a pushover for him."

GEORGE SIMON, *critic*: "He's been the jazz world's foremost barker . . . a press agent's delight."

BUD SHANK, *saxophonist*: "He's just like he was twenty years ago—magnificent! A beautiful person! Straight ahead!"

ANONYMOUS, *recording executive*: "Stan is laughable."

ZOOT SIMS, *saxophonist*: "He was always a gentleman. After we finished a job he would always say, 'Thank you, thank you very much for the gig.' Then he would go get drunk."

VIOLET FOSTER (*Mrs. Stan Kenton #1*): "Stanley was one of the most *tender* people I have ever encountered."

MILT BERNHART, *trombonist*: "The hard knocks, the traveling, it's made him insensitive after all these years."

BUDDY CHILDERS, *trumpeter*: "Stan is The Man of La Mancha."

FRED CARTER, *trombonist*: "He's the General Patton of the music business."

ANN RICHARDS (*Mrs. Stan Kenton #2*): "He's not a very generous man."

JO ANN KENTON (*Mrs. Stan Kenton #3*): "Stan is not a generous man."

BOB GIOGA, *saxophonist*: "He brought me a four-thousand-dollar Porsche from Europe."

PETE RUGULO, *composer-arranger*: "He's a dear friend."

JO ANN KENTON: "He does nothing to sustain a friendship."

BOB FITZPATRICK, *trombonist*: "If the bus wouldn't start, he'd be the first one pushing it. Unloading baggage, getting people into airplanes, always helping—help, help, help."

IRMA KENTON HOPKINS, *sister*: "He *must* be the strong one, sometimes to the extent that he's inclined to rob the other person of their strength."

STAN LEVEY, *drummer*: "He's very articulate."

BILL HOLMAN, *composer-arranger*: "He spins these rhetorical webs! If you really listen, a lot of what he says is double-talk. But not too many people do listen—because it's all you can do to withstand that Presence!"

QUIN DAVIS, *saxophonist*: "What he is is a great leader. You see those nine-foot arms come out, and you play!"

DICK SHEARER, *trombonist*: "He's like a father to me."

JO ANN KENTON: "I found my father in him."

BILL HOLMAN: "He was a disciplinary father rather than a protective one. I felt that because of our difference musically, he might straighten me out with a bolt of lightning."

xiii

JERI WINTERS, *vocalist*: "His kids absolutely trompled all over him!"

GEORGE MORTE, *road manager*: "There was a great number of women on his trail. But he didn't encourage them."

ANN RICHARDS: "He's a latent misogynist, and maybe not too latent. Maybe a little overt."

DR. HERB PATNOE, *college professor*: "Stan is a man whom men love."

GRAHAM ELLIS, *trombonist*: "He's a person to worship."

BILL FRITZ, *educator*: "I think of his personality as akin to Christ's."

JO ANN KENTON: "He's some kind of symbol to people. There's something very godlike about him. If he told you to walk across water, you'd try."

VIOLET FOSTER: "He feels he's the second Christ."

JO ANN KENTON: "Basically, he's a man that's always wanted a family."

IRMA KENTON HOPKINS: "He has a great hunger for a home and stability and a relationship. But he has sublimated his life in his music."

JO ANN KENTON: "It's his ego that propels him. It's strong, and it has to be fed."

STAN KENTON: "I don't know what it is that propels me."

STELLA KENTON: "I'm the only one, I guess, that Stanley was close to. He never caused me a bit of trouble."

It is not the intent of this book to establish whether or not Stan Kenton can walk on water. The question raised here is more modest, and simply stated: Can the whole equal more than the sum of its parts?

Straight Ahead, and Strive for Tone.

STRAIGHT AHEAD
The Story of
STAN KENTON

Jazz Orchestra in Residence. 1971.

"Magic is when you've been ridin' the bus all night for four hundred miles after doin' a one-nighter, and the Old Man's drinkin' with you, and we're all havin' a ball. You wake up in the morning and he's in the front of the bus and he's had the same suit on all night, but his suit looks like it's immaculately pressed. His hair is combed, and he smiles. And he's old enough to be all of our fathers—even Willie Maiden's! And you walk off the bus hung over and draggin', and you're like twenty-five, thirty years old, and there he is, handing you your suitcase. That's magic!"

DICK SHEARER, lead trombone

HE enters the small concert hall from the back, unannounced, while the band is tuning up. Assuming the hunched posture characteristic of men who pass the six-foot mark at an age when it can only be embarrassing, he makes his way to the stage. Signs of physical strain are painfully evident. The face, a ravaged relief map charting thirty grinding years on the road, looks flaccid and sallow. Faded, sunken blue eyes peer wearily, warily out from above frighteningly dark circles of fatigue. He looks overweight and undernourished, unhealthily bloated and cadaverous, all at the same time. The profuse perspiration could simply be the August heat, but more likely it's weakness; after all, the man is almost sixty, he's had major surgery twice within a few months' time, he's still got a drainage tube sticking out of an incision in his gut—should he even be ambulatory, let alone conduct an orchestra in this hundred-degree-plus oven?

Stiffly and gingerly, in deference to that obscene tube, he

1

seats himself at the piano. Those gargantuan hands that can reach chords as lush and full as any ever heard on this earth begin the intro to "Artistry in Rhythm" with a sincerity that belies thirty years of repetition. Impossibly, the skin takes on tone and color. The eyes begin to sparkle like a lover's. A radiant smile erases ten years from the face. And when he rises to his full six feet four inches to conduct the body of the piece, you get the unforgettable, powerful, all-stops-out, larger-than-life impact of STAN KENTON, head high, shoulders back, juices flowing, arms flailing convulsively, projecting vibrations of vitality, authority and sexuality that flood the room like a searchlight. Involuntarily, you respond.

Years ago, a young Stan Kenton discovered that music could ease a persistent internal ache, and he willingly became its prisoner for life. Music gave him the realization of his generation's classic success fantasy: fame, fortune, creative satisfaction. It gave him the power to turn on an entire generation, and gratified his voracious ego by making him a legend before he reached forty. In return, it occupied his life like a conquering army, displacing three wives, two daughters, a son, the warmth and companionship of innumerable good people, a college education, well-loved homes, boats and a list of simple, everyday pleasures too painful to recount. Not to mention his youth and his health.

Undoubtedly, Stan considers it a fair exchange. Separated from his music, the man exists only as a frustrated fragment in search of wholeness—a wholeness made possible by a charter bus with STAN KENTON ORCHESTRA on the outside and nineteen musicians on the inside, whether en route to a one-nighter at the Burlington, Iowa, Elks Lodge or a sold-out concert at Carnegie Hall. For him, those moments on the bandstand, sandwiched joyously between his music and his audience, are everything. All the rest is waiting.

❊ ❊ ❊

This is Stan's twelfth full-time band, and the last he intends to build. In a business so abrasive to the sensitive personalities it attracts that a notoriously large number of them shatter under its pressures, the price of survival defies the Straight imagination. What nine-to-five mind can begin to grasp the cumulative effect of thirty years on the road? *Thirty years!* Representing how many punishing one-night stands? How many interchangeable hotel rooms, indigestible meals, interminable interviews? How many loadings of buses, trains, planes, taxis and private cars? How many packings and unpackings of clothing, shaving gear, travel clock? How many timetables, itineraries, schedules, maps, miles, poker hands? How many hands outstretched to be shaken or tipped? How many 3 A.M. revelations and regrets? How many fifths opened at midnight and emptied by dawn? How many fans demanding to be stroked with a word or a smile? How many mornings of waking unsure of the day, the time zone or the town? How many sleepless nights in a bus seat designed for short-term occupancy? How many sneak attacks of heartburn, backache, boredom, piles, insomnia, allergies, migraine, depression? How many unobserved birthdays, anniversaries, Christmases? How many requests for "Eager Beaver"? How many choruses of "Peanut Vendor"? How many downbeats?

Knowing this to be Stan's last band, its members share a heavy sense of responsibility. They see the band as a kind of institution that began before most of them were born, and to judge from the way they're playing, they're determined to give the Old Man's career on the road one hell of a finish. In casual conversation, they come across more like disciples than employees. "The people out front all remember the big tall gray-haired fellow with the long arms," says bass trombonist Graham Ellis, "with his beautiful music that we're playing. To the guys in the band, he is a person to worship—because he's so dedicated, so devoted, such a beautiful person."

3

At thirty-five, Ellis is one of the oldest members of the band. The average age is thirty, a statistic skewed somewhat by Stan's fifty-nine years. Many are barely old enough to vote. And on this sweltering night at the University of Redlands, next door to the Mojave Desert, they present a motley image of hairy faces, colorful and mismatched shirts and physiques that reflect the most sedentary occupation next to proofreading.

The audience consists of a hundred and fifty music students, average age seventeen. Most are attending this week-long music clinic, formally designated "Jazz Orchestra in Residence," at the behest of a persuasive school-band director. Others are here courtesy of scholarships, or their parents' largesse; and for a few, the tuition and travel expense represent a substantial personal investment in terms of dishes washed, lawns mowed, papers delivered, short-term loans negotiated. The majority are Southern Californians, but many are from as far away as Phoenix, Oakland, Seattle—and one piano student has motorcycled all the way from New York. But their attitude during registration this afternoon was curiously indifferent. Asked what they thought of Stan Kenton's music, nine out of ten responded with a vague shrug or fakeout, "Oh, he's okay, I guess." Born after Korea, weaned on rock 'n roll, raised on hard rock and in all probability never exposed to a big band any hotter than that of their local college—what would they know of Balboa, of Progressive Jazz, "Artistry in Rhythm," "Eager Beaver," "City of Glass"? Who are Maynard Ferguson, Anita O'Day, Gerry Mulligan, Lee Konitz, Bob Graettinger, Shorty Rogers, Art Pepper, Shelly Manne, June Christy, Stan Getz, Zoot Sims to them? Stan Kenton? An unknown quantity. Someone whose music their parents once listened to in a Neanderthal, pre-TV world totally outside their never-look-back frame of reference. If the name connects at all, it's only because they've seen it on their school-band arrangements.

And how could it be otherwise? To these children of electronics, if you haven't made it on the tube (or at least the top forty), you haven't made it. Lawrence Welk may be a musical joke to them, but at least they know who he is and what he stands for. But . . . Stan Kenton? Shrug.

Now that he's got their attention, Stan steps to the microphone and in a voice emanating from some subterranean source delivers a few brief, low-keyed words of welcome. One oblique allusion to his illness—"I guess you all know I've just gotten out of the nuthouse"—and flashing that dazzling smile, he gives the downbeat for "Rainy Day."

"Rainy Day" is a ballad that begins like a dirge, with the five trombonists playing slower than trombonists were ever meant to play, thus requiring a degree of control that sends all the trombone students in the room into paroxysms of awe. As the full band joins in and the number gains momentum and intensity, the students' eyes begin to widen and their jaws to drop. And by the time the arrangement builds and swells and climaxes, without ever perceptibly picking up tempo, the audience is beginning to levitate right out of its collective seat. "Ooooooooh," moans a seventeen-year-old trombonist in the front row, "that does my heart good!"

As a concession to his physical condition, Stan delegates the conducting of the next number, "Chiapas," to its composer, Hank Levy. Levy is a musician's musician whose particular genius lies in musical prestidigitation—unorthodox time signatures. To the untrained ear, his work evokes images of cyclotrons gone berserk, sending shattered melodies and countermelodies somersaulting crazily over each other in dynamic, driving rhythms with no apparent pattern. What does a layman know of 5/4, or subdivided rhythms? But these students know something of the intricacies of writing, playing and *thinking* in such literally offbeat time signatures; hearing such a piece performed with the full virtuosity and power of the

5

band for which it was written gives them a mind-blowing, exhilarating glimpse of the hoped-for result of all those practice hours, and the sudden and subdued ending of "Chiapas" leaves the kids turned on like strings of Christmas-tree lights.

Saxophonist Willie Maiden conducts the next number, shamelessly milking the last drop of theatricality out of his arrangement of "Hey, Jude." He cues each solo with a broad flourish—a jive game, Willie calls it. But the kids love it, particularly the six flashy horn solos. By the time the band reaches the pretentious big finish, the eyes of Kenton's trombonists are bulging out of their sockets; the kids are cheering, whistling and exchanging hushed "Wows." And in the makeshift wings, for all the world like an adulation junkie getting a fix, Stan Kenton, resident Legend, smiles.

Redlands is less than a hundred miles away from Balboa, where it all began—but for Stan, it's been a matter of thirty years and God knows how many miles. When his first band opened at the Rendezvous Ballroom, it was the most exciting thing to hit Balboa before or since that summer of 1941. The gangling, painfully self-conscious young man who led that band was idealistic to the point of fanaticism; he *believed*, and his fierce enthusiasm carried musicians and audiences along with it like a tidal wave. Every performance was an exercise in sustained hysteria. His intensity, his total commitment to the music was awesome to behold. The vulnerability on his face was like a public confession. Had Stan appeared on the stand stark naked, with a bag over his head, he would have been less exposed.

That young man has undergone considerable changes in the intervening years—but in the rarefied atmosphere of this music clinic, he lives again. No wonder Stan prefers these clinics to all his other endeavors, even though the financial rewards are nil. In this environment, reality gracefully withdraws. Surrounded by eager students who approach him with just the proper mixture of respect and adoration, he feels young. They ask, he answers. He gives, they take. There is much exchanging of bits and pieces of evidence indicating a resurgence of jazz, maybe even of big bands! Rapport is expedited by a vocabulary with built-in exclusivity: embouchures, charts, chord progressions, phrasing, triplets, time signatures, section work, intonation, improvisation, chops. For this brief time, music is all there is.

To an impressionable young musician, a week of studying and performing with this band is the experience of a lifetime. For most of them, this is the closest they'll ever come to a professional band—although music as something less than a lifetime calling may still bring them tremendous gratification. For a few, this may be the first serious step toward a vocation. One or two may even possess sufficient promise to warrant a job offer from Stan. He has hired a number of sidemen out of these very clinics. Their enthusiasm almost makes up for their lack of experience, and it keeps operating costs down; and operating costs constitute the basic fact of life for a road band these days.

"Jazz Orchestra in Residence" means precisely that. Musicians and students live on campus for the duration of the clinic. The musicians make themselves accessible not only during the scheduled classes and rehearsals, but at virtually any waking hour—and students aren't shy about requesting private lessons.

On the surface, the interaction between Kenton and kids is an ideal teacher-student relationship, in which Stan and all the members of his band willingly share everything they know about technique, theory, composition, arranging, improvisation and, basic to all of this, professionalism of approach. To both teachers and students, the experience is rewarding.

On a deeper level, there is a strong feeling of *family*—an almost exclusively male family, to be sure—with all the

7

hierarchy thereof. Stan is apparently incapable of saying "Good morning" without involuntarily projecting a quality that inspires instant allegiance. No effort is spared to win his approval. In this father role, he is perfectly cast.

The musicians function as older brothers to the students. Other clinic staffers, administrators and such, are stern but helpful uncles. At the pyramid's base are the student-sons. There are a few favorites, a few scapegoats. Sibling rivalry is intense but controlled. The family appears to be totally self-sufficient. Everyone has his clearly defined role to play, his assigned work to do. Life is simple, clear-cut, black and white—just like a sheet of music.

On the final afternoon of the clinic, parents begin arriving to reclaim their children and appraise their investments. The students are in a last-day-of-camp mood, charged with nervous energy, anticipating the loss of something precious but ephemeral. All assemble in the concert hall for a marathon demonstration of what the week has wrought.

Each of eight student bands performs two numbers. The students, sweaty but starry-eyed, blow as they've never blown before. The last group to play is the "head band," so called because unlike the other bands that played standard Kenton arrangements, its music is improvised. Their wildly spontaneous performance is aptly critiqued by an excited alto player: "It sounds like shit, but it sure is fun!"

By the time the Kenton band takes its place to conclude the concert and the clinic, a representative (read "middle-aged") group of Redlands citizens has joined the audience. Along with the parents, they make up an interesting generational cross-section. Members of the respective age groups respond, as though programmed, to the elements of the music that push their respective buttons. The students turn on to the immediacy, as well as the mechanics, of the more demanding, experimental concert numbers, while most of the

8

oldsters remain irrevocably in the "Artistry" bag. The latter group applauds politely enough for the Hank Levy charts, but it's "Peanut Vendor" that sends their eyes rolling back in their heads, accompanied by sighs of, "*That's* the Stan Kenton I remember!" It's not necessarily a reflection of their musical sophistication; it's a simple matter of nostalgia, an emotion Stan abhors. Never Look Back is his credo; the past is best forgotten. Period. And yet . . . Stan Kenton provided the background music for the coming of age of a generation. And if the reprise of that music recalls a time when idealism was high, options open and responsibilities minimal—who can resist the pull of *that* Paradise lost? And so the yellowing sheets of "Peanut Vendor" remain in the book.

In the wake of the exhausting decibel volume created by the students, Stan shrewdly shifts the mood. "We're going to assume that you, the audience, collectively, is a beautiful woman," he announces, "and we're going to go about the process of making love in a very easy and quiet manner." Screaming brass may be his trademark, but nobody can get the emotional mileage out of a sentimental ballad like "Love Story" or "MacArthur Park" that Stan can. So that the final encore leaves the audience satisfied, relaxed, ready for nothing more taxing than a good night's sleep. While the band faces the prospect of loading the bus and getting underway, hopefully by midnight, toward tomorrow night's job in San Francisco, four hundred fifty miles away.

Barring blowouts, mechanical failures and acts of God, they'll get a few hours' sleep on the bus and check into a San Francisco motel "on the day sheet," saving the price of a room for tonight. The unprecedented two weeks in Redlands (for two consecutive clinics) has left them bored, restless, anxious to get moving. The first few days were a welcome relief from the pressured pace of one-nighters (they've been known to do seven straight months of them). Only a musician

9

who ran out of clean socks a week ago can know the joys of catching up on his laundry, as well as his sleep. And the respite from one-nighters provides an opportunity to take care of other personal matters for which there's simply no time on the road. For Mike Vax, lead trumpet player, Redlands will be forever memorable as the town where he (1) bought a new sports car, and (2) got engaged. But the novelty of unpacking your bag, of sleeping in the same bed for more than two consecutive nights, begins to pall surprisingly soon. Exiled from the familiar insulation of the bus, there are too many reminders of the deprivations built into the bizarre lifestyle of a road band, and only constant psychological vigilance can guard against questioning the validity of the bus as a surrogate home, the other band members as surrogate family, Stan as surrogate father. Saxophonist Chuck Carter cannot afford to dwell on thoughts of his wife and five children in Indianapolis, and Willie Maiden must at all costs maintain the fiction that he and his chick in Chicago communicate via ESP.

Sexually, one-night stands are infinitely safer than two-week engagements, during which a relationship can develop sufficient potential to deflect a lonely sideman from his single-minded dedication to the band. Once his mind swivels in the direction of a real home and family, his enthusiasm begins to erode and his resignation is just a matter of time.

The members of this band wile away countless hours on the bus weaving elaborate fantasies of a time when they'll have their own road bands. Musicians who put in their time on the road with Stan years ago and have since put down roots in New York, Chicago or Los Angeles view such ambitions dubiously. The road is a young man's scene. Some adapt to it better than others, but all succumb eventually to its merciless pace.

BUD SHANK, *saxophonist*: "I wouldn't ever want to do it

again. No home life. No sleep. Too much drinking. No chance for study. No home. No wife. No home."

MILT BERNHART, *trombonist*: "I developed a chronic cold. All that jostling around, long jumps up to five hundred miles, eating quickly and dangerously, not getting enough sleep. I never felt terribly good, so I was always looking for the time I could break away."

LAURINDO ALMEIDA, *guitarist*: "I like to see the country . . . going through the misty trees at dawn in Oregon, meeting my first snowstorm in New York, seeing the sunrise, beautiful things. But it's so tiresome. Many times we'd vote if we stay in that town or if we go ahead and travel two hundred or three hundred miles that night after the concert. If enough people vote yes, you have to go."

MEL LEWIS, *drummer*: "The bus gets to stinking of dirty clothes, sweat and booze and cigarette smoke and cigar smoke, and the guys have their shoes off and everybody's wearing their socks for two and three days, because we don't always have a chance to get them washed. There comes a time when you have to make up your mind. And my wife had put up with five years of road with me."

JUNE CHRISTY, *vocalist*: "We worked seven nights a week, in a different town every day with no time to rest. If we did have a night off, we'd spend it traveling on the bus. I finally became very ill, and Stan wasn't at all sympathetic because he was holding up and he felt if he was, everyone else should be, too."

GERRY MULLIGAN, *saxophonist*: "Life on the road is murder. It's as though life begins and ends when you have your horn in your mouth. It's like the loneliness of the long-distance runner."

In Stan's straight-ahead view, no allowances are made for those who forsake the road for the comforts of home, family and in many cases a substantially higher income.

11

"They've lost their love for music," is the way he puts it. "When a guy comes in the band and he shows potential, I always feel that maybe there's a possible chance of him developing into a leader himself. And there have been just dozens and dozens of wonderful musicians in the band. And usually when they leave the band, I'll have high hopes of them maybe doing something with their music. But it seems like the majority of them just kind of fall by the wayside and go the path of least resistance. New York is full of them. Hollywood is, Las Vegas, too—guys that've just kind of sold out."

But even Stan admits that it's not that simple. The dilemma has accompanied him through three broken marriages; a basic ambivalence underlies the rationalizations. "The road is our out because when we play, we play our way, without restrictions. Entirely free. And we couldn't be that way if we stayed in one place. So when a musician settles down—and usually they settle down because of family problems; *marriages are the thing that hang musicians up the most*—it's only right that the wife doesn't want her husband wandering around the world and she's left to raise the kids. So they *have* to compromise. They'll go into television [he's tried it] or into recording [that, too]. And most of them are miserably unhappy, but they just can't seem to do anything about it. . . . Sometimes wives will destroy a guy, and don't even know they're doing it! That's one good thing about this band; I think there are only three or four guys out of the whole band that are married.

"Mike Vax told me yesterday that his marriage is not going to affect our relationship whatsoever. He feels that's the way it's gonna be. But it's not gonna be that way. She's not gonna be able to stand bein' away from him; she's gonna want him with her, and she should have him with her. Husbands and wives should be together. And when things keep them apart, there's a great risk of the relationship falling to pieces."

Mike Vax is in love, and his reality is structured accordingly; but Stan's feelings on the subject are no secret, and when Mike broke the news to the Old Man it was with trepidation. "I was almost scared to tell him I was engaged. I felt he might think that I wouldn't do as good a job because I had a woman on my mind—which was part of the reason our last first trumpet player left the band. His wife pressured him. But Sandy would never want me to quit. She fell in love with a musician, and she knew it when she did it."

But Sandy has only just turned twenty, and Mike's self-delusion is colossal. "The only difference between me and a guy who works from nine to five every day," he says coolly, "is that Sandy'll see me once in awhile for a lot of time, whereas that guy's wife never sees him from nine to five anyway, and half the time she never sees him at night because she's at a bridge club or he's bowling, so they say a few words to each other at dinner and that's it. I'm going to stay with Stan until he retires, but after that I'll probably start my own band and Sandy'll just come on the road with me, for as long as she wants to." Never mind the complication of children, or the possibility that Sandy may find a lifetime of waiting, interspersed with road trips which for her will lack even the mitigating satisfaction of playing music, less than fulfilling. Mike and Sandy met three weeks ago in Iowa, where Sandy was the reigning Miss Burlington. Mike is twenty-eight, and has never married. And Stan shrugs and says, "Sure, Mike, your marriage won't affect our relationship whatsoever."

Sandy and Mike take off for San Francisco in their shiny new red Datsun, waving good-byes to the rest of the band members gathered around the bus outside the Redlands dorm. In the vast darkness of the parking lot, the amber lights in-

13

side the bus are inviting; the motor throbs, a reassuringly familiar sound. Stan, with his incision hopefully on the mend, supervises the loading—a conscientious father getting his boys off to camp.

Loading the bus is a ritual so familiar that its participants could perform it in their sleep—and have done so on numerous hungover occasions. In the well-established order of priorities, essentials come first. Luggage, instruments, music stands, all the paraphernalia of the business end of the band is stowed in the luggage compartment, deep in the belly of the bus. What goes into the passenger section is considerably more varied. Everyone has his own seat, and there's a special significance in its location. The back of the bus is reserved for those who want to *cak* (sleep). The front of the bus is Insomnia City, the scene of all-night discussions and drinking bouts. Stan's seat is the second behind the driver.

The last items to be loaded are the most personal. Everyone has his own cassette recorder with tiny earphone, to accommodate his particular musical taste (most prefer the classics to jazz, which creates endless arguments). Trombonist Dick Shearer stashes the self-improvement book he's currently reading. Willie Maiden must have his orange security blanket. Trombonist Mike Jamieson, the only member of the band who appears capable of running around the block without collapsing (and a thrower perpetually in search of a catcher), checks on the baseball and mitt, football, Frisbee and other token sporting gear that he breaks out during food stops, gas stops, booze stops and breakdowns. Like adaptable animals, each man converts his seat into a customized nest, equipped with his particular antidote for boredom: booze; cards; booze; magazines; booze; tapes; booze. Along with such vital accessories as paper cups and ice.

It's almost 1 A.M. Seat backs are adjusted, bodies settled, shoes removed. The door hisses shut. The interior light is switched off, replaced by pencil-thin reading lights. The transmission grinds into gear. The tires crunch through the gravel of the parking lot toward the highway. Moving through the night, the men breathe a collective sigh of relaxation.

They're home.

2 The Road

"I left the band after four years, because I couldn't stand the road any longer. Playing the same music night after night became so boring that I had to get drunk to do it. Year after year . . . you become what's known as a road bum."

BILL FRITZ, *trombone*

THE merciless monotony of the road grinds grown men down into bored, fretful, fidgety children playing endless variations of a continuing game called Filling Up the Time.

While the music fills many of their emotional needs, their intellectual needs, no matter how modest, go begging. Such is the structure of their world that books, television, films, social concerns, wars, families, floods, elections, even sports have little relevance for them. Discussions of any depth are impossible; they have no opportunity to inform themselves on the issues that occupy the minds and tongues of "normal" people. Yet these are men with active, curious minds that refuse to remain disengaged. So that when a sideman packs up his instrument each night, a large block of time looms before him, demanding to be filled or somehow gotten through until he takes his instrument out of its case again. Time is his constant challenge and nemesis.

Poker is a tradition, and many a pot of several thousand

dollars has been won—and lost—during an otherwise dull five-hundred-mile jump. Another favorite pastime, especially use-ful for relieving tensions, is pillaging, a crude form of wrestling in which two men engage in a no-holds-barred con-test in the seat of a fast-moving bus. Pinching and hair pulling are commonly employed. The pillager generally chooses an unsuspecting pillagee; a man attempting to cak is a likely victim. Pillaging has a cathartic effect upon the entire band in times of stress. Toward the end of the four months during which Stan's illness kept him off the road, when tensions became almost tangible, a record-breaking pillage (three hundred miles, halfway through Tennessee), may have averted a more serious explosion.

Cakking is an ideal way to pass the time, but it requires an almost superhuman ability to relax in seats designed for unknowable purposes, certainly not sleep. In cases of extreme exhaustion and/or drunkenness, of course, this does not apply. But even an adept cakker is vulnerable, not only to marauding pillagers but to a variety of practical jokes, ranging from an aspirin tucked into his mouth to an ice cube down his neck. Cakkers also risk awakening to find that their clothes have acquired an assortment of unidentifiable food or booze stains. Not even Stan is safe when cakked. A chronic insomniac, he once was jolted out of a rare moment of sleep by the 185-pound body of drummer John "Baron" Von Ohlen (known in his drinking days as John Von Pitiful) passing out on top of him. Although the Baron disclaims any memory of the in-cident, he gave up juicing shortly thereafter.

Von Ohlen subsequently developed his own ingenious version of Filling Up the Time: Cassettes. The compact tape players are considered regulation equipment for bus dwellers, but Von Ohlen has taken the diversion one step further, into obsession. When the Baron strides through airports, hotel lobbies and restaurants with headphones securely clamped over his ears and player tucked under his arm, his brooding good looks give him the appearance of a turned-on dark angel. "I get a lot of weird looks from people," he admits, "but if they bug me, I just turn the volume up. They think *I'm* weird, but I'm listenin' to beautiful music!"

His unfortunate habit of falling asleep with the player on has resulted in a succession of burned-out motors. When this happens, John is heartbroken. He interprets the mechanical failure as personal betrayal. The offending machine is immediately deposited in the nearest receptacle or outstretched hand, and the Baron eagerly rushes out to buy a newer model that will, hopefully, turn itself off and kiss him goodnight. In this way Von Ohlen has bought and disposed of over a thousand dollars' worth of cassette players in a year.

Reading passes the time, but the forced physical inactivity, combined with the funky atmosphere, discourages sustained concentration and reduces the hardiest attention span. Fleeting diversions are best. Someone is always on the alert for a passing car containing a good-looking chick; a sighting is accompanied by the thudding of noses against windows while bassist John Worster may press his entire body against the glass door of the bus, exaggeratedly mouthing "I LOVE YOU" in his most winning fashion. A rock, a brook, a tree—*anything* that will support a few moments' conversation—will provoke some comment that will be seized and carried to its meaningless conclusion. Running gags are very big. Ever since one sideman observed that a cow on a hillside had at first glance appeared to him to be a hole in the side of the hill, every cow on the horizon has provoked excited cries of, "Look at the hole!"

Every band has its share of comedians. At any moment of the day or night, trombonist Fred Carter may suddenly be inspired to deliver a freewheeling, fundamentalist-Southern-preacher-type sermon on some uplifting topic: "Burn a

Hippie for Christ," "Niggers Are Shiftless" and "Fight, Fight, Fight for Jesus" are a few well-loved favorites. John Worster's fag number is well received by everyone except Chuck Anderson, the driver, when chosen as straight man. Anderson's struggle to keep the bus on the road while Worster plays with his hair and blows in his ear is, unintentionally, funnier than Worster's bit.

Another popular form of Filling Up the Time is gossiping. The world of jazz musicians is a peculiarly inside one, and detailed discussions of the marital and extramarital activities of other musicians, on or off the road, help pass the time. Sex is a favorite topic. The sexual proclivities of various musicians are minutely examined, bragged about, envied, pitied or censured. Predictions are made and judgments passed.

Far better than talking about sex, of course, is having it; and to a jazz musician, the road presents a movable cafeteria of sex.

MEL LEWIS: "There's always chicks that'll hang around bands and look at who's handsome and who's a soloist. If a guys knows how to give some chick the eye from the bandstand, he can end up with that chick. They're there, they're laying it out for you."

MIKE JAMIESON: "The times I've come closest to quitting this band are the times I've been the horniest. Fortunately, that hasn't been too often."

ART PEPPER: "What I miss most about the road is, I really enjoyed making love to a different woman every night."

FRED CARTER (*patiently, to a hustling hooker*): "Honey, you are just wasting your time. Don't you know musicians get all they want for free?"

To many an unsophisticated girl with a craving for action, a traveling musician represents the ultimate in accessible glamour. "Girls would write notes," recalls one-time superstar

19

saxophonist Art Pepper, "saying, 'I'm so-and-so,' and they'd describe themselves and say, 'Would you like to come home with me?' Usually they were girls who wanted to show off to their friends that they had one of the musicians. Sometimes they'd have like a party, or a couple of girls, you'd make love to them both. It was sort of a status-type thing. I don't know whether they thought that the musicians would teach them something that they didn't know, or the fact that they would be there for a night and then they would be gone, and they wouldn't have to get involved."

Band chicks predate groupies (and, possibly, recorded history). There are band chicks who ball only trumpet players, or drummers, or whatever instrument pushes their particular buttons. There are band chicks who set out to ball every sideman in a given band, possibly in one memorable night. And a small subcategory of band chicks, known as Starfuckers, ball only leaders.

Some band chicks are young and inexperienced, some notso-young. Some are merely nonprofessional whores; others take pride in their loyalty. For sheer ingenuity, none can surpass a chick Fred Carter once acquired, who attempted to prove her devotion by having I LOVE YOU FRED tattooed on her rear end—in red, white and blue ink!

A band chick may remain unilaterally faithful to her Old Man, even though she may see him only three or four times a year, knows his relationship with her is one of many, and has no assurance of permanence or even, in some cases, love. If she does manage to marry the guy, the chances of its lasting are negligible. Four months after the Redlands clinic, five out of the nineteen Kenton musicians were in one stage or another of a divorce, most of them messy—and Mike Vax's engagement was off.

For years, long after other big bands discontinued the policy, Stan allowed wives and band chicks to travel on the

20

bus, making every effort to make them comfortable and even, on two European tours, paying their travel expenses. Since the breakup of his last marriage, he has set a limit of four traveling days for any woman to spend with the band. At such times, the men without female traveling companions tend to resent the intrusion into their "home," and have been known to express their relief at the women's departure with a nonstop barrage of the obscenities proscribed by the unwelcome presence.

Contrary to popular myth, jazz musicians are neither sex- nor dope-crazed fiends, and although the density of their brain tissue may decrease appreciably through years of heavy juicing, it is impossible to imagine a musician committing an act of violence without extreme provocation. They are simply a group of desperately bored men who, if the truth be known, are oftentimes propelled by their egos into bed with a chick with whom they would as happily have spent the evening talking, over a bottle of wine or pot of coffee. For despite the constant presence of their fellow musicians, road life is a continuing confrontation with loneliness. Only on two limited levels are relationships possible: music and sex. Regardless of the intensity of these relationships, their potential for growth is slight, their satisfactions frustratingly fleeting.

It is the morning of December 17, 1971. The band has been on the road for 328 days. On 32 of those days they did not work, but 10 of the days off were spent traveling. They have logged over sixty thousand miles on the bus, and additional mileage on planes. Each man makes a point of laying these statistics on you, like a war veteran displaying his scars. In two days they will break for the Christmas holidays.

On the bus, tension and exhaustion mingle, jangling exposed nerves and tightening the atmosphere. Two days ago, in Denver, they squeezed three clinics and eight concerts into forty-eight impossible hours. Yesterday afternoon they had a rare opportunity to rehearse some new music they'll record next month. Last night they played a naval officers club dance in San Diego. Tonight they'll play another officers club, this one at Vandenberg Air Force Base, three hundred miles away.

Although dances provide a good 20 percent of their bookings and keep the band solvent, the men dread playing them almost as much as they dread doing clinics. The clinics are physically draining and rarely break even, but the excitement of the concert pieces and the enthusiasm of the kids offer some compensation. At dances, they play an entirely different kind of music. The difference between playing concerts and playing dances is the difference between a fair fight and a fixed one. To the spectators, the difference may not even be noticeable. To the performers, it's crucial.

The routine of the next twenty-four hours, then, is familiar and 99 percent predictable. They will drive all day through the brown, dry California countryside, enjoying an occasional glimpse of the ocean. There will be a supermarket stop, rather than a proper lunch stop at a restaurant. Everyone will buy more than he can eat, and eat more than he should. Willie Maiden will disdain the food but replenish his beer supply. Sustained conversation, if any, will concern either music or Where I'm Spending My Christmas Vacation. At least six different individuals will be heard to ask, at various times, "Where we playin' tonight? What time do we start? What are we wearing, suits or the elf uniforms?" This last in reference to red knitted vests and trousers, also known as fairy outfits, a misjudgment road manager Mike Vax will never live down.

At around five, they will reach the Lompoc Travelodge. Mike Vax will handle the checking-in procedures and distribute room keys. There will be just enough time to have dinner at the only convenient restaurant, shower, shave and dress (in the red suits, which they hope will be interpreted

as concessions to the Christmas season) before returning to the
bus for the short trip to the base. They will unload their instruments. Chuck Anderson will help the band boy in setting
up the bandstand, or whatever makeshift playing area they
will be using. The musicians will ferret out a men's room, cor-
ridor, alcove, storeroom or corner of the kitchen in which to
warm up.

At precisely eight, Stan will give a straight little speech
of welcome before kicking off "But Beautiful" or "Sunny" or
"It Was a Very Good Year" or "September Song" or "Girl Talk"
or "Days of Wine and Roses" or "Close to You" or "My Old
Flame" or a similar selection from their dance book. The floor
will fill up quickly with fox trotters in their forties and fifties,
sporting crew cuts and corsages. The women's dresses will in-
dicate a partiality toward turquoise, true red and black, and
their wearers will enjoy themselves more uninhibitedly than
their husbands. One such wife, in her fifties, wearing shoes
carefully dyed to match her pink dress, will indefatigably
samba, partnerless, all evening long.

They will play an arrangement of "MacArthur Park" that
is danceable enough through the part where the sidemen softly
sing the "There will be another song for me" verse, gazing
longingly into each other's eyes and always getting a laugh
out of the audience—and when they suddenly swing into the
wild second chorus with its erratic, indecipherable beat, the
dancers will doggedly jitterbug. "Eager Beaver" and "Peanut
Vendor" will be requested, played and enthusiastically received. Altogether, they will play four forty-five-minute sets.
The club will get its money's worth.

At midnight, Stan will give the downbeat for the theme.
As the last strains of "Artistry" fade away, he will make another straight little speech, thank-you-and-goodnight, and the
ritual of packing up will begin. Naturally, the smaller the
instrument, the simpler the procedure. Von Ohlen's job takes

23

the longest, which explains why drummers often complain about getting the leftover chicks. But at this job, there will be no chicks.

Back at the Travelodge, most will "hang out" in groups of varying sizes, juicing or discreetly smoking grass to facilitate the process of winding down from the performance. Critiques of what was played tonight, how it was played, what *wasn't* played, *why* what wasn't played wasn't played, the new music soon to be recorded, or someone's newly acquired cassette by Don Ellis, Chicago, Blood Sweat and Tears or some more obscure group will continue until everyone's exhaustion threshold is reached. At 9 A.M., back on the bus for another three-hundred-mile drive.

This year's tour was an exceptionally frazzling one. The Old Man's enforced absence exacted a heavy emotional toll, and there were times when neither his nor the band's survival seemed likely. While Stan underwent one of those freak misfortunes in which the cure does more damage than the symptoms—exploratory surgery, retroactively judged unnecessary, resulted in peritonitis, which necessitated further surgery—rumors were rampant. He had cancer. He was dying. They would disband next month . . . next week . . . tomorrow! Arriving at a job after a drive of several hundred miles, they would be greeted by irate ballroom or club owners who had booked and advertised Stan Kenton and His Orchestra, declaring, "I don't want you without Stan Kenton!" To Mike Vax fell the disagreeable task of persuasion.

"You convince them that they gotta have you! You say, 'Look, we have a band on the road, and it's a very expensive proposition. We can't afford to drive as many miles as we've driven to come here and have you tell us you don't want us 'cause Stan isn't with us.' And sometimes they'll say, 'Well, we don't care about that!' Or they'll refuse to do anything to make the band sound good in their club! Or sometimes there isn't a very big crowd, but you can tell from talking with the people that it was because the guy didn't publicize it. And the guy comes up to you after the first set and says, 'See, Stan isn't here! And I think we should take off x amount of dollars.' So I'd say, 'You do and we don't go on for the second set!' And he says, 'I have a contract!' And you say, 'So do we!' And the guy goes off muttering something like, 'I knew I shouldn't have hired Stan Kenton, he plays weird music!'

"The absolutely worst club in the United States is the Losers Club in Dallas, Texas. That guy decided he wouldn't pay us the money he owed us and he tried to pick a fight with me, called me every name in the book, just because I was trying to collect the money, as I normally do every night!"

Vax hastily rounded up Fred Carter, the biggest member of the band, and four other musicians. Carter will remember the scene as long as he lives. "We went downstairs to the owner's office. It was a typical Mafia place, with big plush rugs and elephant tusks on the wall and all kinds of guns and *tools* on the wall, chains, with balls on the ends of them. The owner was sitting behind his desk, feet propped up on it, with two bodyguards or triggermen behind him. We started arguing and I thought for sure there was going to be a fist fight. Then Willie Maiden, who weighs about a hundred pounds, runs into the room and walks real briskly up to the guy and sticks his nose in the guy's face and says, 'You son of a bitch, you mean you're not going to pay us, you dirty son of a bitch?' And the guy says, 'That's right!' And Willie says, 'Now I know how this place got its name!' And he turns and leaves, and everybody started to laugh. But they didn't pay us."

There was also the delicate problem of dissuading the audience from demanding its money back when it became aware that the star was missing. Their tactic was to play a big, flashy, impressive opening number before announcing that "Mr. Kenton won't be with us this evening, but we have a

25

great show for you," etc. To their credit, the audiences proved more understanding than the owners.

Before Stan's illness, there were lighter moments. If the band's humor lacks subtlety, so do most of its audiences; so that when Stan pretends to hide behind a potted plant, or conducts by waving an American flag or seems about to swing from a chandelier, it gets a big laugh. At an Elks Lodge in Pennsylvania, Graham Ellis disrupted the traditional Saturday night tribute to departed Elks (an ultrasincere rendition of "Auld Lang Syne") by jumping up on his chair and yelling, "Happy New Year!" At an amusement park ballroom in Cedar Lake, Indiana, after struggling to play a prehistoric piano that not only was hopelessly out of tune but had some keys that didn't play at all, Stan crumpled a piece of paper, tossed it inside the piano and lit a match, and proceeded to sing and play gospel music while the paper blazed away.

Even disasters serve the purpose of breaking the monotony. When the band arrived to open a beautiful new nightclub north of Chicago, the place was burning down before their eyes, brand-new grand piano, sound system and all. Stan was so appalled to discover that the insurance hadn't yet gone into effect that the band played a benefit that night, in another hall, for the near-bankrupted owner.

The most difficult job they played all year was in the spring, at Disneyland. It was billed as the official celebration of the thirtieth anniversary of the Stan Kenton Orchestra—and on that night Stan was in the hospital, prognosis unknown. It was a poignant evening, with June Christy emerging from semiretirement to sing a few numbers. Just when the evening threatened to deteriorate into a sentimental pudding, Dick Shearer introduced the musicians. When he got to Graham Ellis, Graham coolly let his pants fall down—and equilibrium was restored.

The extraordinary loyalty Stan inspires in his musicians

was demonstrated by the fact that during the entire four months of his absence there was no turnover of personnel— even though several men had already planned to give notice. Stan credits Dick Shearer and Mike Vax for keeping the band intact. Privately, the men confide that they stayed together in *spite* of Vax, who, like many trumpet players, has an apparently indestructible ego. Actually, the only person who kept the band together was Stan himself.

MIKE JAMIESON: "Everybody loved Stan so much that he may have been gone bodily, physically, but everybody still saw him up there."

FRED CARTER: "Stan is an idol to all of us. If he told you to run through a brick wall for him, you would not even question it."

WILLIE MAIDEN: "This isn't just a job—it's a dedication!"

CHUCK CARTER: "I've got a family, five children, in Indianapolis. Stan's is the only band I would leave home for."

KEN HANNA, *arranger*: "Nobody wants to see this band stop. It belongs to too many people."

Three hundred twenty-eight days on the road, however, erode any devotion. Underneath the horseplay, an ominous tension has been building. Griping, grumbling and petty jealousies proliferate. When the Road Sillies give way to the Road Crazies, practical jokes take on a hostile edge: wakeup calls left in another guy's name for 5 A.M.; food disappearing from restaurant tables, to be thrown, ruined or shoved in someone's face; obnoxious remarks to waitresses. In these final days of the tour, their behavior is dangerously volatile.

Stan feels the strain, and shows it. Like a parent who suddenly realizes that discipline has been gradually deteriorating to a point where drastic measures are required, he has cracked down unexpectedly, inconsistently, arbitrarily. Without warning, Mike Vax was demoted from lead to section trumpet player, a significant comedown in this caste-conscious society. Willie Maiden, who lives on beer and fantasies and asks no more than an occasional word of appreciation for his music, was suddenly jumped on for "looking like a fuckin' vagrant! Buy yourself some new clothes," Stan demanded, "or leave the band."

Willie was shocked and hurt. "What's more important," he asked, "the way I play or the way I dress?"

"The way you dress!" Stan said flatly, and walked away.

At the Vandenberg dance, Stan even lost his cool to the extent of yelling at the saxophone section for coming in late, chewing them out furiously in front of the astonished crowd. (His anger is awesome. "If you ain't been screamed on by Stan Kenton," says Fred Carter, "you ain't been screamed on at all!")

He is bone-weary from the strain of pushing his physical endurance to its absolute limit. He has a persistent cough, and catarrh, and a restlessness he tries to ease with alarming quantities of vodka. While the musicians scatter over the holidays to their assorted destinations, he will spend long days and nights at his Beverly Hills office, catching up on a mighty accumulation of details that require his attention, and filling in the thousand last-minute technicalities of next month's European tour.

A great deal is riding on this tour. The last time Stan took a band overseas, in 1963, it was an unmitigated disaster. In 1970, a planned European tour fell through a scant thirty days before they were to have left. Since a road band cannot exist without bookings—Stan pays his musicians an average of three hundred dollars a week regardless of whether they play every night or not—they were forced to fill in, on impossibly short notice, the weeks they were to have spent overseas. Desperate, Stan grabbed at whatever bookings he could get to keep the band alive. For two dismal weeks in Three Rivers, New York, they accompanied an assortment of acts that must have been old Major Bowes rejects. On some nights, not more than fifty people showed up. After Three Rivers, there was a succession of hit-and-runs, so far apart that they drove all day and night, stopping only to play and to eat. In Topeka, after seventy-two straight hours on the bus, they checked into a Holiday Inn for one hour, just to shower and shave with hot water. Conversation slowed, then stopped. Everything had been said.

The year 1972 will be different. The deposit has already been put up; the six-week tour is assured.

Two weeks from now, when the band reassembles in San Francisco on New Year's Eve, Stan will look younger, feel more relaxed, sound very much in control. On the first night of a tour, morale is always high. Despite the layoff, the band will be hot and the capacity audience will be responsive. He will regret leaving Dana and Lance, the teen-age children of his second marriage, but "as soon as I get back with the band and start hearin' those sounds again, the sadness leaves." At such times, it scarcely matters that "I don't know where the hell I'm goin', what will happen, what the hell I'll do." All that matters is that in the morning Stanley Newcombe Kenton will be back on the bus, standing in the well by the door, gazing through the windshield—staring intently, impassively, unswervingly, straight ahead.

3 Stella

"Stella has always been the most important woman in Stanley's life."

VIOLET KENTON FOSTER

IN the beginning, there was Stella.

Even as a handsome young woman on her father's Colorado ranch, Stella Newcombe had the expression and attitudes of a Western pioneer. In 1911, at the age of twenty, she abruptly left the University of Denver to marry Floyd Kenton. They had known each other since childhood. Only after their marriage did they become strangers.

The marriage began badly and went steadily downhill, in a time when connubial misery was infinitely more acceptable than divorce. Stella and Floyd were opposites that attracted but were no more capable of mixing than oil and water. He was all dreams, charm and gossamer; she was logic, down-to-earth, granite. He was a drifter, pursuing variety; she was a nester, needing stability. Within a year of the marriage, Stanley was born. Their parenthood was unplanned, if not unwelcome.

Stanley's birth aggravated dormant symptoms of an injury Stella had suffered in a girlhood riding accident, and this limited her physical activity during her son's early years.

Nonetheless, she produced two additional children during those years—both girls. Stanley's first memory is of his father coming home and telling him, when he was two years old, "You have a baby sister. Her name is Beulah."

Stella came into a moderate inheritance early in her marriage. This she invested in a succession of ventures at which Floyd invariably failed: a grocery store, a meat market, a car agency, a garage. In later, leaner years, he worked for other people as a roofer, a mechanic, a carpenter, even a tombstone salesman. Nothing stuck. Floyd was always more concerned with being well-liked than with getting the job done. As a businessman, he was popular but never prosperous. No matter what he tried, he simply never connected.

Floyd Kenton was an unlikely failure, with all the external requisites for success. He was a good-looking man, tall and Lincolnesque, with a quick, innate intelligence and a personality that was capable of persuading anybody to do just about anything. It was a curious case of the personality overshadowing the person. Floyd was expert at capturing people's attention and admiration; but once he had it, he never knew where to go with it. The potential was there—the *magnetism* was there. But magnetism wasn't enough, and Floyd somehow never was able to get it together.

Every time Floyd would get a new job, the family would be jubilant, thinking that at last they would have a steady income, some financial security. Each time, they were disappointed. He was a hard worker, compulsively so, but so unfocused was his enormous energy that rarely was there any payoff. He would knock himself out setting up a roofing job, lining up the job and getting all the supplies ready—but somebody else always wound up actually nailing on the shingles and getting paid for it. When Floyd did earn any money, he was liable to give it away to some casual acquaintance he might run into on the street on the way home.

If Floyd's financial contribution to his family was negligible, his emotional contribution was nil. With strangers, he was so warm and demonstrative that neighborhood kids openly envied Stanley and his sisters their ideal father. But on those rare occasions when he was at home, and not out working or playing the role of local raconteur and all-around nice guy, he was an emotional cipher—distant, erratic, stubborn. "He was a hard guy to get next to," his son charitably understates it. "I tried . . . but it was impossible. We couldn't communicate."

In the meantime—in all the meantimes that made up Stanley's youth—there always was Stella. Stella the strategist, manipulator par excellence. Stella of the irreproachably good intentions. Although there were stormy scenes with her husband, yelling and spanking were never Stella's style with her children; her methods were subtler, and far more effective. Silent disapproval. Withdrawal. "She would just stop talking," Beulah remembers, "and you felt that somehow you had transgressed. She always got what she wanted, and with the utmost finesse." The tactic failed with Floyd, who countered by spending less and less time at home; but with the children, it was eminently successful. There was never a moment's doubt as to who was in charge. If her domination created any resentment in her growing son, he never expressed it—not even to himself. It was Stella upon whom the children depended, to whom they turned in a crisis, and whose attitudes and platitudes they absorbed like obedient· little sponges. "Finish what you begin." "You don't get anything in this world for nothing." "The world doesn't owe you a living."

As Floyd gradually relinquished his responsibilities at home, Stella delegated them to young Stanley. He was a conscientious child, cooperative and eager to please. When he was five years old, his sister Irma Mae was born, and the family moved from Colorado to California; by the time he was seven, they were living in Huntington Park, a Los Angeles suburb. It was here that Stanley was first cast in a role he would come to play to perfection: surrogate father.

STELLA KENTON: "His father being gone so much, and paying so little attention to the children, Stanley kinda became my standby with the younger children. He used to go to the store, buy the groceries, take the little girls to the toilet, ride them on his bicycle to school and bring 'em home that way."

IRMA KENTON HOPKINS: "I was always very proud of my big brother. He always looked nice; my mother dressed him nice. I can remember standing out in front of the kindergarten class, waiting for him to come along to pick me up—and I remember feeling so proud when he came on his bicycle and I would jump on the handlebars and the other kids would see me as I rode away."

BEULAH KENTON JORDAN: "One of the things that shaped Stanley was this terrible embarrassment financially. We didn't have any money at all. We had to charge groceries and he had to go down and get the groceries and put it on the bill; and the man didn't want him to have the groceries, and he *knew* the man didn't want him to have them. It was *pain*ful."

Beulah was a classic middle child, overserious and something of a misfit in the family. Stanley was much closer to Irma Mae, whom he treated like a kid brother. The two of them frequently ganged up on Beulah, teasing and tormenting her with the innocent cruelty of childhood. Irma Mae idolized Stanley and would do anything to please him. They played Tin Can Hockey in the back yard and Run, Sheep, Run. There were endless sessions of Stanley pitching to Irma Mae. "I see him throwing balls at Irma Mae so hard," Beulah recalls, "it would just about burn your hands! And she never flinched. He'd throw 'em that hard at me and I'd scream and run in the house!"

Stella ran a tight ship—sufficient unto itself, and solidly

33

middle class. There were always three meals a day, even though they were often meatless, and two pair of shoes, for school and for "good." Long before Norman Vincent Peale became a household word, Stella was instructing her children in the power of positive thinking. At the dinner table, everything from the carryings-on of the family down the street with nineteen children to a complaint about a teacher would be relentlessly analyzed, categorized and adjudged good or bad, right or wrong, black or white. Stella's mind did not accommodate shadings.

Stella Kenton has been on a lifelong head trip, and all three of her children have pursued that course. All are introspective and hyperanalytical in an often convoluted, circular way. Irma Mae believes that "We all grew up with a liking for the field of psychology because as youngsters we were all so intent on figuring my Dad out! We tried so hard to understand him. But we never really did." Beulah, now a psychologist, refers to her parents as "my first case. When I was four years old, I was a marriage counselor. I failed."

After corrective surgery alleviated Stella's ambiguous ailment—she had "dislocated some organs," according to Beulah—she took a job at the local Jell Well plant, boxing Jell Well on the assembly line. Soon afterward the family acquired an old upright piano, and Stella, who had studied the instrument as a child, augmented their income by giving lessons. Naturally, she tried to teach her own children to play. Just as naturally, they resisted. Beulah vividly remembers "sitting on the piano bench and trying to play the piano, with my mother talking in this ear. It made me very nervous." Stanley, then in his tenth year, was equally turned off—although he had always enjoyed listening to music, and in fact often fell asleep with the headset of their primitive radio clamped to his ears. For two years, he passively resisted his mother's efforts to make a pianist of him.

Stanley was not against learning the instrument, but he preferred a trial-and-error approach. It delighted him to pick out tunes "by ear," a method that horrified conventional music teachers of the day. A boy could pick up all kinds of bad habits that way. Stella finally recognized the futility of her efforts and found another teacher for the boy . . . and another . . . and still another. A succession of spinsterly, uninspired and uninspiring teachers came and went; to Stanley, they merged into a frustrating blur. Finally, the lessons were abandoned.

Stanley's recollections of his early childhood are remarkable chiefly for their absence. Characteristically, he worries that such a blank masks a block. He can remember nothing in the least traumatic, nothing at all exceptional. There are only the expected memories of family picnics, outings to the beach, an occasional movie. His father's increasingly frequent absences are scarcely mentioned, as though every family has a father in absentia. One summer does stand out: "I was about eleven. Pop took care of a fleet of trucks for a big trucking company. That summer, he let me help him tear down the motors, and he would fix them. He paid me twenty-five cents an hour. It was the closest I ever felt to him."

Up to his fourteenth year, Stanley's life was singularly uneventful. He had a fleeting ambition to become a minister, later a railroad engineer. He joined the Boy Scouts, but was quickly turned off by a Scoutmaster who was "a real Prussian. He was always yelling 'Attention' and 'At Ease' and all that kind of crap. I just walked out one night and never came back."

He was a timid, quiet boy with no identity apart from Stella and, more tenuously, his sisters. His rapid growth sapped his energy; he had an enormous appetite and ate huge quantities of food, yet was extremely lethargic. Beulah remembers him going about his chore of feeding the chickens and pigeons in the back yard, almost in slow motion. "We would watch him through the window, and it seemed like he was hardly moving." Even Stella grew impatient with what she considered to be laziness when, instead of applying himself to the devil-grass rake in the yard, he would sit for hours in a state somewhere between daydreaming and a catatonic trance.

In his young mind, Stanley was desperately trying to justify his existence. "I had a very hard time becoming a part of anything. I felt I had no right even to *be* here. I was afraid of people. I was very awkward and clumsy, uncoordinated. I couldn't run or play basketball. I was no good at baseball. Scholastically, I was no great shakes. But I wanted so terribly to *be* somebody, to do something important. Then the music thing came along, and I went after it desperately, was really *driven* into it, because I was so hungry to identify with *something*. Music seemed to give me an identity, and I really hooked to it. At that particular time, it could have been anything. It just happened to be music."

"The music thing" was a serendipitous coincidence. By now the family was living in Bell, another Los Angeles suburb, in a three-bedroom frame "tract" house that would be the most permanent of all their homes. It was to this house that two of Stanley's cousins came to stay during the time of their mother's, Aunt Georgie's, funeral. Stanley and his sisters slept on the floor and gave their beds to the visiting relatives. Billy and Arthur Kenton were only sixteen and eighteen, but they were already earning money as musicians. During their brief visit, they played a kind of music Stanley had never heard before. It had a freedom and spontaneity about it; defiantly, it shattered the rules Stanley had so steadfastly resisted. In a language he had never learned but somehow always known, it spoke to him, direct and compelling. An inner circuit he had not known existed flashed ON, and something within him awoke and responded with a rocking shock of recognition, catapulting him into a world in which he might, after all, *be somebody*. The world, and the music, were jazz.

"From the time I was fourteen years old, I was all music. Nothing else ever entered my mind."

Within weeks, Stanley had found someone who could teach him to play jazz piano. Frank Hurst, the organist at the local theater, was stunned by his new pupil's enthusiasm. Now the piano dominated the Kenton household. For six, eight, often ten hours a day, Stanley practiced, trying to emulate his new idols: Gershwin, Earl "Fatha" Hines, Benny Carter, Louis Armstrong. Like a space traveler who happens upon an atmosphere capable of sustaining his life, the boy grabbed at, fed on, clung to the music. The frame house vibrated to the strains of the popular tunes of the day and, later, as he became more accomplished, *Rhapsody in Blue*. At fourteen, Stanley had achieved something that had eluded his father all of his life. He had connected.

Floyd was ambivalent about Stanley's music, sometimes acting the proud father, at other times advising the boy to get into "something secure, like civil service." Fireman, policeman and postman topped Floyd's list of preferred occupations. But Floyd's absences were of longer duration now; away for months at a time on gold mining and other ventures, he was phasing himself permanently out of the family. Stanley scarcely seemed to notice. The music consumed him.

He played in a few school programs, and word of his talent soon got around. Now, for the first time, he was popular, sought after; he was elected president of his class, invited to parties and asked to play. He went to a few, but was painfully shy. At seventeen he was a stringy, self-conscious six feet four inches, as sensitive about his complexion as he was about his playing. An imagined slight would send him bolting out the back door, never to return. He felt he had only been invited for his playing. He could not conceive of anyone wanting him around just for himself. With relief, he gave up parties.

With three other Bell High School sophomores, Stanley formed The Belltones. They played at school dances and

37

parties, and finally lined up a real paying job, at a local miniature golf course. The music, or so the proprietor reasoned,
would attract customers. But when the Belltones showed up
in their best blue serge suits, so did their competition: a frantic
black combo, heavy on brass, promoting the miniature golf
course across the street. Volume being the main consideration,
the Belltones never had a chance. Not only did the proprietor
intimidate them by shouting, "Louder, for God's sake!" at them
all evening; when the job ended, he refused to pay them! Hurt
and humiliated, the boys stole as many golf clubs as they
could stuff down the legs of their pants.

From such an inauspicious beginning, Stanley's professional star could only rise. He began "jobbing" or free-lancing.
In a Los Angeles hamburger joint, he played for fifty cents a
night, tips and all the hamburgers he could eat. At the Chicken
House, in East Los Angeles, he did a little better: two dollars
a night and a chicken dinner. At each job, he dreaded being
asked to play something he might not know. His expectations
of himself were impossible. No matter how well he played, no
matter how much he improved or how much money he could
command, it was never good enough. It was never perfect.

By his last year of high school, Stanley had outgrown
Frank Hurst. At Hurst's suggestion, he began studying with
arrangers and listening, listening, listening to the records of
Earl Hines and other masters of jazz music. That big, warm,
all-embracing sound was what Stanley was after. In the process
of attaining it, he acquired a versatility that enabled him to
play virtually any style of popular piano, to the extent that
when he graduated from high school he was perfectly capable
of earning a living, though meager at first, playing music.

College being a financial impossibility, Stanley continued
jobbing. When he wasn't working or practicing, he was de-
vouring trade journals or hanging around outside the union
offices, often missing a meal on the chance that a real live

professional musician might stop and talk with him for a minute or two. Although it was 1930, with the economy in chaos, five dollars a night was now his price; even so, he often had to slip homemade cardboard inner soles, painted black, inside his shoes so that the dancers, looking up at him on the bandstand, wouldn't see the holes. Then an offer from Art and Jack Flack lured him away from home for the first—and almost the last—time.

The Flacks were two xylophonists whose dwindling vaudeville bookings had forced them to develop another source of income. They were forming a six-piece combo, and they already had a job lined up: The Green Hat Café, a walk-down speakeasy in San Diego. What the job lacked in class, it made up in security. It paid what was to Stanley a small fortune: thirty dollars a week. He jumped at the chance.

Musically, the job was undemanding and valuable experience. But the wrench of leaving home was more than Stanley could bear. He was achingly lonely, miserably homesick and unable to feel any rapport with the other, more mature members of the group. After six wretched weeks, he gave it up and went home to Bell. But in that six weeks, his consciousness had been irreversibly altered. It seemed to him that everyone had changed. After his brief glimpse of a wider world, the old surroundings appeared colorless and dreary by comparison. And Stella's silent disapproval of his default (mingled, perhaps, with a certain dismay at his realization of his dependence upon her) added to his discomfort. Home could never again be the refuge it once had been. Irresistible forces had been set in motion, and it was only a matter of months before he left again, this time with a trio, headed for Las Vegas.

Vegas was raw and wide open in 1930, and piano players were in demand in speakeasies, beer bars, gambling joints and whorehouses. Stanley played them all. He went on the road with a couple of "turkey shows"—so called because "they folded up and you had to bum rides home." He spent most of 1932 with the Francis Gilbert Territory Band. Gilbert wore a top hat and played banjo; his six-piece group traveled the copper mine area of Arizona in a succession of dilapidated buses and limousines. As pianist, Stanley made forty dollars a week.

As Stanley's versatility broadened, his confidence failed to keep pace with his capabilities. He remained a loner. Neither alcohol (it might jeopardize his precarious self-control) nor gambling (money was too dearly come by to be used for games) appealed to him. Tentatively and superficially, he investigated various religions and philosophies, searching for answers with which to shore up his sagging self-assurance. Then came a jolt that demolished what little confidence he had managed to acquire.

He had returned to Los Angeles to take his first job with a "big band"—the fourteen-piece aggregation of Nick Pontrelli. His first appearance with Pontrelli was at the Palace Ballroom in Ocean Park. (Irma Mae, refused admittance because she was under sixteen, peered through a salt-air-encrusted window thinking proudly, "That's my brother up there on the stand!") The music was more difficult than what Stanley had encountered in his previous jobs, although well within the range of his ability. But in his nervousness, he rushed the tempo. After two weeks, Pontrelli peremptorily fired him.

Stanley was devastated. Instead of blaming Pontrelli for his high-handedness, he turned his anger inward, flagellating himself with imaginary guilts and shortcomings until he became physically ill. The very foundation of his identity was shaken. Bob Goodrich, a Pontrelli sideman on whose recommendation Stanley had been hired, feared that he contemplated suicide. An outraged Stella conducted long phone conversations with Goodrich's mother. Stella fumed. Mrs. Goodrich commiserated. Stanley's depression deepened.

Only economic necessity ultimately pushed him out of the house and back on the road for a three-month tour with Frank Whitney's ten-piece band. He welcomed the exhausting one-nighters; they left him little energy for reflection on where his career might—or might not—be going. When the tour ended, there was another turkey show, followed by another speakeasy job, this one in downtown Los Angeles. Financially, it was a windfall. The singer Stanley accompanied split her tips with him, and some weeks he earned as much as $150 —a fortune in 1933. Then one day that summer, in the middle of his twenty-first year, Stanley got a call from Everett Hoaglund. His band was rehearsing in an hour. Would Stanley come down and audition?

"Hoaglund had the only real jazz band in Southern California, and it was all of us young musicians' ambition to play for him, because he was considered *it*. We all used to haunt the ballroom where he played. If you got a chance to play with Hoaglund, you felt you had really arrived.

"I wanted to play in that band more than anything in the world. At that rehearsal the band sounded so wonderful; I felt so inferior to it, I almost ran out of the place. Then he asked me to play something. I couldn't think of anything to play! All the white keys looked black and the black keys looked white! I was terrified. He said, 'Run an arpeggio! Anything!' So I stumbled around and played a little bit. And he said, 'Why don't you come down and play with us Friday night?' So I got off my speakeasy job, and that first night I played clear over my head. Everybody was just thrilled, asking me, 'Where'd you *come* from?' Then the next night I went back, and it was *awful*. I made one mistake after another."

When that evening ended, Stanley was sure he had

blown it. He was headed for the door when Hoaglund, a quiet, gentle man mature in both years and perception, intercepted him. "It's going to take us a little while to get acquainted," he reassured the visibly trembling Stanley, "but don't worry about it. You're hired."

It was the first of many fateful moments Stanley would live through in this ballroom. Situated in Balboa, forty miles south of Los Angeles, it was only one of hundreds of ballrooms that dotted the California coast. But this particular ballroom was destined to be the scene of euphoric heights and abysmal failures in Stanley Kenton's career. In this ballroom, his fortunes and spirits would soar and plummet. In this ballroom, he would fall helplessly in love with one wife and hopelessly out of love with another.

Prophetically, it was called the Rendezvous.

4 Violet

"There is one talent that I have: I can see talent in other people. And this I think is what Stanley felt. Because when we started out, because of his family background, he was scared to death, and he didn't see what he had. And I wasn't afraid. I think that I had as much drive, maybe more, than Stanley."

VIOLET KENTON FOSTER

IF Violet Peters hadn't had such an unmistakable air of class about her, she might very well have been called a tease.

Violet was tall, blonde and attractive enough that persuading a date to take her to the Rendezvous every Saturday night was no problem. During the week, Violet was just a rather shy, anonymous young cashier at a Los Angeles grocery store. But on Saturday nights, she came into her own. The weekly ritual had originated back in her high school days when, dressed and coiffed with great care, she would allow that week's favored young man to escort her to the ballroom and dance *every* number (unless someone cut in) with her. Violet was never one for sitting anything out. If at the end of the evening the young man was so foolish as to expect more than a token goodnight kiss in return for his services as chauffeur and dancing partner, he was given a hard time and the gate. There was always a willing replacement for the next Saturday night.

If life does imitate art, then it was in imitation of a corny B movie that Stanley went home from work one night and informed his mother, "Tonight I saw the girl I'm gonna marry."

"Really," said Stella, humoring him. "Who is she?"

"I don't know. But I'm gonna find out."

Stanley had gone through some profound changes since joining the Hoaglund band. Unlike many bandleaders of the time, Hoaglund was neither a drunk nor a "stick waver," but a real pro—the first Stanley had encountered. He had made his reputation as a jazz clarinetist; he truly cared about the music and had a fine, smooth, swinging band. And he had style. He was a suave, meticulous man with a little black moustache (perhaps in imitation of Paul Whiteman, whom he greatly admired), and an impressive manner on the bandstand. He demanded self-discipline and impeccable conduct from his musicians, and insisted they show respect for the bandstand. Through observation and osmosis, Stanley absorbed much of Hoaglund's professionalism.

He was becoming more and more accomplished as a pianist; still, the self-consciousness and feelings of inferiority persisted. A friendly overture, especially from a girl, would send him into a panic of embarrassment so acute that finally, in desperation, he confronted the problem and worked it through:

"I was twenty-three years old and I was scared to death of everything. I would never speak to anybody unless they spoke to me first; I had the feeling that nobody wanted to speak to me in the first place. And one day I said God damn it, this isn't right! There's no earthly reason for me to be timid and afraid all the time! And as childish as it sounds, I said I'm gonna speak to people and say hello to people, and I'm not gonna be concerned about whether they answer back or not! If they don't answer, the hell with 'em. I started gradually doing that, and I found out that most people were just as timid as I was! And I began to have a feeling of confidence with people. It delighted me! It was just like a treasure somebody'd given me!"

He was still a little giddy from that revelation when he noticed the tall, girl-next-door-type dancer whose shiny, scrubbed, un-Hollywoodlike appearance and intent fascination with the band set her apart from the crowd. Violet scarcely noticed the awkward, nervous piano player; she had eyes for one of the sidemen in the band. But Stanley, in a fog of infatuation, saw only the girl and what he interpreted as her deep feeling for the music. After several weeks of watching her from afar, he consolidated his newfound courage and asked her to dance—forgetting that, like most musicians, he had never had an opportunity to learn to dance, being always on the bandstand. After stumbling around on the dance floor for a few minutes, he had the presence of mind to suggest that they have a coke. From there, the relationship progressed through all the conventional stages: intense conversations through all the intermissions of that and subsequent evenings, then his driving her home after the dances, finally his asking her to go steady.

Violet didn't believe in going steady—or in being engaged, for that matter. She lived in Los Angeles, and Stanley had moved, shortly after meeting her, to Balboa. During the summer season the band played six nights a week and Sunday matinees, and he had soon grown tired of commuting from Bell. He and two of the saxophone players shared a little two-bedroom, fifty-dollar-a-month house on the peninsula. Stella, Irma Mae and Beulah frequently rented a nearby cabin for the weekend.

Violet explained to Stanley that going steady wouldn't make sense because she *knew* she was going to have dates with other men. So for more than a year they saw each other once or twice a week, but not exclusively. Meanwhile, Stanley was making the most of his musical opportunities. Deadly serious about his music, as always, he spent his free time in the ballroom, writing experimental arrangements on the piano, while the other musicians were on the beach thinking only of sun, beer and girls. Hoaglund was impressed by Stanley's dedication as well as his arrangements, some of which he used. He gave Stanley an inside view of the considerations and compromises a leader faces. It was through Hoaglund that Stanley first became aware of the psychology of leadership, that crucial quality that separates the leaders from the stick wavers. Occasionally, he would let Stanley rehearse the band. With Violet's enthusiastic encouragement, Stanley began to consider alternative means of achieving that *something* that had tantalized him since childhood.

At the end of 1934, Hoaglund decided to organize a new band with a more commercial appeal, more society than swing. Stanley chose to remain at the Rendezvous, playing piano for Russ Plummer, a pleasant enough stick waver whose musical reputation was neither good nor bad, but nonexistent. Stanley appears to have shouldered the brunt of the responsibility for Plummer's band. After seven forgettable months at the Rendezvous, the band sank quietly into oblivion. By this time—July, 1935— Stanley had acquired a wife.

Since neither of their families volunteered any financial or moral support for their wedding, he and Violet simply went to the home of a local minister one afternoon and were married. That night, Stanley played at Balboa. After the job, he told Violet it was the band's last night; they had received their notice two weeks before, but he hadn't mentioned it for fear she would call off the wedding.

They moved into an apartment in Hollywood, one room with a Murphy bed, and there the Depression caught up with them. Stanley scrounged for work, haunting the studios and the musicians' union. They lived on beans until both became ill. Stella gave them forty-five dollars to buy a radio; they bought food instead. Finally Stanley landed a job with the Hal Grayson Orchestra in San Francisco, where they were just getting accustomed to eating regularly again when two uninvited houseguests arrived: Pop, who by now was divorced from Stella and living on a chicken ranch in Petaluma, California, and Irma Mae. Stella had sent them both to visit Stanley and his new bride. In their one-room apartment it was, to say the least, cozy.

When the visit had extended to three weeks and threatened to become a permanent arrangement, Violet informed her husband one morning that they were taking his sister and father home. All piled obediently into the car, and they delivered Irma Mae back to Stella in Los Angeles, dropping Pop off in Petaluma with the chickens.

"When we took Irma Mae home," Violet recalls vividly, "Stanley went over and sat in a chair and his mother went over and sat in his *lap* and said to me, with tears in her eyes, 'Violet, you're taking my poor baby boy away from me!' I was twenty years old! I didn't know how to deal with it! Stella just bugged the bejesus out of me all the time! And Stanley, he always defended her—until he went through analysis, and then he knocked that off."

When the job with Grayson ended, they moved back to Los Angeles, where Stanley again made the rounds looking for work. He remembers it as "a very happy existence, scuffling as it was. Violet was a little bit jealous of my feeling for my family, but it wasn't any big thing." Violet's recollection is somewhat different:

"His mother really wrapped him around her finger. She used to check on me every day. She was always negative, filled with all sorts of superstitions. You don't sit in a draft, because you'll catch cold. Or take a bath every day, for the

47

same reason. When she found out we slept in the nude, she just about fainted!"

A number of musicians in similar straits lived for twenty-five dollars a month in the apartment house on West Adams, with a phone down the hall that rang all too seldom with job offers. Finances were tighter than ever, and an evening spent at the nearby ten-cent movie house was a rare treat. When Stanley wasn't worrying about his seemingly stagnating career, he was trying to keep peace between his wife and mother. He became so moody that Violet was afraid to go to sleep at night, for fear he might harm himself in some way. Then, providentially, came a job offer from Gus Arnheim, and Stanley was again on the road. But this tour would be different. Violet would be with him.

Gus Arnheim had risen to fame at Los Angeles's Cocoanut Grove in the twenties, playing a highly polished brand of dance music and featuring young singers such as Bing Crosby. Now, in 1936, he had decided to form a jazz band. Arnheim was wise enough to know his limitations in the jazz field, and hired Stanley as much for his familiarity with the jazz scene as for his skill as a pianist.

To Stanley and Violet, the trip east was a happy time of discovery of themselves, each other and the country. Neither of them had been out of what Violet called the cow country before. They went sightseeing whenever possible, and were goggle-eyed at all the tourist attractions. A closeness developed between them that communicated itself even to casual observers. Often they thought and spoke as a unit, finishing each other's sentences as naturally as their own. The romantic side of Stanley's nature, long suppressed by fears of rejection and ridicule, was given expression at last. To Violet, "He was one of the most *tender* people I ever encountered. He was so very, very sensitive and aware of the way I felt. He used to do very soft things, like bringing me a glass of water every night before I went to sleep—whether I wanted it or not. He was always that way with me. That's why I was so appalled at the stories I heard later, after we were divorced, about how he'd changed, the cruel things he was supposed to have done."

They began building air castles—air ballrooms, more precisely—housing wildly successful jazz bands playing Stanley's then unwritten music. One of Stanley's fantasies was of a band that would play concerts instead of dances. Violet shored up his fantasies with practicality; she bought a calendar bank in which they had to deposit a quarter each day to change the date, and they began saving money. "Nothing is impossible," she assured him repeatedly. He began to believe it.

When the band played a date in San Antonio, Stanley and drummer Marvin "Pee Wee" George heard about an old Negro musician who knew all the mysteries of jazz. They found "Nigger" George Foster in a cellar, lecturing on rhythm and demonstrating on his old piano that emitted no notes, only the sound of the keys cracking. Foster's theories were a kind of musical Rosicrucianism. He told Stanley his left side was spiritual and his right side worldly, and the music had to balance the two. They even lured the sedate, reserved Arnheim down to Foster's cellar one night; but unlike Stanley, who hung on Foster's every word, Arnheim was politely unimpressed.

They took an enforced vacation when the Denver ballroom into which they were booked burned down, leaving them with four empty weeks. They rented cabins in nearby Estes Park where, like children discovering summer camp, they delightedly roamed the hillsides, rode rented horses and played at roughing it. Jack Ordean and Bill Covey, two talented saxophone players, found the nights uncomfortably chilly, but were too juiced most of the time to figure out how to go about finding wood for the fireplace; so in the evenings

49

they resourcefully heated their cabin by burning up the furniture, piece by piece. Violet's first and last attempt to cook breakfast for everyone aborted when she tried to heat the wood stove by burning the wood *inside* the oven, and nearly burned the cabin down. Nothing was taken very seriously. It was perhaps the most carefree time of Stanley's life.

They spent over a year on the road with Arnheim, during which time Stanley received his first official recognition in print. When critic George Simon reviewed the Arnheim band for *Metronome* magazine, he commented that "Stanley Kenton plays not only good rhythmic piano, but interesting fill-in figurations as well." Shortly after the review appeared, Arnheim disbanded.

Stanley and Violet returned to Los Angeles with a plan. They would live on their savings and what he could make playing "casuals"—local parties and intermittent free-lance jobs—and he would not look for steady work; instead, he would find a good teacher and study, filling in what he felt were serious gaps in his musical education. A year or two of study would qualify him to play in one of the motion picture studio orchestras, a lucrative, secure and respected job.

He began studying technique with John Crown, a concert pianist, but soon realized that the scope of his ambitions, unformed though they were, called for expertise beyond just technical skill. Crown introduced him to Charles Dalmores. "He was a wonderful old guy in his seventies, so excited over music. He spoke eleven languages, he had a repertoire of six operas. He was a virtuoso of the French horn and the cello, and he could play the bejesus out of the piano. Sessions with him didn't last just thirty minutes or an hour; sometimes they'd go on all afternoon. I'd leave there totally inspired, just walkin' on air."

Dalmores taught him solfeggio (voice exercises that develop pitch) and the technical and psychological intricacies of conducting. The wise old European gentleman was amused and appalled by the impatience of his student, who seemed determined to compress ten years of learning into each lesson. He was equally dismayed by Stanley's lack of confidence in his obvious ability. "Dalmores did much to break down my feeling that I was not as gifted as many other people. We used to sing solfeggio; I might be off pitch a half a tone and God, I'd get mad at myself! And he'd always say, 'Mr. Kenton, *nobody* can do that!' And I'd say, 'Yeah, Mr. Dalmores, but you're *supposed* to do it!' 'No,' he'd say, 'you're *not supposed* to do it!' I was obsessed with the idea of having everything right and proper, doing things the way they're supposed to be done. One time he was showing me something on the piano and I said, 'Mr. Dalmores, that isn't exactly proper, is it?' He slapped my hands, and he said, 'Nobody worries anymore today whether a thing is right or wrong, proper or improper! The important thing is to play music! You play music with your knees, your elbows, your feet, your head, everything you can, but you must play! Create!' "

After more than a year with Dalmores, Stanley had an opportunity to put into practice some of the theories he'd been studying. He had worked with tenor saxophonist Vido Musso many times—with Arnheim, Plummer, Hoaglund, even as far back as Nick Pontrelli. It was Vido, in fact, who had suggested to Hoaglund that he audition Stanley. Vido was the Primo Carnera of the jazz world—a hulking Sicilian whose unschooled but exciting playing had made him a reputation with Benny Goodman's band. The mysteries of the English language always eluded Vido, whose references to boats that drowned and Cadillac conversibles kept his fellow band members entertained. Once when on the road with Harry James, he remarked, "If somebody don't open a window on this bus, we'll all get sophisticated!" And it was Vido who was once heard to observe, to nobody in particular, "Music is a very hard instrument."

In 1935, Vido had briefly had his own band and had

used some of Stanley's arrangements. In August of 1938, Vido asked Stanley to help him reorganize, and also play piano. For months, the eighteen-piece band played sporadic local jobs, each man making perhaps five dollars a night. It was largely a "pickup" band; for each job, Vido would round up whatever musicians were out of work. Then with the backing of Al Jarvis, a local disc jockey and promoter of big bands, they were booked for a road tour.

For all his lovableness as a warm and eccentric "character," Vido's manner was as crude as his speech, and he frequently wound up in a fight with some customer who felt Vido had insulted his date. He had a habit of combing his thick black hair and removing the hair from his comb during the floor show, while people were eating their dinners. And he was always just a little distracted, searching for a reed for his saxophone when he should have been taking care of business. The pull of the leadership vacuum upon Stanley was irresistible. Eagerly, he stepped into the breach.

Whether the men felt Vido was deliberately dishonest or innocently irresponsible, none of them trusted him. They insisted that Stanley handle the money, collecting from the ballroom owners and paying them their five dollars a night. Through some inexplicable blending of genes and circumstance, Stanley had begun to project a quality to which the men responded with respect and admiration. It may have had something to do with his towering height, or the penetrating resonance of his voice or the earnestness with which he tactfully made suggestions and performed his various tasks. It was more than conscientiousness, more even than a growing proficiency at manipulating people. It was . . . charisma.

It was not, however, enough to salvage Vido's band. Bookings were too sparse and low paying to sustain eighteen men on the road, and after a few months the band was taken over by Johnny "Scat" Davis, a comedian-trumpeter-singer.

Once again, Stanley headed back to Los Angeles. His future seemed as uncertain as ever. The idea of settling into a studio job had lost its appeal for him, and he began giving more thought to composing and arranging. He did some free-lance motion picture scoring and worked briefly in the house band at NBC. In 1939, he went to work in the pit band at Earl Carroll's Vanities.

Earl Carroll was the acknowledged Flo Ziegfeld of the West Coast. The inscription above the entrance of his theater on Sunset Boulevard read, "Through these portals pass the most beautiful girls in the world," and the claim had enough truth in it to pack the place with tourists and natives alike, month in and month out. It was Stanley's job, as assistant conductor, to play piano and rehearse the band. In terms of financial security, it was the best job he had had, and for the first time since their marriage he and Violet were able to enjoy the luxury of an apartment with a separate bedroom. But he was growing increasingly disenchanted with the Holly-wood scene—the overriding commercialism of the music, the politics, and the cynicism of the musicians at the theater who ridiculed his enthusiasm, didn't talk music and "thought only of getting through playing so they could get home and cut their lawns. I felt I was going around in circles, not getting anywhere. I almost felt I should quit music and get into something else."

Instead of quitting music, in August of 1940 he quit Earl Carroll's. "I decided God damn it, I guess a band is the thing. Go for broke." It was a terrifying but inevitable step. He had written enough experimental music to know there was a definite sound that he wanted, a new and, he felt, totally dif-ferent jazz sound he knew he would never hear except from a band of his own. But before he could organize a band, he had to have music.

He and Violet rented a cabin in the mountains where,

in two months, he arranged some standards like "Body and Soul" and "Stardust" and wrote a number of original tunes, including an untitled piece he thought might make a suitable theme. A theme song was mandatory for every band, and if it was based on some classic such as Tchaikovsky's *First Piano Concerto* (Freddy Martin's "Tonight We Love," or Von Weber's *Invitation to the Dance* (Benny Goodman's "Let's Dance"), so much the better. The resemblance between the opening bars of "Artistry in Rhythm" and those of Romberg's "Softly, As in a Morning Sunrise" may have been coincidental but was never detrimental. The arrangements were based on the sound of the saxophone section, and the saxophone section was based on the sound of Jack Ordean, a fine alto player with whom Stanley had played in Hoaglund's band and many times thereafter. Every week Stanley would drive down the mountain to deliver a batch of arrangements to Bob Gioga, another old friend and a saxophone player, who would copy the individual parts from Stanley's master score.

The tiny mountain town in which Stanley and Violet's cabin was situated was called Idyllwild; but in their cabin, all was far from idyllic. For one thing, they were practically starving, living on their meager savings and eighteen dollars a week unemployment. Their relationship was also suffering from a severe case of malnutrition. Stanley truly loved his wife, but the constant exposure to The Most Beautiful Girls in the World had undone him, and he had fallen in love with a tall, stunning and bewitching showgirl. But Stanley was no gay deceiver. Filled with guilt and confusion, he confessed to a not wholly surprised Violet. His timing could hardly have been worse. After five years of marriage, Violet had just become pregnant.

"He was very honest about his feelings for this girl, and he told me he felt we shouldn't have this child, that I should have an abortion. So I said, 'Well, you go on your way, but I'm gonna have this child.' But he didn't."

They moved back to Los Angeles, determined to make a success of both band and marriage. With Ordean, Bob Gioga, drummer Pee Wee George and ten additional sidemen, Stanley formed a rehearsal band. (Unemployed musicians willingly played in such bands for nothing; none could individually afford a rehearsal hall, and if they practiced in their apartments, even with muted horns, they risked eviction.)

From the beginning, it had been Stanley's idea to have somebody else front the band, with his contribution limited to writing the music and playing piano. Initially, he led the band only until such time as he could find a more qualified leader—one with good looks, personality and glamour. For months, they rehearsed two or three times a week, with the personnel constantly changing depending on who was available. Stanley continued to revise, polish and experiment with different techniques to make the band sound bigger, fuller, more powerful. Squeezed into the tiny back room of a record store that doubled as a recording studio, they cut six "dubs," demonstration records with which Stanley hoped to persuade booking agencies to find them work. It was a frustrating, frenetic, hurry-up-and-wait period. He would rush over to MCA or GAC or another of the half-dozen agencies in town that handled bands with his latest dub and most winning sales pitch, only to be told, "You'll have to leave the record with us for a few days before we can make a decision." Sometimes months would go by before they would give him a definite answer. Invariably, it was no.

Although in that year of 1940 each issue of *Downbeat* listed an average of eight hundred ballrooms, theaters, hotels and other facilities across the country that engaged name, seminame and local bands, the competition was fierce, and Stanley was unable to find enough work to keep his personnel stable. Bill Leahy, a vital member of the saxophone section, left to join Johnny "Scat" Davis's band on the road. "I had no confidence at all in our chances," says Leahy. "It was like bringing out a miracle that we'd even be considered! I hated to leave, but I had to make a living!"

Still, the majority agreed with trombonist Harry Forbes, who felt that "Stan imbued everybody else with his enthusiasm. The first couple of jobs I had with him, I had the feeling that if I never got paid, what a wonderful thing just to have done it!" Only Violet knew the blackness of Stanley's moods when, after having been left to cool his heels all afternoon in some agent's waiting room, he would ask her, bewildered, "Why won't they just *listen?*" and talk about junking it all and getting a studio job. But Violet continued to argue that nothing was impossible, and now her morale-building efforts were reinforced by the members of the band. Early in 1941, after months of beating his head against a wall of indifference at the agencies, he set out to line up his own jobs. Through sheer persistence, he persuaded the owner of a ballroom in Huntington Beach to engage the band for one Saturday night. It was their first public performance, and they were well received by an audience that hadn't known who would be playing that night, but dug it just the same.

Their next job was at the Diana Ballroom in Los Angeles, where a hip young crowd felt it had "discovered" an exciting new band. Word of that success reached Bob Murphy, the proprietor of another ballroom. Murphy hastily arranged to audition this unknown band that seemed to show promise and could be had for considerably less money than the "names" he usually booked.

Quicker than Violet could say, "Nothing is impossible," Stanley Kenton and His Orchestra were booked into the Rendezvous Ballroom for the summer of '41.

5 Balboa

*"We were wired, that first summer at Balboa. We were
glued in. We all had houses or apartments down there; my
wife and I lived within sixty yards of the ballroom for
thirty-six dollars a month. I was so wrapped up in the music,
I didn't even know I was married! We used to follow Stan
around. He was like a god to us!"*

HOWARD RUMSEY, *bassist*

NEVER again in America would there be a summer like '41.
It was a bright, innocent, halcyon summer of cheerful self-
centeredness, especially if you were young. The ridiculous
German paperhanger was considered laughable, if he was
considered at all. *"Deutschland Uber Alles"* didn't have a beat,
and Japan was as remote as Mars. The important thing was
to have a date on Saturday night, to catch the local appearance
of Goodman or Dorsey or Miller or Thornhill or Lunceford or
Ellington or Shaw or James or Basie or Herman or Krupa or
Barnet or Martin or McIntyre—or Lombardo, or Sammy Kaye.
Nowhere was this more true than on Balboa, a convenient,
sunny playpen for the thousands of exuberant high school and
college students who invaded the tiny peninsula and island
every spring vacation, known as Bal Week, and all summer
long. Simply being there induced a glorious natural high, compounded by record-breaking beer consumption. Balboa was a

Utopian blend of sand, sea, sun, sex and swing—a fantasy realized. And the Rendezvous was the hub of it all.

The band opened on June 6 and was an instantaneous success—the right band in the right place at the right time. Trumpeter Chico Alvarez recalls that "Every time Stan would lift those long arms and give the downbeat and we got into the first strains of 'Artistry,' the audience's mouth would drop open and their eyes would pop out. There was nothing to match that first musical thrill. You felt you could reach out and touch that sound."

Every member of the band believed fiercely in what he was doing. They all played over their heads, better than they had dreamed they could play. Their excitement was contagious, the raw energy of the music irresistible. It was characterized by its sharp, offbeat syncopation, improvised solos and frequent, frantic, screaming brass fanfares. Everything was played as though they were fighting the Battle of Jericho. There were no shadings or subtleties; all stops were out, all the time. The three trumpets functioned as an alternate rhythm section, while the five saxophones and two trombones played riffs and rhythmic phrases. The result was a vibrant, driving sound that demanded GOD DAMN IT, NOTICE ME!

Stanley's exertions on the stand were frenzied; arms swooping, hands jabbing, sometimes leaping into the air and yelling like a cheerleader, perspiring profusely and gasping for breath when he had to make an announcement, he used every means short of a whip to exact more sound, more power, more abandon. "What Toscanini does with his head in conducting," wrote reviewer Del Bodey, "Kenton does with his whole body. He's a show in himself." One customer who stood incautiously close to the bandstand was knocked cold one night when Stanley's downbeat hit him on the head. He redoubled his efforts to find a more capable leader after Al Jarvis, an influential local disc jockey and promoter of bands, told him bluntly, "I haven't seen the band yet, but I've talked to a lot of people who have, and they tell me you're very awkward and you don't seem to know what to do. And besides that, you perspire too much. I think you'd better find somebody to front the band."

"Christ," Stanley replied miserably, "I can't *find* anybody, and until I do, I guess I'll just have to keep doin' it myself!" Thirty years later, a fan still remembers him "half-standing, half-crouching at the piano, flailing wildly with his arms as he and that band seemed to be reaching for some chord, some sound that was forever beyond their grasp."

The Rendezvous was typical of the hundreds of beach-front ballrooms built during the twenties. The rectangular building occupied half a city block and easily accommodated three thousand people. From the bandstand, the musicians had a clear view of three distinct groups: the dancers, who all did an identical little shuffle step called The Balboa, as though staged by a choreographer; the watchers, who gathered around the stage as though mesmerized; and the no less avid but possibly claustrophobic watchers in the balcony. Night after night, the place was packed. On a Monday morning after a holiday weekend, the management had to haul the receipts to the bank in gunnysacks.

Once the Balboa engagement had been set, Stanley had been able to stabilize his personnel. He had selected young, unknown players he felt were receptive to new ideas, in preference to established (and higher priced) "names." Except for drummer Pee Wee George and saxophonist Bob Gioga, every member of the band was under twenty-one.

The rhythm section consisted of Stanley, Pee Wee, guitarist Al Costi and bassist Howard Rumsey, a skinny, naive country kid who had played in Vido Musso's ill-fated band. Rumsey attacked his then-unorthodox electric bass with such convulsive ferocity that he was dubbed The Flying Spider. The saxophonists were Gioga, Bill Leahy, Ted Romersa, Red Dorris and

Jack Ordean. Ordean's alto had a haunting, chilling, penetrating sound, and he played with an impeccable natural beat. On the stand, Ordean was all business, demanding, "Get with it, man! Throw some more effort in there!" of anyone he suspected of loafing. Off the stand, he was a proficient juicer with a peculiar taste for warm ale. He kept a supply of the stuff on the windowsill of his room and drank it for breakfast, along with a Benzedrine tablet. Then he would lie on the beach all day drinking whiskey. He initiated his roommate, Chico Alvarez, into this routine, but Chico literally hadn't the stomach for it and wound up with an ulcer at the age of twenty-one.

Bob Gioga was a tenor player who filled in on baritone one day when nobody showed up to play that instrument, and remained a baritone player from then on. He was Stanley's anchor man—reliable, energetic, always on hand with his little Singer automobile when somebody needed transportation.

Bill Leahy's experience belied his years; he had been playing professionally since he was twelve. On tour with Scat Davis in the Midwest, he had listened longingly to radio broadcasts from the Rendezvous. "I felt bad about having left, because the band was sounding so great. I was dyin' to be back with it. Then Stan called me up and asked me to come back, so I got to Balboa before the summer ended."

Red Dorris had been playing in a little Santa Ana nightclub with Pee Wee George and Chico Alvarez one night when Stanley walked in and hired all three of them. Red looked like a young athlete and was known for his way with the tenor saxophone, the jazz clarinet and the ladies. He also sang ballads and novelty numbers in a mellow, Herb Jeffries voice, alternating with the several female vocalists they tried out. Stanley finally settled on Kay Gregory, a competent enough blonde, whose most memorable number was "Hawaiian War Chant." Often, it would be the *only* number she would sing all night; Stanley was so busy keeping the band playing at top pitch, he would forget to play any vocal numbers, leaving Kay to sit like a wallflower beside the piano.

Ted Romersa and trombonist Harry Forbes had their wives and children with them for the summer, thus eliminating themselves from extracurricular activities. But the other members of the group were inveterate ballers; "We never close" was their motto.

Trumpeter Frankie Beach was, at seventeen, the youngest member of the band. He and fellow trumpeters Earl Collier and Chico Alvarez, a cigar maker's son just a year older than Frankie, had studied the new nonpressure system of blowing, which enabled them to play up in the high register all night long without injuring their "chops."

Everyone in the band was an instant celebrity on the island, with fans trailing him day and night. On some afternoons they would hustle up business for the night's dance by marching around the little town playing their instruments. Every Saturday afternoon they would walk the short distance from beach to ballroom to broadcast, on the Mutual Network, "The Balboa Bandwagon—coming to you from the Rendezvous Ballroom on the shores of the blue Pacific with dancing America's next king, California's gift to modern dance music, Stanley Kenton and His Orchestra." In the heat of the afternoon, most of the band and the audience wore bathing suits.

Stanley had no time for the fun and games of his musicians. He worked like a man possessed. Howard Rumsey remembers, "We'd walk by the ballroom at two A.M., coming back from the Bamboo Room, carrying our instruments, and there Stan would be—composing and writing out a chart, and not a soul in the place. The whole ballroom all dark, with just a piano light. And you could hear him playin' in there, and see that little white light."

With almost inhuman energy, Stanley was attempting to

61

function simultaneously as leader, pianist, composer, arranger, copyist, booking agent, manager, husband and father—in approximately that order. His daughter Leslie had arrived two weeks after the Rendezvous opening. In addition, there was the harrowing task of borrowing from Peter to pay Paul. The band was making union scale, but no allowance had been made for a vocalist. And a vocalist, even if only for window dressing, was standard equipment for a dance band. Consequently, Stanley's thirty-five dollars a week went to pay Kay Gregory, all summer long.

He and Violet were heavily in debt to the local radio station that fed the network, as well as to their landlord, who finally evicted them from their apartment. They moved into the converted garage of Violet's parents, in Long Beach. When Leslie was born, Stanley was forced to borrow forty dollars from the musicians union. It was a humiliating, "hell of a wrangle. I had to go before the Board and tell 'em what I wanted the money for, to get my wife into the hospital, so Leslie could be born."

They survived only through the generosity of Violet's mother and stepfather Pat, who each morning thoughtfully filled the tank of Stanley's old car with gas from the refinery where Pat worked nights. With an infant to attend to, Violet rarely got to Balboa, but would wait up for Stanley until the early morning hours. Sometimes he would arrive home with Clinton Romer, a young ticket taker from the ballroom, in tow. Clinton was an aspiring copyist. He and Stanley would sit all night at the dining room table, copying and writing arrangements in preparation for the band's first recording sessions for Decca. At dawn, Stanley would retire to his bed and Clinton to the couch, arising three or four hours later to rush off to a rehearsal.

Money was a constant worry. One of Stanley's first actions after forming the band had been to seek out potential financial backers—standard procedure for a fledgling band. All his efforts failed dismally, including a somewhat surreal meeting with Julie Colt, the Colt gun heiress, whom Stanley had heard was desirous of helping a band get started. She had summoned him to her sumptuous apartment and, after letting him in the door, sprawled on the plush carpet while he played his demonstration records and surreptitiously checked out his surroundings.

"There were horses everywhere. Pictures of horses, statues of horses, lamps shaded like horses. After she'd heard the records, she said she'd like very much to become a part of it. I said, 'How do you think you could become a part of it?' She said, 'Well, I sing.' I told her I had heard that she did. She said, 'I wouldn't clutter up the stage or anything, I'd just like to come out a couple times a night, you'd introduce me, Julie Colt, and I'd sing a few tunes.' I said I didn't think that was too much to ask. But then she said, 'I'll buy all the uniforms, but I'd like the fellows to have a horse on their coat. And I'd like the music racks to be horses' heads. . . .' I listened to that crap as long as I could, then I just walked out."

He consulted with Gus Arnheim, who gave him perhaps the best advice of his life. "Never take money from anybody," said Arnheim, "even if it means you have to write your own music and copy it and make your own uniforms. You don't own yourself, and you have to answer to a lot of people. It just lets you in for a lot of trouble."

Arnheim's warning proved invaluable when word got around about the exciting new band at the Rendezvous. Booking agents who only recently had exiled Stanley like an ugly duckling to the wastelands of their waiting rooms suddenly saw him as a goose harboring a possibly golden egg. GAC (General Artists Corporation) zeroed in on him with heady promises and heavy rhetoric. With one corporate hand, they dangled before him the country's most desirable bookings; with the other, they reached for 50 percent of the band.

Stanley held out for a contract that would assure his retaining financial control of the band, and eventually such an agreement was negotiated and signed. But far from abandoning their avaricious objectives, GAC simply switched their tactics. Their strategy was classic: starve him out.

When the Rendezvous season ended in September, the musicians were broke but in high gear, eager to get to their next job. For two weeks, the agency stalled and made excuses. Finally, they told Stanley the band was booked into Jantzen Beach, Oregon. Could GAC advance some money for transportation, he inquired? Sure, if he would care to renegotiate his contract. No? In that case, how he got his band the twelve hundred miles up to Jantzen Beach was *his* problem.

Undeterred, Stanley borrowed three hundred dollars from a sympathetic sound engineer and bought an aging eight-passenger Buick, complete with jump seats, and a two-wheel trailer, the latter intended for instruments and luggage. Those who couldn't squeeze into the Buick traveled in the antiquated jalopies of a couple of the musicians and, caravan-style, they headed north. After countless blowouts, they arrived at the amusement park known as Jantzen Beach just in time to set up in the ballroom and play for a receptive Friday night crowd. They were a hit that night, and the following night as well. On Sunday, their GAC man showed up. "You're doin' just great, fellas," he assured them, "and you'll be playing here again next weekend." "Terrific," said Stanley, "but what are we going to do during the week?" The GAC man shrugged. (Later, Stanley was to learn that his booking agency had been turning down job offers practically since the day they signed him; the less money the band made, they figured, the better their chances for a piece of that golden egg. If challenged, they had an inexhaustible supply of excuses, and Stanley was too busy to trouble himself with the details of booking. After all, that was what he was paying GAC its 10 percent for!)

The band moved into the cheapest rooming house they could find, and spent the next four weeks rehearsing, playing football and eating peanut butter and crackers, playing only on weekends and an occasional one-nighter in the area. In November, they headed back to Los Angeles, playing a one-nighter near Oroville, in northern California, en route. Howard Rumsey remembers that after driving through wilderness all day long, "all of a sudden this ancient building materializes out of nowhere, just sitting in this flat space with nothing, *nothing* else in sight. And the signs says COCOANUT GROVE! The place looked as though nothing had been touched since the last band left, maybe twenty years before—chairs turned upside down, just a shambles. Ghost City! We set up at nine o'clock, figuring that if anybody showed up at all it would just be some miners with their burros. But by nine-thirty, there were at least eight hundred people there—and they kept coming! It turned out that the band played as good that night as I can ever remember—we all went away completely content and satisfied, feeling we had just played one of the most important engagements of our lives!"

The most important engagement of their lives was, in fact, exactly three weeks away.

6 Changes

*"When I left the Earl Carroll Theater, the guy who was my
boss said, 'You're out of your head to start a band!' And I
said, 'Well, I've gotta do it.' And he said, 'Well, I'll hire
a substitute for a year, and you can come back.' And just a
little over a year later, we were playing across the street,
at the Palladium."*

WHAT Broadway's Palace was to vaudeville, the Hollywood Palladium was to big bands. Its opening, in the fall of
1940, was one of the most publicized events of the year. Built
at an unprecedented cost of over a million dollars, located
on Radio Row between CBS and NBC, patronized by movie
stars, publicized by columnists, it was generally conceded to
be the classiest, swankiest, most glamorous ballroom in the
country.

The Palladium had no corners. The dance floor, the bandstand, the tables, the terraced balconies, the constant movement of the colored lights, all were curved, variegated arcs in
a prepsychedelic rainbow. The sound, lighting and ventilation
systems were superb. The dressing rooms were clean. The
clientele was well dressed and well mannered. Every night
the music was broadcast coast to coast. The Palladium was
unmistakably Uptown, and only the top name bands appeared
there.

During its two weeks of GAC-enforced inactivity between Balboa and Jantzen Beach, the Kenton band had played one Saturday night at nearby Glendale Civic Auditorium. It had been a wild, chaotic mob scene, with the auditorium jammed beyond its two thousand capacity and nearly twice that number lined up around the block. Witnessing this phenomenal turnout for a new and relatively unknown band, Maurie Cohen was impressed. Maurie Cohen had been lured to the concert by GAC. Maurie Cohen owned the Palladium.

The strident sound of the music was not to Cohen's liking; but where Cohen's personal taste conflicted with Cohen's business sense, it was no contest. On the spot, he booked them into his ballroom for a five-week engagement. They opened on November 25, 1941.*

Thanks largely to the loyal Rendezvous fans, they drew record-breaking crowds. People swarmed around the bandstand requesting "Two Guitars," "Arkansas Traveler," "Eager Beaver" and the freewheeling novelty arrangement of "St. James Infirmary" that featured Stan himself on the vocal. ("Am I a Stan or a Stanley?" he had seriously been asking himself and others. On the Palladium's marquee, he publicly became Stan—but privately he was and remains Stanley.) Those who preferred to dance would stake out a two-foot square on the dance floor level, where they would revolve until exhaustion or the call of nature removed them from the crush. Never had they seen a band work so hard. At the end of each set, the musicians were wringing wet; the sleeves of Pee Wee George's coat shrank so much just from perspiration that he could barely bend his elbows. Stan played with such force that strings

---

* At the same Glendale Civic Auditorium concert, Stanley also had the satisfaction of receiving an apology from Al Jarvis for having questioned his leadership ability. "Forget everything I said," Jarvis implored. "You are absolutely dynamic fronting the band. Don't ever doubt yourself. Just keep going straight ahead."

would pop inside the piano. When the piano bench collapsed underneath him one night, he just jumped up and started conducting as though nothing had happened. He began consciously to develop his showmanship, experimenting in ways that led one critic to remark that Stan Kenton did everything on the stand except sell peanuts. He began to feel more secure as a leader than he ever had felt as a pianist, and even went so far as to hire an excellent pianist, Ted Repay, so that he could turn all his attention to conducting.

Then came December 7.

HOWARD RUMSEY: "We had had a big Saturday night; we had all gone home feeling real excited, happy, tired. I woke up Sunday and heard the newscast that Pearl Harbor had been attacked, and I felt that somebody had pulled the ladder to success right out from under me, just as I was reaching for the top rung. I took it as a personal affront."

CHICO ALVAREZ: "When we went to work that night, the whole town was blacked out. They had put blackout curtains up in the ballroom. We played, but there were hardly any people. I remember three: Bullets Durgom, Tommy Dorsey and Lana Turner. They were dancing, getting drunk and having fun. They both danced with Lana."

JACK ORDEAN: "I think I got married that day."

Marriage, war and acts of God all paled into insignificance beside their total absorption in the music and the future of the band. Ironically, those first few days of the war launched them into national prominence. People were glued to their radios around the clock, and while they waited for the latest bulletin on the war, the networks filled in the time after normal broadcasting hours with remote hookups from ballrooms around the country. Since the Palladium was in the last time belt, the Kenton band was the only one still playing when New York and Chicago had signed off for the night. In the general pandemonium that followed Pearl Harbor, there were times when

Stan Kenton's music was being aired simultaneously over all three networks!

The prestige of playing the Palladium greatly exceeded the monetary rewards. Cohen was no philanthropist giving a worthy new band a chance to be heard. He was a shrewd, hardheaded businessman and, as such, signed Stan to an iron-clad five-year contract that provided minimum union scale for fifteen men. Stan had no way of foreseeing that during the next five years he would add three trombones, two trumpets, band boys to set up, and salaried, staff arrangers. Cohen also retained the option of booking the band into the Palladium twice a year on a month's notice, which meant that if the band happened to be in the East, Stan had to come up with the cost of transportation. So that for the duration of that contract, every appearance at the Palladium cost Stan up to three thousand dollars a week.

It was becoming glaringly evident that Stan needed a personal manager—someone he trusted, who could protect him from profiteering vultures, interpret microscopic contractual print, advise him as to the desirability of the various offers that trickled in through GAC, and generally look out for his interests in the jungle of club owners, operators, press agents, music publishers, song pluggers and professional hangers-on. Nobody was better qualified for the job than Carlos Gastel.

Born in Honduras of German parents, Carlos was a suave charmer of overwhelming persuasive powers, unmatched gregariousness, and a vast capacity for food and drink. Carlos had two obsessions. One was alcohol, the probable cause of the perspiration that constantly drenched him, in summer and winter, at times even spurting around him, creating a misty halo. The other was music. He had no talent for creating or performing it, but he had a natural genius for promoting it, which he did with such brilliance that the careers of Peggy Lee, Nat Cole, Mel Torme, June Christy and Nellie Lutcher were largely products of his management. But that was later. Carlos's first big success was Stan Kenton.

When Stan first met The Happy Honduran, as Bing Crosby called him, Carlos was sleeping on the couch in Vido Musso's living room (a promotional feat in itself, in view of Vido's wife, child and tiny three-room apartment), and attempting to promote jobs for Vido's band. Whenever Carlos managed to line up a one-nighter, he would advertise it with an enormous sign reading VIDO MUSSO, LAST CHANCE BEFORE HE GOES EAST WITH HIS BIG BAND. Prior to this time, he had somehow persuaded former heavyweight champion Max Baer that his good looks, imposing stature and national reputation qualified him to lead a band. Carlos got some musicians together, had one of them teach Baer how to wave a baton without falling off the stand, and booked Max Baer and His Livermore Playboys into a few clubs. Carlos's assumption that the fighter's name would draw proved correct. What he failed to consider was the fact that word of how the music sounded would, inevitably, get around. When it did, Max Baer's short, happy career as a bandleader ended abruptly.

The next milestone in Carlos's career was the promotion of an appearance by the popular Jimmie Lunceford band at Los Angeles's Shrine Auditorium. Owing to Carlos's strenuous efforts, the concert was heavily oversold; a riot ensued, from which Carlos barely escaped with his skin—and several apple crates full of money.

His next client was Sonny Dunham, a high-note trumpet player who, after making a name for himself with Glen Gray and the Casa Loma Orchestra, formed a Lunceford-style band of his own in 1940. Playing sporadic dates on the East Coast, Dunham's income always fell a little short of his payroll—a situation Carlos remedied by means of an ingenious book-keeping system known as kiting checks. In those days,

Carlos paid the band in New York with checks drawn on an empty California bank account, having figured out exactly how many days' leeway he had in which to wire the money to cover them. He even managed to enlist the cooperation of an employee of the bank, who when necessary actually held the checks until the money arrived!

One day late in the summer of 1942, Carlos appeared in the office of Dave Dexter, a writer for *Downbeat* magazine. At that time *Downbeat* was a wild tabloid, filled with sensational stories, lurid headlines and pictures of seminude chorus girls. Every musician read it. "Dex," he announced momentously, "I've got a new band out on the Coast that's better than Sonny Dunham! It's better than anything! You've gotta come out and hear 'em!"

"Sure," Dexter promised, "next time I'm on the Coast."

"No," said Carlos, "I mean right now!"

When Carlos had a specific goal in mind, he hurtled toward it like a freight train. Three nights later, after a hairraising cross-country ride in Carlos's Cadillac convertible (Carlos insisted on stopping every hour, day and night, for a "blast," and miraculously turned the car over only once in the three thousand miles), they were at the Rendezvous. After Dexter returned to New York (via train), every issue of *Downbeat* mentioned the new California band with a ready-made angle: controversy. It seemed that for every avid new Kenton fan, there was at least one equally avid detractor. The main criticism was that the band didn't swing as freely as, say, Lunceford's, or Basie's. Reviewing a broadcast from Balboa, critic Barry Ulanov had compared the sound to "a moving-man grunting under the weight of a concert grand." *Metronome*'s George Frazier hated the band, called it "neither fish nor flesh, but pretty foul. It seems to me pretentious," Frazier wrote pretentiously, "artistically phony, and without any attributes that might even charitably be called jazz. The band plays too loud, it has no exciting soloists, its intonation is deficient, it lacks light and shade, and it never, never relaxes. By all rights it should be ready for the ash can. But it isn't. It's going to be the Glenn Miller or the Jimmy Dorsey of next year or the year after that. It's going to be the Whiteman of the 40's (but no Beiderbecke up there in the brass section to blow lovely stuff). It's going to be terrific. I sort of wish it wasn't." It made for good copy.

By the time the band closed at the Palladium, Carlos had booked them into New York's Roseland Ballroom. It was definitely a coup. Roseland, like the Palladium, booked only established bands—and while Kenton was beginning to be talked about, he was a long way from being established.

It was an optimistic little group that set out from the Greyhound bus station in Hollywood one foggy night in January of 1942, in search of fame, fortune and adventure. A group of about fifty loyal fans, stalwart song pluggers and well-wishing relatives went down to see them off. Into the bus Stan had hired, with its motor in front and spare tire stuck on the back like a bustle, clambered an amazing assortment of musicians, wives, children and pets. Everyone but Beach (The Kid), Dorris (The Swinger), Collier and trombonist Dick Cole was married, and Stan felt the men would be happier (and, therefore, play better) if their wives were with them. Violet even left Leslie with her mother in order to make the trip. Frankie Beach's parents were at the station, imploring Stan to take care of their boy on the road. Harry Forbes, Ted Romersa and Pee Wee George all had children with them, and Jack Ordean's new bride carried her kitten in a little basket, like Dorothy and Toto in Oz. Stan had no objection to the excess people or paraphernalia; he thought only of getting the band to its destination. Had all else failed, he undoubtedly would have teleported the entire entourage to Roseland by the sheer force of his will.

They worked their way across the country playing one-nighters. Overzealousness landed them in Las Vegas a day ahead of their scheduled job there, giving them twenty-four hours in which to be beaten by the odds and reproached by their wives. By the time they reached New York, a number of the couples were speaking only through intermediaries. Dorris and Ordean had been drunk in the back of the bus for days, and Ted Romersa's kids had the chicken pox. It was, recalls Pee Wee George, like one big unhappy family.

Their spirits revived, however, when they played a fraternity house at Cornell University, in what seemed to the young Westerners exotic surroundings: Gothic architecture, and snow. It was such a rare evening that Jack Ordean can recall with remarkable clarity, thirty years later, how "It seemed like from the first note we hit, the harmony was so great, so strong, that the rafters shook. I expected the whole place to fall down. There were kids all over the place—the stairs, the hallways, and right at our feet. It was a sensation you only come by a few times in your life; you're playing, but it's *effortless*. It is just happening. You used to hear people talk about getting in the groove, but most people really don't know what that's about. But that was it. Beautiful."

Two nights later, they opened at Roseland. It was an unmitigated, humiliating, ego-shattering disaster.

The publicity that had preceded them had been greatly exaggerated, promising more than any relatively inexperienced band could possibly deliver. When they walked into the ballroom on opening night, the first thing they saw was a sign that covered the entire length of the enormous ballroom. It said, FRED ASTAIRE SAYS HE'S TERRIFIC! A capacity crowd turned out to hear them—music publishers, bandleaders, musicians, critics—everyone wanted to witness the first New York appearance of the new band said to have created such a sensation on the West Coast. What they witnessed was the laying of a colossal egg. And it wasn't golden.

The fiasco was basically a result of unwise booking. Roseland was a glorified dime-a-dance ballroom where patrons came to dance rhumbas and the "Businessman's Bounce" with hostesses who sat in a semicircle behind velvet ropes that were dropped to signal the start of the evening's festivities ("Unchain 'em!" Earl Collier would shout from the bandstand). When Stan's brass blared out at them, the dancers froze. They hadn't yet learned to jitterbug, so the tempos were too fast for them to dance to, and the volume was too loud for them to talk with the hostesses.

BILL LEAHY: "We might as well of been workin' the Cinderella Roof, with a bunch of ribbon clerks and shoe clerks! All they wanted was a tango! What a place to book a band that's got somethin' to say!"

HOWARD RUMSEY: "Dolly Dawn and Her Dawn Patrol Boys was the intermission band, and they sounded so good to us, they frightened us! Even Stan was nervous! The bandstand wasn't big enough for him to be in front of the band, and he was tryin' to decide whether to put a box down on the floor of the ballroom or work from the side, which is what he finally had to do. Out of fright and nervousness, the band started to stutter. The dancers seemed to be saying, 'Dig us! We're the best dancers in the world!' And the band seemed to be saying, 'Dig us! We're from California and we're the greatest!' Earl Collier and Jack Ordean started changing their parts around, and I found myself putting in extra notes. We all just fell apart!"

BOB GIOGA: "One guy came up, a New York Latin type with a pencil-thin twirled moustache, and asked for 'La Cumparsita.' He wanted it in the traditional, soft, Latin, New York society style. It was one of the heaviest pieces in our whole book! So I said, 'Yeah, we're gonna play it this set! The first number, in fact!' He was standing right in front of us, and it blew him back about four steps! He looked at us as though we had crucified his beautiful piece of music!"

74

CHICO ALVAREZ: "When we would play after Dolly Dawn finished, everyone would walk off the floor! They just weren't the kind of people who would listen to our music."

Before the evening was over, the management gave Stan his notice—the ultimate humiliation for an artist. Instead of the eight weeks contracted for, they would remain only until a replacement could be found. Stan and Carlos and Dave Dexter were the last people to leave the ballroom that night. They walked down the steps of Roseland into bitter cold, well below zero.

DAVE DEXTER: "Stan and I were huddling in our overcoats and blowing on our hands, waiting for a cab to take us back to the Pennsylvania Hotel. It was three o'clock in the morning. We stood there on Broadway with despair all over us, 'cause we knew we'd just died in there. It was so frigid, air was coming out of our mouths in big enveloping clouds. And Carlos stood there with sweat just *popping* from his face, undoing his tie and his shirt. But even then, as depressed as Stan was, he said he was more determined than ever to keep the band going."

There followed a series of marginal bookings, with money so scarce that instead of paying the musicians weekly, Stan doled out five-dollar bills whenever he had them. Nobody complained, even when the payment was accompanied by a fatherly, "What'd you do with the five dollars I gave you *last* night?" Raised holy hell, was what. As soon as their last show ended at 12, 1 or 2 A.M., most of them would break out the booze and/or grass; Jack Ordean would have a Benzedrine tablet for breakfast and start all over again. In their behalf, it must be said that some of the places they played required some fuzzing around the edges. At a theater in New England, they shared the bill with Sharky the Seal; at the Flatbush Theater, with Wee Bonnie Baker, whose "Oh, Johnny!" was dated even then. The stage of the Flatbush had been unused for so long that when an ancient Irish clog dancer came on as the opening act, clouds of dust rose from the cracks in the floor and enveloped him. This unfortunate ex-vaudevillian doubled as emcee and, with four shows a night, managed never to introduce Stan the same (or correct) way twice. "Here he is," he'd announce, "Cant Standit"—or Sam Felton, or Stan Newton, or Kent Standing—"and His Orchestra!" At another theater, the extra added attraction was the Duncan Sisters, making their umpteenth comeback. Part of their act involved their throwing doughnuts to the audience; on some nights, the audience threw them back.

Carlos arranged for GAC to book them into the Shribman circuit, a string of New England ballrooms. Money and morale were dwindling, the war was becoming increasingly difficult to ignore, and Stan's certainty about the music grew wobbly. He began to experiment, playing more pop tunes and fewer of his own compositions, trying to please everyone, with the predictable result. Critic George Frazier called him the poor man's Paul Whiteman. "The Kenton band," wrote Frazier, "has everything . . . singers and soloists and pretentious arrangements. But I don't like it. To me, it's terrific in a revolting way."

For all its excitement, the music was heavy and ponderous. They were trying too hard—and the more Stan tinkered with the arrangements, the less satisfying they seemed. He was undergoing a kind of musical identity crisis, along with a financial crisis that was more critical than ever. Carlos turned up in Dave Dexter's office one night, perspiring and nervous. "Stan can't meet the payroll," he explained. "He's in terrible trouble." Stan and Violet had long since hocked everything they owned, and Carlos's mother had even hocked her new dining room set and sent him the money, but it wasn't enough to keep them going. Dexter made sixty dollars a week, but he had eight hundred dollars in a savings account. The next morning, he loaned Carlos his entire savings; thirty days later, the band was playing Frank Dailey's famed Meadowbrook in New Jersey, and the loan was repaid.

Their eight weeks at the Meadowbrook were a qualified success. Dailey liked the music, but found it "too loud"—by now a familiar complaint. After each small step forward, like the Meadowbrook, they seemed destined to take three-quarters of a step backward. By August, Stanley thought they were finished. He wanted to borrow money to get the men and their wives back to California, but his collateral was exhausted. While the men traveled from one dismal one-nighter to the next, the wives were stranded in Baltimore, with no money. Three of them got jobs making malts at a carnival, in order to eat. There were times when Stan didn't know how he would pay for the gas to get the bus to the next town. But whenever prospects looked bleakest, there would be an eleventh-hour rescue from some unexpected source. Trombonist Harry Forbes, who wore a money belt and had a reputation for stinginess in both his playing and his personal habits, was moved to offer an unsecured loan; Stan kept the offer in reserve, as a last resort.

Late in August, during a nerve-jangling heat wave, they opened at the Summit Ballroom in Baltimore, billed as "The First Band with a Sound All Its Own Since Glenn Miller!" Everyone was feeling the pressures of monetary and marital strains. Musically, they felt they were running in place—with their respective draft boards breathing down their necks. Tempers were short, and some of the more uninhibited revelers began bending Stan's fundamental rule: no juicing on the job and no dope, not even marijuana, at *any* time. Stan had no intention of jeopardizing the band's future with any sensational headlines of a bust in the ranks, and the musicians were all on notice that any infraction of that rule would mean instant dismissal. When Stan came upon a group of his musicians one afternoon, thoroughly juiced, in the kitchen of the board-inghouse where they were staying, he exploded. "This drinking has gotten 'way out of hand!" he raged. "No more drinking if you want to play in my band! The next guy that takes a drink is *fired*!" In the stunned silence that followed, Pee Wee George looked up at Stan, then down at the bottle in front of him, and poured himself a shot of whiskey. "Here's to you, Stan," said Pee Wee, downing the whiskey—and passing out cold at Stan's feet.

Pee Wee kept his job, but not for long. It was a difficult band for a drummer; the intense beat that was required to keep the music from sinking into its own heaviness demanded enormous expenditures of energy each night. It was Pee Wee's responsibility to "keep 'em movin', shove 'em along," and the strenuous physical challenge was compounded by constant dissension in the rhythm section. Howard Rumsey was forever turning up the volume on the amplifier for his electric bass, and guitarist Al Costi was forever turning it down. More serious was the fact that Howard heard the sound of a different drummer than Pee Wee George. Pee Wee was always a little on top of the beat, and Rumsey a shade behind. By the time they got to Baltimore, Rumsey's habit of keeping time—*his* time—with his heel had become a sore point with Pee Wee, who began complaining to Stan.

One night at the Summit, with the place packed with dancers, the band became conscious of a new sound, strangely like . . . amplified taps! In a way, it was. In a fit of perversity, Howard had had taps put on his shoes and put a piece of plywood under his feet; he was tapping the plywood so he wouldn't have to listen to Pee Wee's drums! "Take that piece of wood away," Stan repeatedly told him. "You're bothering the drummer!" But Howard played on dreamily with his eyes tightly shut, oblivious to any earthly admonitions. "Get with it, Howard," Stan warned, "or I'm going to throw you off the

78

bandstand!" Receiving no response, he marched over and snatched Rumsey's music from his stand, hurled it beneath the piano, picked the bewildered bass player up by his belt and the back of his collar and made good on his threat. "Take your bass out to the parking lot," he yelled. "I'll talk to you after the dance!" A thoroughly chagrined Rumsey proceeded to make his way through thousands of people, trying to manipulate his bass over his head without hitting the unusually low ceiling or the heads of the customers.

In the parking lot, Stan gave Rumsey bus fare back to Los Angeles and wished him luck. With Rumsey went the last vestige of the esprit de corps that had seemed so invincible at Balboa. No one had wanted to be the one to break up the original band. Once it was a fait accompli, there was almost a mass exodus. Ordean and Pee Wee were gone before they left Baltimore, the former having received his draft notice and Pee Wee so exhausted that he didn't care if he ever played again. Pee Wee firmly believed that, what with his shaky marriage and excessive boozing, the band would be better off without him and that Stan would be in a position to hire better musicians when he no longer felt obligated to carry anyone because of the "family thing." But Pee Wee and Stan had been together back in the Gus Arnheim days, when Stan had first begun to dream of someday having a band of his own. It was an emotional leave-taking—"like a bad marriage breaking up. Necessary, but painful."

By early 1943, all that remained of the original band were Red Dorris, Bob Gioga and Harry Forbes. Most of the departed members were in the service. And a popular catchphrase that had been echoing faintly around the periphery of Stan's consciousness for some time was suddenly ringing insistently in his ears: "Don't you know there's a war on?"

7 The War

All right, everybody, clear the way and let these brave marines through!"

BOB GIOGA, *in a thousand train stations*

THE basic problem confronting a dance band in wartime was one of supply and demand. Military bases, civilian defense workers and servicemen on leave clamored for entertainment, and were willing to pay generously for it. Hounded by draft boards and scorned by ration boards, Stan was hard put to fulfill the commitments that suddenly flooded in through Carlos and GAC. Tire and gas rationing made bus travel impossible, and train travel was little better. Sometimes the band would arrive on time to find that their library of music had been diverted to a later train. Sometimes they played with no rhythm section—just a few horns, and Stan at the piano. Obtaining hotel accommodations for the entire band all in the same city, let alone the same hotel, was a continual hassle.

The band became a revolving door through which new sidemen entered and left in bewildering profusion, as their draft numbers came up. Some were hopelessly inept and left even before their uniforms, now with cuffless "victory pants," were paid for. When that happened, it was road manager Gioga's task to persuade the *next* replacement to pay thirty-five dollars for a uniform that had cost the band forty-five dollars. "Why should I pay thirty-five dollars for a used uniform, when I can get a brand-new one for forty-five dollars?" the guy invariably asked.

"This one's right *here*, we'll just have the sleeves shortened and you can wear it tonight!" Gioga would explain.

"But it doesn't *fit* me, man! It's too big all over!" the guy would protest.

"You'll see," Gioga would promise, hustling the poor sideman in the direction of the nearest tailor shop, "from the front, nobody will be able to tell the difference!"

Card games became more ferocious with the addition of saxophonist Boots Mussuli and bassist Bob Kesterson, both gamblers of near-professional caliber. The only member of the band invulnerable to the draft was vocalist Dolly Mitchell, who had succeeded Terry Harlan and Eve Knight and Helen Greco, who had succeeded Kay Gregory—who, by the end of the Palladium engagement, had sewn peplums on her gowns to camouflage her advancing pregnancy. Of the three drummers and nine trumpeters who played with the band in 1943, only Buddy Childers remained in '44. In all, Buddy spent the better part of ten years with the band. It was his high school, college, fraternity, honeymoon, basic training, and nearly his undoing.

Buddy's mother had a habit of leaving him different places for indeterminate "visits." In 1942, he was staying with his grandmother in Bridgeport, Illinois, when he heard that the Kenton band was playing in nearby St. Louis. He had just turned sixteen.

CHICO ALVAREZ: "Playing the Tunetown Ballroom, this kid walks up in front of two thousand people, with a trumpet in his hand, and asks Stan can he sit in. Stan doesn't bat an eye—

81

okay, he says. Buddy asks for 'Lady Be Good,' and he starts playing. He had tons of enthusiasm and guts, but he didn't know one chord from another. But shortly afterwards Buddy joined the band. And a year later, he was playing first trumpet."

BOB GIOGA: "He stepped right in making the same money that everybody else was making—$125 a week. He'd order two breakfasts, and some of the guys who had families to support were half-starving. Buddy hadn't had to go through the school of hard knocks, so I think a lot of the guys figured they'd better give him a few. Oh, how they used to take his money in poker!"

STAN KENTON: "It's a wonder Buddy didn't destroy himself. He'd check into a hotel and to tip the bellhop, he'd just reach into his pocket and say, 'Here.' He didn't even know what he was handin' the guy."

Buddy never connected his extravagance with the treatment he received. He only knew that his dream of playing for Stan, whom he idolized, turned out to be a nightmare. "When I drove to St. Louis to hear the band, I was a super-hayseed Polack, right off the farm. Those guys had all been my idols—I just wouldn't believe they would do anything bad to me. I was so dumb, I played into everyone's hands. It got so I was afraid to fall asleep on the train, 'cause if I did, they'd come around and drop Anacin in my mouth. Ever taste Anacin after it's almost melted? Then to make sure that it worked, they'd get a straw and a cup and drop a few drops of water in my mouth to make sure it dissolved good.

"I bought some new shoes, the first good shoes I'd ever had in my life, in Canada. As soon as I fell asleep on the first train we were on, big fun—hotfoot! They took two books of matches and stuck 'em down in with the points down, and lit the other end. It exploded. I had blisters on my foot. They destroyed the shoes.

"Whatever I'd say or do, they'd make fun of it. If I'd wake up groggy and say, 'What'd you do, put a bennie in my mouth or something?' they'd just laugh at me. After three months of that, I was like a basket case. I couldn't play anymore. I was falling apart."

He lined up a job with another band, and gave Stan his notice. Stan hired a replacement. The day Buddy was to leave, he got a wire: "MAN DECIDED TO STAY. SORRY. REGARDS." Practically in tears, he showed it to Stan. "It's all right," Stan assured him, "you're staying."

"But Stan," Buddy reminded him, "you've already got somebody else!"

"So we've got five trumpets now."

The realization that there were other jobs available to him, even though that particular one had fallen through, somehow turned Buddy's attitude around. He not only stayed with Stan, he got his playing and his thinking under control. "I got so I could say 'Screw you' to those guys and just do my job."

Another sixteen-year-old player, saxophonist Stan Getz, was just as unpopular as Buddy—but for a different reason. Where Buddy was a dumb country boy, Getz was a smartass city boy on an intergalactic ego trip. On his third night with the band, Getz, sitting in the front row in the sax section, ostentatiously put his music stand behind him. "What's the idea?" asked Stan, noticing the obvious gap in the row of racks. "I don't need it," said Getz smugly. In two days, he had memorized all the music. "You might not need it," said Stan, irritated, "but we want a picture here in front. We don't want people looking at your shoes! Just put the music rack back where it belongs!"

Getz pouted—and practiced. He desperately wanted to play the tenor solos, but they were all assigned to Dave Matthews, one of the outstanding tenor men of the day, who would weave all sorts of creative little embellishments into his solos. After only six weeks, Getz was so impatient that he told Stan he was quitting "because I want to play solos."

"Dave is so good," Stan told him, "the studios want him to do scores for pictures. Just hold on."

Soon afterward, Matthews did leave for a studio job and Getz moved into the solo chair. The first night, he was even better than Matthews; he had memorized every note Matthews had played, and added an extra little brilliance of his own. But a jazz soloist is, by definition, an improviser, not a memorizer. Arrangers write only the chords for the solos, a frame inside which the player is free to extemporize. So that at the first rehearsal of some new charts, came time for the tenor solo and very little came out of Getz's horn. Still, the rest of the band cheered the ballsy little sixteen-year-old for his nerve.

The band played a succession of one-nighters in Indiana, Michigan, Wisconsin and Illinois, then up into New England and Canada. After the jobs in the smaller, cabless towns, they often had to walk ten or fifteen blocks to the railroad station after midnight, carrying their luggage and instruments, often in subzero temperatures. If the stationmaster had already swept out his station for the night, he was likely to lock the door when he saw them coming. They would wait on the platform in the piercing cold, spreading out in groups of two and three as the train approached. (If the engineer spotted just one big group, he might not even stop, but just slow down enough to yell, "We're too crowded!")

Boarding the train was no guarantee of getting a seat. The more adaptable musicians learned to sleep on their feet, or became adept at curling up in baggage racks. There always seemed to be at least one squalling child in the car, which prompted Bob Gioga to walk down the aisle announcing officiously, "There are no children allowed in this car. Please go to the following car."

In June of 1943, they returned to California to play four

weeks at the Palladium, followed by their first theater date: The Orpheum, in Los Angeles. In September, they received an attractive-sounding offer—engineered by Carlos—to replace the band of Skinnay Ennis, who had enlisted, on the Bob Hope radio show. It meant traveling with Hope, broadcasting from military bases. Because they would be entertaining the troops, everyone in the band would be exempt from the draft. Besides, twenty million people listened to the Hope show every Tuesday night—exposure that would make for powerful bargaining leverage when future bookings were negotiated. Convinced that this was the only way to keep his band intact, Stan signed a thirty-nine-week contract. Within two weeks, disenchantment had set in.

As Stan understood it, the band was hired to play the theme, cues and accompaniment for Frances Langford and other guest singers and would also be featured in a spot of its own on each show. Every week they rehearsed a number, but by the time Jerry Colonna did his comedy and Langford sang her songs, something would have to be cut. It was always their number. Stan had envisioned the job as a showcase; instead, they were merely providing background music. After the second show, he called Hope. "I gotta see ya," he said.

"Now?" said Hope. "In the middle of the night?"

"Yeah," said Stan. "I'm comin' over."

"Okay," said Hope, mystified.

Tact has never been Stan's long suit. "This thing stinks," he told Hope. "Langford is acting like an idiot, Jerry Colonna is out of his head, they're both trying to undermine everything we do. We're music, and you're comedy. We don't fit into this. I don't want to have fun made of me, like Skinnay Ennis, how skinny I am."

Hope was equally blunt. "We're stuck with each other," he said flatly.

"How do you mean?"

"I'm a lot older and more important than you are. If you walk out on me, the whole trade is gonna say that I gave you the ax. You don't want that, and I don't want it, either. So let's you and I shake hands and agree to put up with each other for thirty-nine weeks."

Hope's logic was irrefutable. Stan sensibly swallowed hard, took a deep breath—and held it for thirty-nine weeks.

In November, Stan was approached by Glenn Wallichs, who was forming a new record company in conjunction with Johnny Mercer. Wallichs had already hired Dave Dexter away from *Downbeat*, and Dexter was constantly urging Wallichs to sign Stan. For his part, Stan was almost as disenchanted with Decca Records, for whom he had cut a few sides in 1941 and '42, as he was with the Hope show. At Decca, he was a small, unknown fish in a large, long-established pond. Wallich's offer tugged at his ego; his company, Capitol, would see that Stan got the recognition he deserved. They would all grow up together.

When Stan's contract with Decca expired, he signed with Capitol and immediately recorded "Do Nothin' Til You Hear from Me," "Harlem Folk Dance" and "Eager Beaver." The latter quickly became a hit. So did a fourth side, their theme song, which had been variously titled "Nameless Signature," "Hoboken Concerto," "Sunset on a Hairpin Farm" and "Topaz," and was finally, formally christened "Artistry in Rhythm."

As president of Capitol as well as its only A & R man, Johnny Mercer was Stan's boss. Mercer loved "Eager Beaver," and was constantly after Stan to record more such melodic— and therefore, he felt, salable—selections. Stan was determined to record what he by God wanted to record, which led to many a pitched battle in Mercer's office with Glenn Wallichs, Paul Weston and Carlos Gastel fruitlessly attempting to mediate. Finally, Wallichs agreed to an extraordinary compromise:

in exchange for autonomy in the recording studio, Stan would function as a roving public relations representative. A plug for Kenton would be a plug for the company. "I will do everything I can to build Capitol Records," Stan promised Wallichs, "if they'll just stay out of the studio when I'm recording." True to his word, in years to come he talked up the company and all its artists in his personal and radio appearances and even carried cartons of records by Peggy Lee, Jo Stafford, Margaret Whiting and other Capitol artists in the back of his car or the bus, opening accounts and making personal deliveries to astonished record dealers in the cities he played. Capitol's sales executives, unaware of the deal with Wallichs, marveled at his willingness to go miles out of his way to plug someone else's records and called him their ambassador. And disc jockeys, flattered by his availability (a welcome change from the self-important performers who condescendingly gave them little more than a hard time), knocked themselves out to play his records.

Red Dorris had long been a mainstay of the band when, in February of 1944, he was drafted. Dolly Mitchell left with him (and, eventually, married him), leaving Stan with neither male nor female vocalist. He hired Gene Howard, a vocalist-arranger, and looked around for a complementary girl singer.

Anita O'Day had acquired a substantial following singing with Gene Krupa's band and was anxious to try her luck as a single. To guide her career as a single, she hired Carlos Gastel, who naturally saw her as a potential asset for the Kenton band. To give him his due, he undoubtedly also felt the association would be advantageous to Anita. In persuading her that a year with Kenton would greatly enhance her future prospects as a single, Carlos negotiated the truly marvelous mismatching of supersquare Stanley, who could barely bring himself to say *damn*, and superswinger O'Day, whose favorite adjective was *fucking*.

Of all the vocalists who ever sang with Kenton—and quite possibly with any other big band in the forties—Anita was the most natural and original talent. Gene Krupa compared her husky sound with that of a jazz horn; other musicians called her the *blackest* white singer they ever heard.

Anita was never influenced by other singers, only by instrumentalists like Art Tatum and Buddy De Franco, from whom she learned how to get the absolute most out of every bar. She was brighter than she gave herself credit for—but she was street-smart and crude, and she regarded the band's middle-class morality with a mixture of awe and disbelief. "Gene's band was a *drinking* band; they swung. It don't take thinking to swing. Stan had a *thinking* band. They sent their money home, saved their money, made payments on property!" As for Stan, "He was such a gentleman—a *college* man," she assumed. "Someone would come up behind me and take my suitcase, and it would be Stan! He was a good piano player, too. He accompanied me very nice." Still, she could not resist blowing his mind on occasion—such as the time he took her to a department store to help her select some more appropriate costumes than the mannish-looking outfits she preferred. "Come see how you like this outfit," she called to Stan from the dressing room. Obediently, he pushed aside the curtain—and there was Anita, stark naked.

Not surprisingly, she had a reputation as a wild, freakish, anything-goes chick. "If ya hear of anything new," she'd tell the musicians, "be sure and let me know—I wanna try it!" In dress and behavior, she was predictably unpredictable, as likely to show up in men's clothes with the fly open as in a long, slinky evening gown. It seemed to Bob Gioga that "It was a game to her, being a different person every night." Apparently nobody ever took the trouble to wonder what might have prevented her from just being herself.

Anita conceded that "The band was great—but it wasn't

a swing band! I learned how to sing on the upbeats, but it's hard to sing upbeats when the brass is playing downbeats." Since the departure of Pee Wee George, Stan had not been able to keep a satisfactory drummer. "He must have had ten different drummers in the ten months I was with him. They had to look at me to know when to cut it off. I never heard of any of 'em again—I think it must've scared 'em out of the business!" For her first record date with the band, she asked Stan if she could bring in Jessie Price, a drummer she had heard the night before who had impressed her, "just for my part. I thought it might save the session." Stan agreed, and according to Anita, "That was the first time the band ever swang." The tune was called "And Her Tears Flowed Like Wine," and sold over a million records.

Jessie Price was as much of a misfit in the band as was Anita, but for a different reason. He was black.

Price was the second black Stan hired; the first was Karl George, who was playing second trumpet when Price joined the band. But George was a light-skinned *Negro*, who coolly opted for expedience; if he had any qualms about road manager Gioga telling desk clerks, "This is our Cuban drummer," he kept them to himself. (One such clerk, unconvinced, beckoned George over to the desk to ask, "Are you really a Cuban?" "I sho' is," George replied.) Jessie Price was a funky, nitty-gritty, down-home, let-it-all-hang-out black who came on just as strong off the stand as on. He made no secret of the fact that, sexually, he drew no color line. This was more than guitarist Bob Ahern could bear. "He told me he couldn't even stand the *thought* of black musicians bein' in the same band he was in. That stinker said I was always playin' the wrong things, even though the records I made with them turned out real good. That guitar player just made my life agony, and I didn't stay too long.

"Stan's attitude was altogether different. He told me he

felt a man was a man. He treated me like I was the same as he was. Stan's a wonderful person. Wonderful. Real wonderful. He just didn't know how to handle the situation. So I left the band in Omaha, Nebraska."

Stan has periodically been accused—notably by jazz critic Leonard Feather—of discriminating against black musicians. He has. But in their haste to label him racist, his detractors reveal their own ignorance of the Gestalt that is Stan Kenton.

No man can be expected to be any more or less than the environment that shapes him. Stanley is his mother's son. From early childhood, he was indoctrinated with Stella's philosophy of absolutes: right-wrong, good-evil, black-white, democracy-communism. Scratch the superficial veneer of sophistication and you find, at the core of the man, the provincial, chauvinistic, myopic, unshakable values of the quintessential WASP. Stan is a lifetime product and prisoner of the Puritan ethic; therein lies his strength and his weakness, his drive and his hangups, his greatest achievements and his most humiliating defeats. Abstractions carry more weight with him than people. He believes in Motherhood, hard work, goodwomen and badwomen, the power of reason, the dangers of emotion, the free enterprise system and the American flag. Morally, he has no peripheral vision; a social conscience is "that liberal crap."

During the years in which Stan was serving his musical apprenticeship, two magazines, *Downbeat* and *Metronome*, reflected the prevailing attitudes of the jazz world. When *Metronome* profiled the members of Stan's first band in 1942, it was perfectly acceptable for its reviewer to say of Red Dorris, "He sounds colored when he sings and when he plays tenor sax. That's because Red Dorris has always studied and admired the music of negroes. Dorris is an Arkansan . . ."

Waspishness is, perhaps more than anything, an ability to tolerate contradictions. Stan's support of a George Wallace can and does coexist with his sincere belief that "a man is a man." The data with which he was programmed "in front" simply cannot accommodate an appreciation of the implications of being black in America.

Beyond that, the music was Wasp music; *it didn't swing.* Buddy Childers contends, "It's not that they weren't technically able—they were—but I didn't know any black cats who wanted to be in a band that didn't swing. A lot of white guys felt that way, too. Accuracy and precision is what our band was during those years. You can say Duke Ellington's band has played some really wild things, but he had some of the most undisciplined people—Duke would write something down, but however the guys played it, that's what they accepted. But we didn't have that kind of a band!"

The Jessie Price episode occurred in June of 1944, just as the contract with Bob Hope expired. The band immediately went back on the road, headed for a booking in Miami. Before Stan left California, Carlos had begged him to let him arrange a defense job in the Valley. "You won't have to work there," he explained. "You'll just be listed there with the draft board." Stan told Carlos that his conscience wouldn't allow it. As a result, his induction papers were waiting for him in Miami.

He took the papers to the Miami draft board for further instructions. They were brief: "Be here tomorrow morning at seven o'clock for induction," a clerk told him.

"Look, lady," he protested, "you don't understand! I got a band I gotta get rid of! It's gonna take me about ten days to two weeks to do it! I got wives here and everything else!"

"I don't care about your band!" said the clerk. "You be here in the morning!"

All Stan could think of was that if he didn't show up on the job the next night, the promoter wouldn't pay them. Panicked, he grabbed his papers from her desk and bolted out of the office with the clerk in hot pursuit, yelling, "We're coming after you! We'll get you! Uncle Sam's job's bigger than your job!"

He returned to his hotel and, after consulting with Violet, called his draft board in Hollywood. This woman was more sympathetic. "Where are you going next?" she asked.

"Detroit."

"What hotel?"

"The Statler."

"Fine," said the woman. "I'll send your papers there."

Much relieved, Stan made plans to disband in Detroit. At the Statler, sure enough, he received another communication from his draft board. Resigned by now to his imminent induction, he opened the envelope to discover that he had been reclassified to 2-A; he had just passed the draftable age limit.

Each such crisis that was resolved seemed to be followed by two new ones. The intensity of their music drastically limited their bookings. Bob Gioga insists, "If Stan could've compromised just a little bit, he could've been bigger than Glenn Miller, Tommy Dorsey, everybody combined, because of the infectious quality that he had. But he would refuse to make concessions!" In sophisticated places like the Pennsylvania Hotel in New York, where patrons expected appropriately soft music, at least at the dinner show, Stan would keep the volume down for as long as he could stand it and then, nudged by some private perversity, would have the band hit a chord that would knock the people's forks right out of their hands. Not surprisingly, they were thrown out of quite a few places.

During a theater date in Providence, Rhode Island, Stan got a phone call from Carlos: Tom Rockwell, president of GAC, wanted to see Stan in his New York office. Stan was to take the train down there the next morning.

"Christ," recalls Stan, "all the way to New York I was shakin' all over, wondering what the hell he wanted to see me about. I had never been to Rockwell's office. He had a private reception room and a huge office, with a view overlooking the Hudson. He told me to sit down. Then he said, 'I've got something to explain to you. We're your agents, and we want to book you. But the trouble is, every place we book you, you either get thrown out or, when you leave, they close the door behind you; you can never play there again. The music's too loud, and you don't play what the people want to hear. We're coming to the end of our road.'

"I sat there lookin' at him, and all of a sudden my eyes started to fill up, and I started to cry. He noticed that I was in trouble, so he offered me a cigarette, then he got on the phone and made a few fake phone calls and turned his back to me and looked out that window. When he saw I had regained my composure, he turned around and he said, 'What do you think we can do about it?'

"I said, 'Mr. Rockwell, I don't really know what to do. If I knew how to play that kind of music that you're talking about, I'd play it—but I don't understand it. I don't know whether I'm dumb, or what—I just don't know how to do it!' And I started to cry again!

"Rockwell turned his back on me *again*, and made some more fake phone calls. When I got hold of myself, he said, 'Well, you're gonna blow your first show if you don't get back to Providence. You'd better go. But before you do, I want you to know one thing: I've had the same God damn trouble with all you guys. I went through the same thing with the Casa Loma band, I went through the same thing with . . .' and he named off all these bands. 'They're all too God damn loud; the music was screwy. But I want you to know that we are your agents. We'll book you.'"

It was years before Stan could bring himself to call Tom Rockwell anything but "Mr. Rockwell." He was profoundly in awe of Rockwell's style and consciously attempted to emulate his psychological finesse, his ability to deal with any situation without blowing his cool. If any man ever served as a model for Stan, it was Rockwell.

By the spring of 1945, Anita O'Day was convinced that her career was at a standstill; also, she was fed up with the road. In Grand Island, Nebraska, they were stranded in a flood and spent three days on a crowded train with no air-conditioning. On another train, the only space available to them was in the baggage car, which they shared with a donkey. Transportation between army camps was often supplied by the air corps, which sometimes meant sitting in the pitch-dark bomb bay of a B-25 bomber surrounded by airsick musicians and wives (when one wife vomited into a sack, Stan pushed a section of the door open and threw it out, so that they completed the flight with the back of the plane wide open). At the Oriental Theater in Chicago, Anita tore up her contract and left the band. The next day, on the basis of a test record she had sent him, Stan hired a seventeen-year-old country girl from Illinois. Shirley Luster had had little experience, and her style was a watered-down, third-rate imitation of Anita's. But Stan was in a bind; they were booked into Indianapolis the next night, and he had to have a singer.

"On the train to Indianapolis, Stan gave me a sheet of music and said, 'This is what you'll be singing tomorrow.' I stared at the music, and I was petrified! This was my lifelong desire, and I was too frightened to tell him I couldn't read music! It was horrible—I wrote some of the lyrics down in the palm of my hand, and I faked it! I don't know how I ever got through it—I must have looked like a zombie!"

At Stan's suggestion, she listened to Anita's records every chance she got. By June she had shaped up into a *first*-rate imitation of O'Day, and Stan decided to keep her. He rechristened her June, in honor of the month, and Christy, because he liked the sound of it.

In July, they were booked into the Paramount Theater in New York for the first time. They had played other theaters, but the Paramount was the theater most universally identified with dance bands, and in a way it meant they had Arrived. At least, so they thought—until everything that could possibly happen to prevent their Arrival happened.

En route to New York from Ohio, they had a three-hour layover in Pittsburgh between trains. Three members of the brass section imprudently took this opportunity to score some grass and were busted and thrown into jail. The rest of the band continued on to New York, where the guitarist and the bass player were greeted, respectively, with an induction notice and an ultimatum to get off the road *now* or face divorce proceedings. When rehearsal began the next morning (they were to open that night), both those members of the rhythm section were gone and a third, drummer Bob Varney, was incapacitated with ptomaine poisoning. As a capper, three of the remaining brass players had overslept.

With their opening only hours away, Stan was forced to abandon his policy of hiring unknown (therefore inexpensive) musicians in favor of signing the best New York studio men available. The men he hired at this time—they included trombonist Kai Winding, trumpeter Ray Wetzel and bassist Eddie Safranski—gave the band a reputation for musicianship it had not previously attained. *Metronome* headlined "STAN STUPEN-DOUS," and added, "To proclaim that Stan Kenton's band is one of the finest, most original and musicianly dance organizations in the nation would be understatement."

Stan's "Concerto To End All Concertos" had already become a "Kenton classic," and Christy's first recording, "Tampico," was an immediate success. In August, they scored a big hit at the Sherman Hotel in Chicago and negotiated a lucrative contract with the Palladium where, in October, they drew thirty-seven thousand people their opening week, again breaking a house record. In November, the band was featured in a Columbia picture, *The Duchess of Broadway*, and a Warner Brothers short subject, *Artistry in Rhythm*. By the end of the year, it was apparent that survival no longer need be Stan's primary consideration.

(Parenthetically, the war ended.)

8 Paying Dues

"As the band grew, Violet started realizing that she'd built a monster. She became harder and harder to BE with; she even got to where she hated music. She just couldn't understand that I loved music more than any woman."

IF the ascendance of Stan's career and the decline of his marriage were plotted on a chronological graph, the lines would intersect at the year 1946.

When Stan was doing the Bob Hope show, he and Violet had bought their first house. It was on Hollyridge Drive, high in the Hollywood Hills; it had two stories and a panoramic view. They had moved in with apple crates for furniture, and for a while Violet had occupied herself decorating the place. Then the band went back on the road full time. Violet left Leslie with her mother and went along with Stan, but she missed Leslie desperately and was ridden with guilt. She tried taking Leslie along, and wound up spending her evenings sitting on lids of toilet seats in hotel bathrooms, so the light she read by wouldn't wake the child. Staying at home with Leslie was little better. The separations lengthened as the band prospered; the music, and everything connected with it, became the enemy.

BUDDY CHILDERS: "I never felt anything but a freeze from Violet. Even when she was smiling and talking to us, we were still the riffraff, the servants. That was the feeling most of the guys got."

IRMA MAE HOPKINS: "Violet wanted to be a star herself, and she felt like she was shuttled into the corner."

BOB GIOGA: "When we were at a spot for a month or so, like the Meadowbrook, Violet would join us occasionally. But Stan was so wrapped up in the music, it always came first."

VIOLET FOSTER: "Stanley and I used to talk about creating a dynasty. And we *could* have. But somehow we got mixed up along the way. And finally, when you get to the point where you can have a dynasty, you've lost something and there's no point in it."

Faced with the Hobson's choice of being a wife or being a mother, Violet opted for mother. She was miserably unhappy, and Stan's assurances that somehow they would work it out were scant comfort during the long, solitary nights on Hollyridge. Still, she was not ready to accept the inevitable— not yet. The only real meaning in her life had come about through Stan; giving that up would require a strength that was beyond her resources in 1946.

Stan had little time for introspection. He had pushed the band so hard, for so long, that by now it had a momentum of its own that swept aside any personal considerations in its path. In January of 1946, *Look* magazine named it Band of the Year. By spring, they were breaking records wherever they played. By summer, not even Stan's detractors could deny that he had the hottest band in the country.

Stan no longer had the time to sit in theaters writing and arranging all night (although the dark circles under his eyes from the years of doing so remained), and began, little by little, buying outside arrangements from Ralph Yaw, Joe Rizzo and Ken Hanna. In July of 1944, he had hired Gene

Roland as his first full-time staff arranger. Roland's assignment was to write "up" tunes for Anita O'Day; his early contributions included "Gotta Be Gettin'" and "Are You Livin', Old Man?" Roland's arrangements truly swung, and the band loved to play them. So did Roland. He liked to sit in with the trumpet section, at that time only four parts, playing a fifth part he would write for himself. It sounded terrific—so much so that Stan began paying Roland for playing as well as for arranging. But Roland's musical versatility was exceeded only by his poor judgment, particularly with regard to booze and women. "All talent and no brains," Bob Gioga describes him. "Why didn't somebody pick up my trumpet?" Roland would shout, upon realizing, on the bus thirty miles out of a town, that his horn was still sitting on the bandstand where he had left it. "You know I'm not responsible!"

In 1945, after a year with the band, Roland, feeling "saturated," went to work for Lionel Hampton. The band sounded so strange without him that Stan permanently added a fifth trumpet. A few months later, the prodigal son returned. All was forgiven, and he began sitting in again—this time, playing a fifth *trombone*. With the five trumpets, it sounded beautiful! And how Roland dug playing! Musically, his instincts were infallible; and when the moon was right, and the mood was upon him, he would jam right on through Stan's solos, even through Christy's vocals.

"I joined the trombone section around November of 1945, in Salt Lake City. We toured the Midwest and the East, and we wound up in the middle of January in the snowbound Meadowbrook, in New Jersey. In those days I was a hot jazz player; I wanted to play solos, and I started getting disenchanted with my position in the band. I figured I was buried among fifteen, sixteen other guys all fighting for a place in the sun. When you're with a big band, everybody wants their share of the blowing, and there's not that much solo work to

99

go around. And I resented the fact that when we went into the Adams Theater in Newark, Stan was billing Vida Musso and Boots Mussuli and Kai Winding, but he wasn't billing me! I was with the band before those guys, I was writing and contributing a lot!

"I've never pulled on a bandleader's coattails with demands. All I ever thought about was writing my best and playing my best, and letting the quality of what I was doing speak for itself, and figure it returns automatically. But it just isn't that way! Stan was as fair as any bandleader I've ever known, but when you've got fifteen or twenty guys to worry about, there's some times when you've got to be a son of a bitch. So I got mad and told Stan I was gonna stay in New York. He said, 'Well, we made a little splash. If you don't do okay in New York, give me a call and come back with us.'"

Without Roland's fifth trombone part, the band again sounded incomplete. Stan hired a fifth trombone player, permanently expanding the section. Then in mid-1946, "I got a call from the Old Man, from Del Mar, California. He says, 'Would you like to come out here? I don't want you to *play* in the band, because it's too much of a hassle. I just want you to write some things for June.'"

When Roland got to Del Mar, Stan described a tune he wanted—an original—and Roland immediately wrote "Ain't No Mis'ry in Me." June subsequently recorded it, and it was included in the original *Artistry in Rhythm* album. But within a week, Roland got the itch to play.

He asked Stan to let him play with the band again, and Stan, intrigued with the idea of having a *sixth* trumpet, agreed. That night, a whole carload of musicians, Roland included, piled into Vido Musso's Cadillac and drove across the border to a party in Tijuana. Coming back the next day, they looked so suspicious in the big black sedan—Vido, driving, looked like a candidate for the FBI's Most Wanted list—that the border guards shook them down for drugs, making the men strip and virtually disassembling the Cadillac. Miraculously, nothing was found. But when Stan heard about the incident, he was furious. He dreaded the notoriety of a drug bust, which at that time could mean instant death to a performer's career. A previous incident had involved his bailing out a group of his musicians, whom he promptly fired, and had been hushed up at considerable expense. The Tijuana caper frightened and angered him, and he gave the band a strong lecture about not caring what they did on their own time, "But if you have trouble with the law and it gets back to me, you're through!"

The next day, Stan stopped by Roland's quarters in Del Mar to pick up an arrangement. When Roland opened the door, a huge cloud of marijuana smoke nearly knocked Stan down. "That's it, Gene!" said Stan, and turned to leave.

"But Stan," protested Roland, grabbing his arm, "you don't want to let me go! I'm going to write a six-trumpet book for you, and you're going to have the greatest band in the world!"

Stan relented, but Roland's reprieve was brief. "I called his hotel room," recalls Roland, "and I said, 'Stan, if I'm gonna play in the band as well as write, I'd like to get a little raise, so I can take care of my family a little better.' He was in a very bad humor, and he says, 'Well, I need a sixth trumpet like I need a hole in the head. As a matter of fact, you're on your notice, right now!'

"I knew he didn't really mean it. Gioga told me not to pay any attention, that something was going on with his wife and daughter that was giving him a bad humor. But I said, 'No, I've been offered another job, and I'm leaving!' And I did!"

Roland's departure did not leave Stan without an arranger. At a rehearsal during one Roland-less period in 1944, Red Dorris had reminded Stan, "How about those arrangements that fellow gave you in San Francisco?" He was referring to a shy, horn-rimmed, bookish-looking Pfc. who had approached Stan backstage at the Golden Gate Theater, shoved a half-dozen arrangements into his hands, mumbled, "If you don't ever get a chance to play these I wish you would somehow send them back because it was so much work for me to copy them," and vanished. As they played through the first chart at rehearsal, Stan's expression was incredulous. "My God," he said when they finished, "he writes just the way *I* do!" When the war ended and Pete Rugulo was discharged, he and his wife Jan immediately joined the band at the Meadowbrook.

Pete quickly became Stan's musical alter ego. He had studied formally with French composer Darius Milhaud, but jazz was his first love, and his rapport with Stan's conceptions and intentions was almost eerie. Their collaborative efforts were so tightly meshed that one could finish an arrangement the other had begun, and at times neither could remember which of them had written a particular portion of a piece. Pete's feeling for Stan was unequivocal: "I worshiped him. I followed him around like a little puppy. It was my big chance. Anything I wanted to write, experiment, he would try it. I don't remember him ever saying 'Gee, that's too wild!' He paid me $150 a week, but I would've done it for nothing."

Not only did Stan play everything Pete wrote—from his atonal, Stravinsky-influenced "modern" works to his melodic, romantic themes—he also made a point of acknowledging, on the bandstand and on his records, the contributions of all his arrangers. This was a rare gesture among bandleaders, many of whom apparently hoped the audience would give *them* the credit for writing, arranging and performing every note their bands played.

As reverse sides of a coin share its center, so diffident Rugulo and effusive Kenton shared an egocentricity that obliterated all but their mutual, straight-ahead objective. To Jan Rugulo (one of the few people capable of telling Stan, in her unadulterated Oklahoma accent, that he was full of *shee-it*), "They were exactly alike: completely self-centered and strong-willed about music and about people. Neither of them had the ability to get close to *any*body! As long as they were doin' what they wanted to do, and were bein' recognized, they didn't give a God damn about how anybody else felt!"

The Band of the Year had a style noticeably looser and more relaxed than the uptight precision of earlier years. As the brass section had grown from five to ten, with the saxophone section remaining at five, there had naturally been a shift of emphasis. When they played the Palladium in 1946, the marquee was crowded with the names of featured soloists: vocalists June Christy and Gene Howard, trombonists Kai Winding and Milt Bernhart, trumpeters Ray Wetzel and Buddy Childers, bassist Eddie Safranski, drummer Shelly Manne, and the two Sicilian saxophonists: Boots Mussuli (alto) and Vido Musso (tenor).

Vido had been doing quite well with Tommy Dorsey; but Dorsey liked to transport his band by plane, and Vido was phobic about flying, even in the big "Consternation." In 1945 he had joined Stan at the Meadowbrook, having crossed the country in a drawing room of "one of those new Consultations." Vido liked to travel in style. He bought one of the first postwar Cadillacs, and frequently Mussuli, Wetzel, Childers and Chico Alvarez, who had returned to the band after the war, rode with him in the long black sedan.

Boots Mussuli rode in front. Smoke from the everpresent cigarette dangling from his lips had reduced his eyes to slits. To Chico, "He looked like a little gangster—and Vido, driving, like the head of the Mafia. And Ray Wetzel looked like Sydney Greenstreet!" They all had heavy beards, and just the sight

103

of them could clear the streets of some little towns. Gas station attendants, fearing a holdup, would yell, "We're closed!" and run and hide.

Late one rainy night after a job in Iowa, on a dark highway, a car speeding in the opposite direction splashed some water onto Vido's car, also speeding, with a loud THWACK. Vido, thinking he'd been hit, turned his car around, caught up with the offender and stopped him. The two drivers got out. "Hey, Jack," said Vido, not unfriendly, "you hit my car!" As he knelt by his fender lighting matches, searching for the nonexistent mark, the other driver hauled off and, with the full force of his two-hundred-plus pounds, punched Vido in the eye. Vido shook his head in annoyance, like a gorilla troubled by a fly.

BUDDY CHILDERS: "Vido keeps saying, 'Wait a minute, Jack! I want to show you something! You hit my car!' Then he realizes something. He says, 'Hey! You hit me! That's not nice! But I'm not mad!' Then: POW! The guy's feet left the ground! He landed six feet away, did a backward somersault, just like in the movies. We thought Vido was gonna kill him!"

VIDO MUSSO: "I knocked the guy *ten* feet! Then—and this I shouldn't have done—I put the heel of my foot right in his mouth, and tore his mouth. Then *another* car drives up, and six guys get out. They look like football players. They say, 'Hey, that guy's our buddy!' And WHAM, I never saw so many fists flying against me! Nobody is helpin' me, so I say, 'Boots, get the gun! Get the gun!' Boots says, 'Where? Where?' I grabbed one guy and kicked him one in the mazzoulas. Then the cops came. I had hurt a man very badly. We were told never to come back to Iowa."

That Vido was honestly unaware of his own strength was demonstrated when a Southern motorcycle gang approached the bandstand one night with the intention of beating up the Yankee musicians. Their leader made the mistake of reaching

104

for Vido who, mistaking him for a friendly fan, took his hand to shake it and twisted slightly, breaking the young man's arm. Later, in the bus, he paced the aisle, reproaching himself. "I broke that kid's arm! I didn't mean to hurt him!" he insisted to one and all, almost in tears. To emphasize his sincerity, he gestured with his fist—clean through the roof of the bus.

For all his bumbling obtuseness, Vido was not without his crafty side. His colorful playing and personality attracted droves of youngsters who felt privileged to provide him with beer and sandwiches, for which he never paid (except with a hearty "This is great, Jack!"). He had a large collection of mouthpieces, acquired from students so foolish as to ask for his opinion ("Leave it with me, Jack, I'll fix it up for you!").

Vido was—Vido. A natural phenomenon, invulnerable to blows and insults, with the physique and sensitivity of a Sherman tank. He played his tenor as though the rest of the saxophone section was there exclusively to accompany him. "Come Back to Sorrento" was his big solo. Everyone in the band hated the cornball number, but audiences clamored for it, and Stan called for it often.

Kai Winding, whose talent as a jazz trombonist was exceeded only by his arrogance, didn't care for the big, fat, wah-wah vibrato tone of the brass section. Instead of that sweetish, melodious quality, he wanted a pure, straight tone, "a tremendous zing," he called it—"a kind of open blare that hit the audience right between the ears." Stan describes Winding's influence on him as tremendous. "In the early days of the band," he explains, "the whole concept was short, almost staccato notes. I can remember an arrangement we had that started with a big TUT at the beginning of it. The whole band was supposed to play this, and then the bass player played a passage and then the band played TUT again. So we kicked this thing off, and the whole band went TUT—but Kai goes BOP! I'd say to him, 'No, Kai, it's TUT!' And we'd kick it off again, and the band goes TUT, and Kai was so God damn headstrong, he'd go BOP! I was so God damn mad at him, I would have fired him—but I had a lot of respect for him, as childish as he was at the time. So we'd try it again, and Kai would go BOP. . . . And gradually, Kai changed the whole God damn conception of the band, and my whole way of thinking. And there hasn't been a short note in the band since!" °

After Pee Wee George, Stan had gone through more drummers than he cared to remember. Then early in 1946 he hired a thoroughly dedicated and experienced musician who looked like a skinny kid (though he was twenty-six), and wanted to be the Charlie Parker of the drums.

Shelly Manne grasped a subtle and crucial fact that escaped Stan's critics: namely, that *there was more than one kind of swinging.* Although Stan's band never swung in the conventional rhythmic sense, Shelly was able to move it by what he calls *sound pulsation.* The *momentum* of the sound made the band swing; it created excitement through sound and dynamics. Shelly demonstrated that "Textures and colors can make drums become really musical, rather than just a percussive thing." Using little triangles, cymbal rolls, unorthodox glissandos on tom-toms and big cymbal flares, Shelly turned the drum chair into a color chair, irreversibly expanding the role of the drummer in the band.

Shelly, a Jewish street kid from New York, was struck by the same manifestations of Waspishness that had blown Anita's mind. Although Shelly was not himself a juicer, it astounded him the way "The guys from California didn't know what it was to get drunk and sleep in their clothes all night! They would buy property, and check the stock market! In New York,

---

° "All styles that concentrate on accenting beats are through," was Stan's typically dogmatic statement to *Downbeat* in 1947.

you don't think about buying property; it all belongs to the landlord!"

Almost everyone in the band had his own fan club, none more determined than Shelly's. Wearing little white bebop hats and sweatshirts lettered O.M.S. (Our Man Shelly), its members would be sitting in the front row of the Paramount Theater from the moment the curtain went up at nine every morning until it fell after the last show, well past midnight. They had resourceful ways of finding out where the band would stay, and when and where the bus would arrive. Thousands of people waited at hundreds of stage doors for autographs, or just for a glimpse of the musicians; the more enterprising would try to sneak into the dressing rooms. Some devoted fans followed the band from city to city, so that the places would change but the faces would not. Much of the music was accompanied by screams from the predominantly young audience.

By the end of 1946, the ratio of supply and demand for big bands had reversed itself. Participants in the scene frantically grasped for explanations, as though in so doing they could somehow halt the decline which, in hindsight, was an inevitable result of collective greed. When wartime price regulations were lifted, operating expenses skyrocketed; the cost of chartering a bus almost doubled from its prewar rate, and $2.50 hotel rooms became history. As bandleaders had tried to outbid each other for available sidemen during the war, salaries had soared. The bandleader's increased costs necessitated his demanding guarantees from ballroom owners, who were squeezed at the other end by a 20 percent cabaret tax. Radio stations, in a necessary economy measure, replaced ballroom remotes with disc jockeys. Television threatened to make theater stage shows obsolete. The public, drained after wartime tensions, wanted sweeter, Jan Garber-type music to dance to—if they cared to dance at all.

107

In December of 1946, Armaggedon seemed at hand for
the big bands. In that one month, no fewer than eight top
bandleaders—Woody Herman, Benny Goodman, Harry James,
Les Brown, Jack Teagarden, Benny Carter, Ina Ray Hutton
and Tommy Dorsey—capitulated to the economic facts of life
and disbanded. With these giants of the business crumbling
around him, and with one of the largest bands and a payroll
of over six thousand dollars a week, there was every reason
for Stan to be concerned. Instead, his band continued to break
attendance records and win polls and began, for the first time
since its inception, to show a profit. It was no accident. Stan
was pushing himself as relentlessly as Shelly's drums pushed
the band. Like a presidential candidate on the campaign trail,
he spent every waking moment promoting the band through
appearances at radio stations, record shops, schools. In January of 1947, *Downbeat* paid tribute to his perseverance with
this inimitable prose:

> The press agents of two of [Stan's] hottest rivals . . . raved
> for hours to *Beat* staffers about the goodwill and enlighten-
> ment program the long, leanster of Leapo has carried on
> during his recent road tours and recent Paramount theater
> date. . . . Every town he goes through he calls on or talks
> to every disc jockey there, and makes sure they have his
> records, and that they get a chance to query him!
> . . . There may be times when we disagree with the
> music, but whatta guy the Stanley is!

To maintain his frantic schedule, Stan had forsaken the
bus for his Buick convertible. Often he drove alone, all night,
arriving in a city just in time to make an early morning interview (after working till three in the morning). His exhaustion
produced some close calls. One night, with Shelly along for
company, the car slid down a hill of ice in Minnesota, completely out of control, its descent broken only by a succession
of mailboxes it knocked from their posts in a zigzag pattern.

Sometimes June Christy went along for the ride and the interviews, which could add up to eight or nine in one day—before, between and after shows. They were seen together so much that many fans thought they were married.

June was married, but not to Stan. Shortly after she joined the band, Stan had hired a tall, gawky tenor player named Bob Cooper. Temperamentally, he and June could not have been less alike. Coop neither smoked nor drank; he was quiet, boyish and virginal, with an absolutely even disposition. Stan had warned June against fraternizing with the musicians; although she was young and appeared naive, a reputation for drinking and carousing had preceded her. In her eagerness to please Stan, whom she adored, June was supercool—until she met Coop. From then on, they were practically inseparable—even though they rarely went out together without three or four other members of the band along for cover. When June wasn't riding with Stan, she was sharing Coop's seat on the bus, sleeping with her head on his shoulder. When they were married in 1946, hardly anyone was surprised except Stan—who by this time was so preoccupied with the deterioration of his own marriage that his startled reaction was, "Are you sure you know what you're doing?"

Coop and Christy were married after the last show at a theater in Washington, D.C., wearing their band uniforms. Shelly and his wife Flip stood up for them. Christy remembers that "The band gave us a party after the ceremony. In a hotel room. It wasn't very romantic. We made the first show the next morning, at ten o'clock."

Christy's voice never had the originality or the purity that she would have liked. Even Stan admitted that she sometimes sang flat. She was not an inventive singer; what sounded like improvisation in numbers like "How High the Moon" had often been carefully written out beforehand by Coop, an accomplished arranger as well as player. Still, Christy's voice

109

had a compelling quality, a smoky, sensuous blending of vulnerability and pain, that went beyond technical niceties and touched audiences in a personal and meaningful way. Their response made her one of the most popular singers in the country. But June was never really comfortable with either her singing or herself. In her early years, she tried to sing her discomfort away. In later years, she tried to drink it away. Bob Cooper tried—with some success—to comfort it away.

In the spring of '47, Christy came down with the flu. She needed rest, but they were in the middle of a tour of one-nighters, with no nights off and long jumps on the bus. "Stan wasn't sympathetic at all," June recalls, "because he was still holding up very well and he felt if he was, everyone else should be, too."

Stan would not, could not admit that he was feeling the cumulative strain of the past months. Buddy Childers remembers the time vividly:

"In 1946 we did ten weeks in the Paramount Theater. Before that we had been doing one-nighters for *months*, just driving and driving. One time I figured out how many one-nighters it had been, and how far we had travelled; the figures, the numbers were just absolutely *staggering*. And ten weeks in the Paramount is like a life sentence. The picture we were with was *Blue Skies*. It had Bing Crosby and Fred Astaire. It was the first big super-duper musical after the war, over two hours long. And on stage were Nat Cole and Nellie Lutcher *and* us. Carlos was handling all of us.

"On regular days, the six-show days, our first show was at 10:02 in the morning—we did fifty-five-minute shows—and our last show started at 1:48 A.M. There's no way we could get more than six hours' sleep. You're afraid to sleep between shows. Ten weeks of that, and you're a basket case. And from there we climbed right back on the bus with only one or two days off—and during that time we rehearsed and made some

110

records—and did like thirty-eight one-nighters, lacing back and forth and down into the South, out to California. The shortest jump was like 350 miles. On the bus at seven in the morning, all day, get there, play the gig, back on the bus until the next morning. We'd check in [to a hotel] every other day. We worked a ballroom in Los Angeles for a couple of weeks, and when we weren't working, we were working. If we had a day off, we rehearsed, 'cause all this time in theaters we hadn't been able to put any new music in the book. Then we got right back on the God damn bus, went clear up to Canada and back down, and at that point I knew I had had it. I didn't really want to leave the band, but it was just too much for me. In April of 1947, I said to Stan, 'I'm gonna have to leave.'

"He said, 'Look, I've decided to disband. But we've got three or four weeks of dates to do, and I'd like you to do 'em. Will you do me the favor?' I got to thinking, well, it's a few more dollars, it'll help. We got out on the road and when we got to Mississippi, just about the time I was supposed to get through, he called a meeting and said he'd decided to go on, not to disband. So I went to him later and I said, 'Stan, I think you're makin' a terrible mistake. I can't make it, and you've been under twice the strain that I have. We get to a town and I can at least fall out and sleep somewhere. You're with the disc jockeys, you're at the radio stations after work—you'll kill yourself! *Please,* for your own sake, you shouldn't do that!'

"He got very angry with me. He said, 'It's none of your business! You get a ticket to St. Louis. That's where you joined the band, and that's where you're goin' back to!'

"I said, 'Bullshit! You asked me in Los Angeles to come out for this, and now you want to give me a twenty-seven-dollar ticket to St. Louis?' We got into quite a thing about it, and I finally said, 'Look, Stan, you're gonna pay me to go back to Los Angeles and that's that, but *please,* you go with me! Like, stop! Don't go through with this!'

111

"He walked away. And within two or three days we were in Tuscaloosa, where it all blew up."

At the University of Alabama in Tuscaloosa, they played without June Christy or Bob Cooper. When June's flu had worsened until she could no longer sing, Stan had reluctantly agreed to let her go to Miami Beach for a few days to recuperate. He was astonished when Coop indicated that he planned to accompany her. Even though Coop had lined up a substitute, Stan refused to let him go.

Coop told him he felt his relationship with June was more important to him than the orchestra because he felt she needed him, and in fact seemed on the verge of pneumonia. Coop's attitude was incomprehensible to Stan, whose intransigence finally forced Coop to say, "If we have to quit, we just have to quit!" They went to Miami Beach, and Stan went on to Tuscaloosa, driving, alone, in his Buick.

"On my way to Alabama, I was so upset I felt I had to throw up. There was all this torment that came about because Violet and I were separated so much, because she refused to go on the road anymore. At one time I saw her for about two hours in a railroad station in St. Louis, out of eighteen months of being apart. I was constantly begging her to come with me on the road, and she'd never do it. We'd have these long God damn phone conversations where we'd start cryin' and carryin' on, all kind of emotions flying. It preyed on my mind, terribly, and all of a sudden I just figured out the hell with it, the band is what's screwin' everything up, so I'm gonna get rid of it, I'm gonna go home and try to straighten out our marriage.

"I stopped alongside the road to lose my cookies. And all of a sudden I saw blood comin' out. And I thought, Oh, Christ, I'm gonna die right here in the bushes! I got back in the car, and from then on to Tuscaloosa, this just sorta took shape in my mind. I said, 'Tonight is the night, I'm gonna junk everything.'

"I got to Alabama. We played the job. After the job, I said, 'Everybody meet at the hotel and get your money, 'cause we're foldin' this thing up tonight!' "

He told them he hoped to start the band up again at some future date and gave them all a month's pay and their transportation home—a sizable amount of money. He got back into the Buick and drove through the night, feeling pursued by Petrillo, by forfeited contracts, by nameless guilts. Without his band as a point of reference, his intentions grew muddled.

"I went to the boss of a lumber yard in Arkansas, and asked for a job. I wanted to spend a few weeks there just working, physical work. He said, 'What do you do?' I told him I could do anything. He asked if I was familiar with such-and-such a saw; I said I wasn't, but that I could learn. He finally said, 'There's no job here for you! You don't know what you're doin'!' "

For days, while Carlos tried frantically to locate him, he drove aimlessly, feeling he had to hide out, lay low. Not even Violet knew where he was. Finally he called her, from Mineral Wells, Texas, and told her he was on his way home, and that she was not to tell a soul.

High with anticipation, he returned to Hollyridge expecting to find a haven of warmth and approval. But Violet had waited years for this moment, and was not about to let her advantage slip away. With so much time on her hands, she had explored the new scientific fad that was attracting Hollywood personalities in droves, and had consequently amended her "Nothing is impossible" philosophy with the qualifying phrase "through psychiatry." She welcomed Stan with folded arms—and an ultimatum. She had already filed for divorce, and she meant to go through with it—*unless* he went to see a psychiatrist.

The idea terrified him. "I didn't know anything about psychiatrists. I thought they were all guys with an eye in the middle of their foreheads who could look at you and tell you everything you've ever done wrong. I said I didn't want a psychiatrist. All I wanted was her, and our daughter."

"No psychiatrist," said Violet, "no me."

9 Progressive Jazz

"Without psychiatry, I'd be dead."

VIOLET won the battle, but she lost the war.

To Jan Rugulo, "That was the era when it was very popular to go through analysis. It was a very expensive pastime. Violet and Stan and Pete and I went to the same guy, Bernie Gindes. They tried to get Carlos and his wife involved, too, but they figured it was a big hoax. They were right. Later on, Gindes was run out of California because he was callin' himself a doctor and he wasn't a doctor at all!

"Then this child psychiatrist got involved, she was practically *living* up at their house during this *analysis* routine, studying *Leslie's* behavior. It just got way out of hand, and finally Violet's *mother* got involved, they wanted *her* analyzed! Everything anybody did was being *analyzed*! I think that was really the beginning of the end of their marriage."

To Violet, "It was productive, because you're not afraid to say what you think. Stanley finally would say 'Damn it!' or 'Go to hell!' In fact, he drove it into the ground."

To Stan, it was a revelation. "After three or four weeks of analysis, I didn't care if I was married or not! The whole thing just straightened itself out that fast! Of course, that made Violet mad as hell. It didn't work out the way she thought it was going to."

Psychiatry grabbed Stan as nothing had since his discovery of music. Since childhood, his thought processes had had an analytical bent. Here was a neat support system for a kind of logic which, if it couldn't resolve your hangups, at least offered endlessly fascinating illuminations of them. Psychiatry legitimized techniques Stan had been using for years. He was a master, for example, at psyching out his musicians. If a fan requested a demanding number when he knew the trumpet players' lips were practically numb, he would tell them at intermission, "I told the guy it would be too tough on you to play that tonight," and they would insist on doing the number if it took their next-to-last breath (the last being reserved for praising Stan's consideration). If a sideman gave notice at a time inconvenient for Stan, he would suggest they "talk it over." Such discussions invariably ended with the sideman convinced not only that staying in the band was in his own best interest, but that he was somehow obligated to Stan for allowing him to reconsider his foolish decision to leave. He had an amazing facility for projecting an authority based on the sheer dazzle of his personality and enhanced by his acquisition of enough psychological jargon to hint at a superior intellect. Even Violet, who should have known better, admits, "He used psychology on me. I thought he knew more than me. He would *analyze* everything, and dump his problems on me, even after we were divorced. He made me cry a lot."

If, as Violet contends, he used people to gain strength for himself, it was neither mean nor Machiavellian. Manipulation was as natural to him as his music. He saw his style with people with disarming naiveté:

"When I was about thirty-five years old, the realization came to me that I really, genuinely loved people. People fascinated me! This was probably the greatest revelation that ever came to me! I could communicate with total strangers, *fast*! It wasn't how to win friends and influence people, or any of that kinda crap—it was another, deeper thing. It was so much fun when I discovered that! Everywhere I'd go, it was like walkin' on top of the earth! Used to go into lonely gas stations in the middle of the night to buy gas, and some old guy would hobble out to give you gas, and there was almost a complete rapport, right away. Didn't even know his name! When you develop a genuine love for people, then there's no fear of anyone."

His rapport with his wife, however, was less than complete. Over the next few months, while he rested and regained his strength, he and Violet uneasily negotiated a cease-fire. He would live his life, she would live hers, and no questions asked. It seemed to them both to be an eminently adult, civilized arrangement.

Meanwhile, repercussions of the layoff jolted Hollyridge daily. GAC was besieged and beseeched by frantic promoters who were counting on Kenton one-nighters to keep them in the black. Faced with a substantial loss of commissions, the agency doggedly campaigned to get him back to work. Rumors proliferated that it wasn't his health that had knocked him out of action, but the fact that his band couldn't make it. Thousands of fan letters begged him to deny that he was washed up. In August, a mere four months after Tuscaloosa, *Downbeat* headlined "KENTON TO REBUILD BAND ON COAST. SEVERAL STARS WON'T RETURN." GAC booked the band into a break-in date at the Rendezvous in late September, followed by a two-week West Coast tour. The music would be "modern," oriented toward concerts rather than dances. Stan called it Progressive Jazz.

Twelve of the eighteen sidemen returned to the fold (Winding, Musso and Mussuli were notable exceptions). With Carlos acting as mediator, Christy and Stan were reconciled, although June's considerations were more practical than sentimental. "I wanted to work as a single, but Carlos thought I should go back with the band for at least six months to reestablish the relationship and make some records before going out on my own, so I went back with just that in mind. In the meantime, Stan had solved a lot of his personal problems and gone through quite a big personality change. He was more charming than ever. Within a week, he won everyone over again."

Sixteen concert dates were set at such prestigious halls as the Philadelphia Academy of Music, the Chicago Civic Opera House and Boston's Symphony Hall, symbolizing a respectability accorded few nonclassical performers. Their appearances outdrew those of philharmonic orchestras; even standing room sold out. The power, precision and unadulterated *Pow* of Progressive Jazz inspired violent critical controversy and attracted the curious along with the converts. A Carnegie Hall performance was scheduled for midnight, to appease conservative concertgoers who felt that jazz at Carnegie was tantamount to whistling in church. Tickets for every seat in the house, including three hundred folding chairs placed on the stage, were sold out within forty-eight hours. *Variety* headlined "KENTON'S CARNEGIE HALL CONCERT A KILLER BOTH ARTISTICALLY AND AT B.O.," and ecstatically described the "dissonant and atonal chords, barrels of percussion and blaring, but tremendously precise, brass" as the jazz equivalent of Stravinsky and Shostakovich. In a different vein, George Simon carped in *Metronome* that "Stan and Pete and the men who play their music so well are deeply shrouded under a neurotic conception of jazz if not of all music. Their stuff is not mellow, but megalomaniacal, constructed mechanically of some of the familiar sounds and effects of modern composers, from Bartok to Bongo Drums, with little apparent feeling for the jazz medium and none at all for the subtleties of idea and emotion which support every roar ever heard in music. . . . Stan and Pete and June and the band and its manager, Carlos Gastel, are among the very nicest people this business has ever seduced," Simon concluded, "but their collective effort, mighty as it is, is not making it. It couldn't have not happened to a nicer bunch of people."

Not all their dates were concerts, and not all their numbers were "progressive." In the ballrooms, theaters and rooms like the Century Room of the Hotel Commodore in New York, they still performed their popular hits: "St. James Infirmary," "Eager Beaver," "Southern Scandal," "Peanut Vendor," "Intermission Riff." With Rugulo, Stan had written a whole series of "Artistry" numbers featuring various soloists: "Artistry Jumps" (Bob Cooper and Milt Bernhart); "Artistry in Bolero" (Bernhart and Ray Wetzel); "Artistry in Percussion" (Shelly Manne); "Artistry in Boogie" (Cooper, Alvarez and Childers). Heavier, concert-type pieces included Kenton's "Opus in Pastels" and "Concerto To End All Concertos," and Rugulo's "Interlude," "Machito" and "Guitar Solo" (Pete's "Cuban period" introduced the brilliant Brazilian guitarist, Laurindo Almeida, to American audiences). Heaviest of all was *Prologue Suite*, a Kenton-Rugulo collaboration in four movements. Christy's segment of the concerts consisted of five numbers, including the cutesy (but commercial) "Rika Jika Jack," and the more sophisticated "How High the Moon" and "Willow Weep for Me," often performed with just a dramatic pin spot on her face.

The band won the *Downbeat* poll as Best Big Band of 1947, at that time the highest distinction a band could achieve. Individual awards also went to Stan, Rugulo, Christy, Shelly and bassist Eddie Safranski. Critics continued to carp. Said

Charles Miller in *The New Republic*, "He is looked on today by his followers, and there are millions, it would seem, as the leader in the frantic avant-garde of jazz. To me, his music is flashy and pretentious, and so what?" Miller conceded that much of Kenton's music was intelligent and imaginative, "but who wants to wade through the bombast to find it? Some piano is played with understatement and taste, but it's surrounded by ensemble choruses that nearly blast you from your seat."

Through the winter and spring of 1948, the band toured the East, Midwest, and South. They played dances only when necessary, and Stan made sure to let the world know what a concession those dates represented. "When it comes to music for dancing," he told an interviewer, "bands like Lombardo, Kaye and Carle are tops. Our band is designed for creating moods and excitement. Our band is built to thrill."

For once, he spoke without exaggeration. At the Chicago Opera House, Shelly received a five-minute standing ovation for "Artistry in Percussion." On one hot June night, also in Chicago, the band was greeted at the Pershing Ballroom by a crowd that so far exceeded the hall's five thousand capacity that the musicians and their instruments had to be passed above the shoulders of the audience to get to the bandstand.

MILT BERNHART: "Everything we did, every move we made was celebrated by people who loved the band. You began to get a little spoiled by it all. I remember being used to the idea of having a big crowd. They were huge. There was never a night without a sellout."

GEORGE MORTE, *road manager*: "Some of the followers of the band were so intense, they just literally would get gassed by the band, and I think this *fed* Stan, motivated him and gave him that drive. Backstage, I had to go out of my way to not antagonize them, to let them know they would have a moment with Stan."

ST. LOUIS POST-DISPATCH: "Neither rain nor heat nor gloom

of night nor anything short of monsoon can stay Stan Kenton's admirers from their appointed rounds when their favorite bandleader is in town."

The musicians were initially awed and a little intimidated by some of the august halls they played, and toned down their bandstand clowning accordingly—but not for long. The broad comedy provided needed relief from the intensity of the music and the concentration it demanded from musicians and audiences alike.

The secret of bandstand schtick is that when the music is sufficiently exciting, the audience actually gets high on it and, like drunks at a party, will laugh uproariously at anything—even lines like, "Hey, Stan, your laundry came back." "It did?" "Yeah. They rejected it!" When trombonist Bart Varsalona slid the bar on his "bone" out to where it seemed about to fly off, only to have it snapped back at the last minute by a rubber band, people fell off their seats. Shelly was irrepressible, capable of yelling, "Everybody into the pool!" and jumping off a riser, holding his nose, on the stage of Carnegie Hall. He would abandon his drums, appropriate Bob Cooper's tenor, and toot the one note he knew on it while lying on his back or running around the stage until Stan would collapse on the floor laughing. Most of the men shared Shelly's feeling that "It was a very happy band, a very special time. We had such respect for each other, and for Stan. Everybody had a direction; it was the time when the personnel of the band was most stable. And the ease with which Stan did it made it easier for us. We didn't know he was cracking up."

What the musicians couldn't see, *Downbeat* did. Its June 2, 1948, issue ran this editorial:

STAN KENTON AND HIS MEN ARE KILLING THEMSELVES
Never before in the history of pop music have so few men worked so terribly hard, physically, to out-blow precedent and herald modernism. Milt Bernhart is considering the estab-

blishment of a small business in Chicago; Buddy Childers and Ray Wetzel are wearing abdominal belts—to hold their insides together when they blow. . . . It is because Kenton is probably the best-liked bandleader in the business that we are concerned. His last breakdown (April, 1947) was preceded by a series of one-nighters which were child's play compared to his current schedule of concerts. When playing for a ballroom crowd, it's usually four tunes to a set, a break, an intermission every half hour, etc. . . . That routine resulted in Kenton's previous forced retirement.

A concert requires at least 1½ hours of steady playing, a 15-minute intermission, and another stint equally as long as the first, possibly longer if encores are generous. How long can Kenton stand it? What is he trying to prove?

Stan had been asking himself the same question. Progressive Jazz had been a chancy undertaking. The challenge had been met, and in the process had lost its appeal. His flirtation with psychiatry continued, through reading and sporadic appointments with Bernie Gindes when the band was in California. He began making statements like, "Jazz is neurotic," and told an undoubtedly bewildered *Downbeat* reporter, "The band reflects me as well as my musicians, and I have within me tremendous aggression and drive which have to be expressed in my music."

In June, the same month in which *Downbeat* expressed its concern for his health, Stan took the band to the Coast for some concert and recording dates. At the Hollywood Bowl, they played to fifteen thousand enraptured fans. Throughout the summer, they played only intermittent concert dates. Stan and Violet bought a modest Steelcraft powerboat on an impulse on the Fourth of July and took off for Catalina the same afternoon, overloading the little boat with Leslie, Violet's mother and their collie, and with no knowledge of navigation or even how to read a compass. To Violet, the boat promised an opportunity to be alone with her husband; but Stan was looking for escape, not intimacy, and was forever inviting the Rugulos or the Gastels or some other couple along for company. In September, the band headed east again. The Steelcraft sat at its dock for months and finally was sold.

The basics of the road are unchanging; there have always been breakdowns and blizzards and band chicks. Only the details vary. When the bus broke down in the dead of winter on a highway near Des Moines, the musicians bundled up in overcoats, scarves and mittens and marched all the way into town playing marching tunes, Shelly riding on Ray Wetzel's broad shoulders. During a blizzard that froze everything in Milwaukee, including transportation, the audience stretched out on the floor and in chairs, the band played as long as it could, and nobody went home until morning. The promoters booked them into warehouses, stables, anyplace that could house a dance. In Clovis, New Mexico, they played a football stadium where the only light came from the headlights of parked cars pointed toward the makeshift bandstand, just boards and bricks, and they all had to drench themselves in evil-smelling bug repellent to avoid being eaten alive. Christy wanted to send Carlos a box of the bugs with the contract torn into shreds on the top. But as it turned out, Carlos was already bugged. His career and Stan's, interdependent for so long, had been heading in different directions for some time. Progressive Jazz had taken them beyond the point of no return.

In spite of his affection and respect for Stan—their only contract had been scribbled on a napkin, which Carlos subsequently lost—Carlos was one of the few people immune to the Kenton charisma. By 1948, he had refined his wheeling-and-dealing techniques to a point where he could transact two deals simultaneously over two telephones, a receiver at each ear. Headwaiters brought phones to his table instead of menus. He kept his boat tied up in front of a Newport restaurant, and it was not uncommon to see a procession of waiters carrying provisions aboard. He was capable of drinking sixteen double martinis before dinner, which he rarely ate before midnight. Any friend accused of having a drinking problem could claim with self-righteous indignation, "*I'm* not an alcoholic! *Carlos* drinks more than I do!" Yet Carlos's hands shook so violently he could not put a phonograph needle down on a record without missing half the selection.

His other addiction was people. He found solitude unbearable and spent fortunes on lavish entertaining and gifts. Like many alcoholics, he was a chronic insomniac, with no qualms about calling thirty or forty people in the middle of the night. "Get here!" he would boom, and by the time they arrived, enormous quantities of food and booze would be en route from Chasen's. He called Stan at three o'clock one morning, demanding, "Get Leslie up! I'm comin' over!"

"You're stoned!" Stan replied. "Stay away!" Undeterred, Carlos appeared at the Kenton door minutes later with a gift for Leslie under his arm—a squalling baby pig!

Stan and Violet, by virtue of their temperaments and training, viewed Carlos's freewheeling style with ambivalence. On the one hand, they admired his quick mind and education and, even more, his ability to handle any situation or individual with ease. "Carlos was so much more sophisticated than we were," recalls Violet. "When Stanley was on the road, Carlos would call and take me out to dinner. I had never been to Romanoff's and fancy places. During the war, Carlos would get the waiter to give me a pound of butter to take home. When he opened his fancy office on Sunset, he invited me to come see it. Waiters from Ciro's would bring dinner and champagne right into his office!"

At the same time, they resented his extravagance with what they felt was their money. "Stanley'd be working so hard for all this money that he'd send to Carlos, and Carlos was flyin' back and forth across the country, chargin' meals and makin' long-distance phone calls, and we're payin' for it! It was always against Stanley's principles, and mine. You don't have to buy your way, you don't have to be buyin' people presents and takin' 'em to dinner. Stanley finally told Carlos to knock it off." Furthermore, Carlos had gradually acquired a sizable stable of talent, including Nat Cole, Peggy Lee, Mel Torme and Nellie Lutcher, all of whom demanded their share of his time and energy.

In the summer of 1948, the gap between the music Stan was playing and the music Carlos was promoting had widened irreversibly. They agreed that, professionally, they had gone as far as they could go together.

JIM CONKLING, *producer, Capitol Records*: "Carlos would book Stan and then Stan would play concert music instead of what was promised, and the bookers would pressure Carlos, 'Can't you get him to do what he's supposed to do?'"

MILT BERNHART: "At the Hollywood Bowl concert, I over-heard Stan and Gastel in the dressing rooms, having a strong set-to. Gastel had created a mystique around the name *Stan Kenton*; Stan could never have done it on his own. Gastel had come up with a radio show with an auto sponsor, Ford or Chrysler, who were willing to do like a Fred Waring-style weekly hour show. A show like that probably would have operated out of New York; the band would have had a place to sit down, and around New York were a lot of places to play, on weekends or whenever, and it would've been very nice for everybody—for Stan, too. I was standing in the hall-way; I heard it all. Carlos said, 'Now all they want from you, Stan, is a couple of pop tunes.' And Stan said, No, I won't subvert my art, or words to that effect, and he made a very strong speech about selling out. So Carlos said, 'Well, Stan, I've done everything I can. This is as far as I can go.' And Stan said okay."

STAN KENTON: "As far as our getting started, I doubt if I ever could've done it without Carlos. But when we started the Progressive Jazz period, a lot of the music was kinda hard to take. He said, 'You're gettin' crazy, I don't want to have anything more to do with it.' So we made a deal and I paid him off. It wasn't very much money, something like fifteen thousand bucks. People like me are very hard to manage. Managers usually are people that guide other people, and I'm awfully headstrong, maybe to the point of being bullheaded lots of times. So it's best, I think, that people like myself maybe take on the responsibility of managing themselves."

Even though the band continued to be the hottest box office attraction in the country and won the *Downbeat* poll for the second year in a row, its audiences were polarizing into the Listeners, who crowded around the bandstand, and the Dancers, behind them. "As a result," Stan told an interviewer, "it's impossible for us to attempt to satisfy more than half the crowd. The fans up front are mad when we play for the dancers. The dancers are griped when we play the style for which we've been fortunate enough to gain some fame." At a college prom in Ann Arbor, a fist fight broke out between the two factions.

In December, during a sellout engagement at New York's Paramount Theater, Stan sent a personal telegram to each of his musicians stating that it had been great working with them, and he was disbanding. "I released a big story to the trades that if we couldn't play music the way we wanted to play, we weren't gonna play it! And I really meant it! I thought, God damn it, I'm through with this hassle with these ballrooms! That night, after the last show, there sat Tom Rockwell in my dressing room—by this time, I was calling him Tom. He said, 'I want you to meet some people,' and he took me over to a beautiful room in the old Capitol Hotel. It had terraces and a balcony and everything.

"Rockwell says, 'You think you could make a jazz club out of this place?'

"I said, 'Yeah, it'd be great!'

"He says, 'You think you can get this place goin' for seventy-five thousand dollars?'

"I said, 'Yeah.' He said, 'I got the money.' He just kinda snapped his fingers and here came this guy, a big man. Rockwell says, 'Here's your seventy-five thousand dollars, and he'll help you run it.'

"I was very elated—but the band was already on notice. About ten days later we folded up and went back to California. The plan was to come back East and open up this club, which would've been the first jazz club in America. But I never did. 'Cause when I got to California, I had already decided to give up music and become a psychiatrist."

10 Innovations

*"I wanted Stanley home, to be a father for his child, and
I kept bitchin' about it, and we could feel that we were
growing further and further apart. We were trying to hang
on."*

VIOLET KENTON FOSTER

IN Stan's confused state of mind, psychiatry seemed a
perfect solution to his dilemma. The subject fascinated him;
it was a lucrative and challenging and *respectable* field; and
it was a way to get off the road for good. That it would require twelve years of study seemed a minor detail. But before
embarking on this bright new life, Stan and Violet decided
to take Leslie on a long-postponed vacation.

They drove to New Orleans and boarded a cargo vessel
for South America, intending to buy a boat down there and
sail it back. As Violet remembers it, "We had a marvelous
time on the boat." To Stan, "It was miserable, no fun at all.
There were about fourteen days when we didn't even see
land anywhere. I just sat on the deck of that ship every day,
thinkin', goin' over everything. And before we ever got to
Bahia, the first stop, I saw that I was makin' a mistake. Here
I was goin' into a strange field like medicine, psychiatry,
when I hadn't even scratched the surface of music. So by

the time we got to South America, I had abandoned the idea of going back to school.

"And Violet was going through the hells. Anybody would even stop me for an autograph, she just flew up in the air, she was so disenchanted with the whole thing.

"We were standing on the deck of the ship in Rio. The docks were full, and the boat was waiting for a place to dock. We had refused to let our names be on the passenger list, so that nobody would bother us. So she and Leslie and I were standing at the rail, looking across the bay, and all of a sudden a launch pulled up and there were a couple of guys on there with cameras, and they asked the first mate if they could see Stan Kenton. My wife had something in her hand, a camera or something, and she said, 'That's *it!*' And she threw it right into the bay!"

Violet remembers the incident but insists, nonetheless, "We had an awfully good time. I remember Winchell at that time printed that I was going to have another baby. We wanted to go across to Europe, but Leslie was real homesick. And I could tell Stanley was restless," she concedes. "He missed the music business."

They returned by way of Florida and some Southern dude ranches and, all told, were away nearly four months. "When we came home from that fiasco, Violet and Leslie and I went down to Lakewood Village. Her stepfather had bought a house down there that he wanted to rent for some income. So we decided we would redecorate it and fix it all up. We were supposed to go down for two weeks and, Christ, we were still there after two months.

"We finally got the God damn thing finished. We went to a drive-in restaurant one morning for breakfast, and Violet told me then that she didn't want any more of the marriage— that she was going to marry Jimmy Foster, her cousin. They'd been seein' a lot of each other, and I didn't even know it. So

129

I said, Okay, if that's it, that's it. That's when I knew I was goin' back into music with all my might. So that's when I conceived the idea of the Innovations orchestra. 'Cause it just got that that was gonna be my life."

In 1948, Stan had emphatically stated to *Downbeat* that the use of string sections by big bands was "a thrilling sound, but not for jazz and jazz bands, certainly not for ours." The Innovations orchestra, a tremendously ambitious, costly and controversial venture, consisted of forty pieces. Sixteen of them were strings.

Stan's announcement that he was forming a forty-piece orchestra that would include such nonjazz instruments as violins, violas, horns and tuba, English horn, oboe and bassoon, prompted Buddy Childers to dub him The Man of La Mancha. "Stan had made an *awful* lot of money from about 1946 to 1950; even after the time he laid off, he *still* had a lot of money. And he proceeded to *blow* it on what I call The Silly Symphony. The only thing silly about it was, it was one of those impossible dreams. It was magnificent—a great orchestra! One of the greatest musical experiences of my entire life! But . . . impossible!"

The dream was to bring about a musical revolution: to bridge the gap between classical music and jazz. It was the natural outgrowth of the daydreams spun by the fourteen-year-old boy who so desperately wanted to *be* somebody, to do something *important.* The musical equivalent of the respectability accorded, say, a psychiatrist, was the concert stage. Stan proceeded to assemble a miniature symphony orchestra, with woodwinds, violins, cellos and tympani augmenting a roaring, red-hot jazz band. The dream caught the imaginations of the top musicians in the country. At auditions, the competition was fierce.

BUD SHANK: "During Stan's layoff, Buddy, Shelly, Coop and Christy were working casuals around L.A. Toward late summer, they got the word that Stan was forming this band and was looking for a first alto player who could double on flute. I'd been playing flute maybe four years, but not very seriously. All of a sudden, I got very serious about it. I spent a lot of woodshed hours with my flute. Instead of taking one lesson a week, I took two. I auditioned with quite a few other guys, most of them better flute players than I was. But a flute and saxophone double wasn't too common at that time; I guess I was the first jazz-oriented musician to get interested in both. And I got the job!"

Both Art Pepper and trumpeter-arranger Shorty Rogers were hired, according to Buddy Childers, through the grace of Buddy Childers. "I would get it in my mind about someone who really needed the gig and was right for the band —people I fought with Stan to hire. I hounded his office almost every day. He didn't want to hire Shorty because he thought there was too much of a connection with Woody Herman. And Art Pepper had gotten drunk a couple of times when he was with the band many years earlier, before Art started his real downhill trek—but at that time, he was a giant of a player. The things I went through in that office—begging and pleading!"

With Shank on lead alto and Pepper handling the jazz solos, the saxophone section was rounded out by Bob Cooper, Bart Caldarell and Bob Gioga. In the trombone section were Harry Betts, Bob Fitzpatrick, Bart Varsalona, Bill Russo and Milt Bernhart, to whom fell most of the solos.

The coping on the wall of brass that was the Kenton trademark was the trumpet section: Chico Alvarez, Buddy Childers, Don Paladino and Shorty Rogers. Perched jauntily atop that wall, Humpty Dumpty with a horn, was the most idealized superstar of any Kenton aggregation, ever: Maynard Ferguson.

Maynard was an unlikely candidate for superstar. He was

raised in Canada in a protected environment, and that environment accompanied him to the United States in the person of his mother, his father and his brother. The Ferguson family followed the bus in an old Ford, in which the entire family, Maynard included, slept, parked by the side of the road. Despite the fact that Maynard was making close to four hundred dollars a week, they considered hotels an unnecessary luxury. Maynard was forbidden to smoke or drink or go out with girls. Off the bandstand, he dressed in wild outfits; his favorite shoes were plaid.

Maynard had served his apprenticeship on the road with Jimmy Dorsey and Charlie Barnet. With the Innovations orchestra, he came into his own. The impossibly high notes he blew had been blown before, but never with such infallible power, clarity and consistency. His solos were meteoric, incandescent, radioactive. Shorty Rogers composed a frenetic, demanding showstopper titled "Maynard Ferguson" to stretch —and showcase—Maynard's phenomenal talent. Maynard could play the number twice in one night, his neck expanding like a glassblower's, and not miss a note. His horn put that soaring, screaming top on the band's sound that Stan had always been after, and changed the complexion of that sound forevermore.

In the rhythm section were Don Bagley on bass, Laurindo Almeida on guitar, Carlos Vidal on congas and the man Stan called the world's greatest living drummer, Shelly Manne.

The size of the band necessitated two buses, which were quickly designated The Quiet Bus and The Balling Bus. Bob Gioga was in charge of The Quiet Bus, which contained the string players—headed by concertmaster George Kast, they considered the jazz players barbarians—and an occasional exile from The Balling Bus, the scene of a perpetual poker game and party. Stan once sent a scout from The Balling Bus to "See what those intellectuals are doin' in there!" The scout came back shaking his head, mystified. "They're *reading!*" he reported. "And *sleeping!*"

INNOVATIONS

If the Innovations concept captured the imaginations of the musicians, it sent composers into orbit! Pete Rugulo, Shorty Rogers, Neal Hefti, Johnny Richards, Laurindo Almeida, Franklyn Marks, Chico O'Farrill and Bob Graettinger contributed to the book. The compositions varied widely, from Bill Russo's moody "Ennui" to Manny Albam's exotic "Samana." Most of the arrangements were elaborate and experimental; many had a Latin beat. Critic George Simon described the programs as "a mixture of atonal concert arrangements, sometimes reminiscent of Bartok, with works that had a tangential relationship to jazz."

When a concert tour was set to begin in mid-February of 1950, the enormity of the undertaking caused Stan some apprehension. He arranged a pretour trial-run performance, primarily invitational, at the Los Angeles Philharmonic Auditorium.

The orchestra performed in street clothes before an audience of young people that overflowed the 2,670-seat Philharmonic. Stan nervously tried to prepare them for what was coming, but the best he could do was to warn them, "If you start looking for melody, you won't find any. . . . We got a great thing out of concocting sound. . . . It's sound concoction." He asked the audience to write their confidential reactions to the music on cards that were handed out, then whirled around and gave the downbeat for the bongos that start off Neal Hefti's "In Veradero."

Time's accounting was typically acerbic:

> The first belt of sound from the brasses pinned the audience to its chairs. Lanky Stan Kenton flapped his arms like a scarecrow in a hurricane as the band blasted out a "montage" of the jazzed-up dissonances that Kentonites have slavered over since 1941: *Artistry In Percussion, Opus In Pastels, Artistry Jumps.* Every once in awhile he gave them a breather. Christy . . . cooed *Get Happy, Lonesome Road* and *I'll Remember April.* Most of the time it was a bewildering battle between the violins, violas and cellos on one

133

side and the bursting brasses on the other. Kenton himself admitted there was room for improvement. "The greatest criticism we had was for the fact that the brass section, when it spoke, it spoke so loud that the string section which it interrupted was so completely dominated that it all sounded disconnected—as if they were playing two different pieces."

He was sure he was on the right track with his main idea. "People hear music and they don't know what the hell they like about it, but it creates a certain turmoil, a certain insecurity, things that are with us today."

Earnest, ever-posing Stan Kenton was set to take his turmoil on a tour of 77 U.S. and Canadian cities, beginning this week.

Most critics were kinder; but the critics were trained and paid to make the effort to meet the music halfway. The audience was not. Droves of Stan's most devoted fans were turned off by the complicated, unconventional harmonies, the flatted intervals, the beatlessness and what they considered lack of emotion in much of the music. The classicists resisted the jazz aspects of the selections, and the jazz fans were turned off by the heavy stuff. For many, many loyal fans, the music of Bob Graettinger was the last straw.

During the band's first engagement at the Hollywood Palladium in 1941, Howard Rumsey spotted a tall, gaunt, intense teen-ager with disproportionately large hands and dark, deep-set eyes, hanging around the bandstand night after night. During one intermission, he shyly introduced himself. His name was Bob Graettinger, he told Rumsey, and he had these arrangements. . . . Did Rumsey think Stan might take a look at them?

The arrangements were amateurish, but ambitious. Stan emcouraged the boy to keep writing, and forgot him.

Six years later, during a rehearsal of the Progressive Jazz orchestra in Hollywood, Graettinger turned up again—taller, thinner, and with a haunted look in his eyes that betrayed the fact that, at twenty-four, he was already wasted. He wore an ill-fitting suit and carried an arrangement under his arm.

Graettinger had by this time played alto saxophone for Vido Musso, Alvino Rey, Benny Carter and Bobby Sherwood, for whom he had also done some competent but unexceptional dance arrangements. Drafted toward the end of the war, he had quickly received a medical discharge—for alcoholism. Shortly thereafter, during a period of sobriety (some lasted as long as a year), he announced to a friend, "I have more to say than I can say with one horn," and gave away his alto, never to play again. He enrolled in Westlake School of Music, in Los Angeles. Westlake was oriented toward scoring for films, rather than the classics, and had a fine reputation. But Graettinger's ambitions were neither classical nor commercial. To him, music was a vehicle—the only one available to him—of expression for the conflagration that raged inside him and would, before his thirty-fifth birthday, destroy him.

SHELLY MANNE: "Graettinger was the kind of guy that, you don't know what to say about him! Even though we were on the road with him, spent time with him, we really never knew him."

BILL HOLMAN: "I felt that Graettinger had a goal with his music, the same as I did with my rhythm and warmness, but I never did find out what it was. His music came out kind of cold, but I never felt that he was like that. I never had a conversation with him. When he came out on the road, he would hang out with management, and I was labor; I think he might have been more pro-labor than management, but he always wound up there. We were kind of in awe of him; none of us understood his music."

VIOLET FOSTER: "He was a loner—very introspective, preoccupied. I suppose he saw all those *notes* goin' by all the time."

STEVE PERLOW, *saxophone*: "When we socialized, we talked about music."

CLINTON ROMER: "As long as he ate and had his cigarettes and his music, that was all he wanted. He lived like the novel or motion picture version of the starving composer living in the garret. Every time you were around him, it was like a chapter out of a book or out of a movie."

JAN RUGULO: "He was a very *weird* person. He had this terrible coloring—sick. He looked like he was just out of the picture all of the time. Just very *weird*. We didn't really have a lot of weird characters on the band, but he was really very *strange*."

GENE HOWARD: "Bob Graettinger was frightening! Probably the world's first hippie. Completely and utterly a nonconformist. He wrote things that I still don't understand, and I think that if Stan would be completely honest with himself, he doesn't understand them either!"

STAN KENTON: "His music is great! I know it's great! No doubt in my mind!"

Graettinger lived like a derelict, in a succession of ten-dollar-a-month rooms over garages or in tiny Hollywood "courts." His possessions consisted of a card table; a couple of apple boxes; a mattress that lay, bedsteadless, on the floor and, except for the bleakest periods, a little upright piano. He had one glass, one cup, one saucer and a frying pan in which he scrambled thousands of eggs. He believed that if he ate enough high-protein food and drank enough milk and took vitamins, his body would withstand any amount of abuse, including lack of sleep. Graettinger literally *hated* sleep. "Sleep in the grave," he'd say. He was shabby and untidy, but clean—obsessively so. He never had more than one suit, a blue one; when his belt wore out or couldn't be found, he simply substituted a length of rope.

While Graettinger's poverty was not, as some suspected,

a pose, something in him must have perversely relished it, for in all the years he was on the Kenton payroll, he refused to accept more than twenty-five dollars a week. "I'd try to force more on him, but he'd say, 'No, I'm straight, I get all my vitamins, I'm all right.' I'd say, 'Graettinger, come on, you're not livin' right! You're too God damn skinny!' He'd say, 'No, I'm straight, don't you worry about me. Twenty-five dollars a week is all I need.'

"Once in a while we'd have to go somewhere where he was going to be introduced, and I'd say, 'What clothes have you got to wear?' And he'd say, 'This.' And I'd say, 'That's not good enough, Graettinger. Come on, I'm gonna buy you a suit.' I'd pick out the material, and tell the tailor how to cut it, and Graettinger would wear the suit."

Graettinger's relationships with women illustrate the peculiarly elliptical romantic entanglements of many musicians. From 1947 to '49, Graettinger lived with Gale Madden, who had appropriated her last name from another saxophone player, Dave Madden, who had also lived with, but never married her. Gale was a frustrated pianist; she saw herself as the woman behind the genius (whomever he might be at the moment). She *looked* even freakier than Graettinger, in mismatched shoes, men's clothes, whatever took her fancy. She shared Graettinger's oblique perspective on life and was one of the few people who could make him laugh. But she was volatile and erratic, if not downright psychotic; Graettinger came home one day to find everything dyed pink—bedspread, towels, curtains, clothes, shoes, everything. Sexually, the relationship was bizarre. Gale had a reputation for being, to use one musician's phrase, "a sexual circus," and Graettinger was impotent; the implications can scarcely be imagined.

When Gale left Graettinger, it was for still another saxophone player—Gerry Mulligan—and there were others after him. Graettinger subsequently became involved, platonically but closely, with Lois Madden, who had married *Dave* Madden after Gale's departure from *his* life.

"I live above the timberline," Graettinger told Lois, "where nothing grows." Truly, that landscape is the visual counterpart of his music: desolate, stark, chilling, terrifying. The influences on Graettinger's music ranged from Beethoven's *Eroica* to Stravinsky, but the notes he made to himself on his incredibly intricate worksheets reveal that the strongest influence was nature. Bars and phrases are described as DESERT SOUNDS . . . RIPPLES, THEN WAVES . . . THE OPEN SEA AND WOODS AND HILLTOPS. PERHAPS A BIG WAVE, THEN BACKWASH DURING WHICH THE CELLO ENTERS . . . THE RAW CHORUSES ARE LIKE BEING THROWN AROUND IN WAVES. And, poignantly, THOSE FOOL BIRDS AGAIN.

Other notes, scribbled in other margins, pinpoint the solitary spot where Bob Graettinger lived. SOME FAMILIAR AND DYNAMICALLY JOYOUS SOUND . . . ALL KINDS OF INNER THINGS POKING THROUGH . . . THINK OF THE BEAUTY OF THE ACTUAL INSTRUMENT . . . A WOODWIND SOARING OVER MIDDLE STRING SOUNDS . . . THIS BUILD UP MUST HAVE ITS JOYOUS ASPECTS. IT IS LIKE SOME FANTASTIC EVENT . . . IN THE OBLIVION, USE THE MIDDLE FLUTE VERY TENDERLY . . . CLIMAX IS AFTER THE PEAK IS REACHED, THEN MAKE IT TO THE OBLIVION THAT YOU SO SELDOM ACHIEVE, THEN GRADUALLY COME DOWN FROM IT . . . BE ADVENTURESOME WITH MELODY; SHOW IT IS LIKE A DAM BREAKING WITH A SHOWER OF ALL THE OTHER THEMES, TOO. . . . And in bright green ink, underlined: *WHAT DO YOU HEAR?*

Then . . . CLEAN ALL OF THIS SHIT UP TODAY!
THE PRESSURE IS ON—RIGHT NOW!
RELAX!

And finally, in the middle of a fragment of a score:
HEAVEN.

The chart Graettinger handed Stan at that afternoon rehearsal was "Thermopylae." It was dramatic, daring, *different;*

138

Stan was impressed, and recorded the piece before the year ended. He put Graettinger on the payroll, even while confessing to friends that "I don't know whether his music is genius or a bunch of crap!" Most of Graettinger's work was unsuited to regular engagements of the Progressive Jazz orchestra and was performed only rarely, during concert dates. The musicians were mystified by his music and his method of working.

ART PEPPER: "Graettinger didn't write just for a band, or for sections; he wrote for each individual person, more or less like Duke Ellington and Billy Strayhorn did. It was so very difficult to play, because you were independent of the guy next to you. If you got lost, you were dead, because there was no way to figure out where you were at. But in order to do this, he spent a long, long time just traveling with the band. We played one-nighters, mostly, and we'd be on the bandstand playing, and he was very tall, and he looked sort of like a ghoul or a vampire or something; he had these strange, haunting eyes, and he stood out. All you'd have to do was look out in the crowd and you could see him immediately, even in the balcony! He would just stand and listen to the band. Then on the next set, he'd be in another spot. He would block everything out, if he could, and listen to just one particular person, and get that person's sound, the way that person played; because even though together it sounds the same, everybody has their own little personal connotations of playing the same thing. He wrote for each person, like as far as the projection of their sound, how the sound carried, what it reminded him of, and he spent months just doing that, just standing and listening to the band."

Circa 1950, the Innovations period, Art Pepper had no way of knowing that his career as a brilliant alto soloist had already peaked, and that what then seemed a harmless flirtation with drugs would lead him to addiction and nine years in San Quentin. In hindsight, however, he recalls wonderingly,

139

"Graettinger perceived my sound as being very mournful and very sad. Very introverted. Very unhappy. Very tragic, very lonely, very unhappy, very turbulent. And he told me this at a time when I was still young and everything was going great. And the way he described my sound is exactly the way my life went.

"It seemed to me that he knew that he didn't have long. He never wasted any time. He was a true existentialist. He was God. There was nothing outside of himself. People were nothing more than things to be used to further his art. He talked of himself as a genius; he was a self-admitted genius. But he *was* a genius.

"I was one of the few people that would spend time with him. We'd smoke pot together and just talk. When he died, I was very unhappy because I always had the feeling that if he had lived he would've been someone that I could've went to and talked to and possibly gotten some direction or understanding or sympathy or whatever it is that you need. . . ."

Instead of composing on conventional score paper, Graettinger used large sheets of graph paper with the tiniest squares available—one hundred to the square inch. In many of the squares, with delicate precision, he drew infinitesimal numbers, letters, circles, squares and hieroglyphics decipherable only by himself. But the bulk of the squares reflected his lifelong preoccupation with color; varying intensities of blue, orange, red, violet, green and yellow formed abstract pictures of sounds. The top line of the graph indicated the notes. The left side, from top to bottom, represented all the instruments in the orchestra, from the highest possible sound—Maynard Ferguson's trumpet—down to the lowest register of Bob Gioga's baritone. And each instrument had its own color. When copyist Clinton Romer transposed the music to score paper,

the notes corresponded to the patterns on the graphs. Graettinger explained the process to Art Pepper after completing
his major work, a four-part suite called *City of Glass*.

"He drew a city, coming into the city, with colors, on the
graph paper. As you would approach the city, there wouldn't
be much, occasionally a little sign or something, and the sign
would be just so many squares of color, condensed, like a block
of sound. Then as you approached the city, more and more
things would happen—more notes, more colors. When it was
daytime, it would be bright colors, depicting a whole city—
buildings and trees and sidewalks and people. A tree would
be like a tree in the picture, and when you saw the score,
there would be all kinds of notes that would look like a tree.
If it was a bright tree, then it would be bright instruments,
like trumpets, that had a high, bright tonality. If it was dull
and dark and dreary, he would use lower sounds, dreary,
subtle sounds—trombones, or bass. For the solos, he used each
person's particular sound, depending on what he wanted—a
sad sound or a bright sound, or dull, or morbid. If you knew
the format, you could actually see the pictures of what was
happening."

Graettinger worked on *City of Glass* for over a year, sitting at the piano twelve to fourteen hours a day, seven days
a week. It was premiered by the Progressive Jazz orchestra
in the summer of 1948, to a capacity audience at the Chicago
Civic Opera House, with the composer nervously conducting.
In Stan's view, "The way to listen to *City of Glass* is to sit
alone or with someone you have an especially good rapport
with, and have a few tastes first. You're not supposed to understand it. It's fantasy. You experience it with your subcon-
scious." But the audience at the Chicago Civic that night was
without benefit of this advice. When the last dissonant, nerve-
jangling notes died away, they sat as though turned to stone

—baffled, confused, silent. After a long, frozen moment, Stan jumped up from the piano, gestured for the musicians to take a bow, and turned to the audience with both arms high in the air, indicating that what they'd heard was something great, and it was *over*. Obediently, they stood and cheered.

The Innovations repertoire included a substantial sampling of Graettinger's music, from the comparatively swinging "Incident in Jazz" to the haunting "House of Strings." *City of Glass* was scored to include the string section, and in December of 1952, Capitol reluctantly recorded that version. Lee Gillette produced the album.

"As Stan's producer, I was his representative, so I'm the one that had the big battle with the people upstairs. Nobody understood *City of Glass*. What were we trying to do? Why were we going to pour money down the drain to promote something like this? My arguments always were, 'I think Stan has proven himself up to now; I don't think we should stand in his way! He may not have had all million record sellers, true, but he certainly was making a big dent in the music industry.' And they would admit that and they'd go along, but they'd always try to slow us down."

When Gillette was arguing for *City of Glass*, he had not yet heard the piece performed. Stan, the flimflam man, had presold him. When the time came to record it, "The engineer and I had a rough time with the scores because of that graph system Graettinger used. It was unquestionably the hardest album that was ever made with Stan. The night that we completed the album, I took the dubs home. We lived out in Van Nuys, in an orchard more or less, and I had a record building off from the house. I went out there about one o'clock in the morning and played this whole album, and when I got through and opened the door, I was afraid to walk to the house!

"Some of the branches [of Capitol] thought we were out

of our minds to record it. Others raved about it. And it didn't sell that much. I don't think we sold ten thousand albums."

Downbeat gave the album four stars; Rob Darrell's review of January 28, 1953, verged on hysteria:

> If your nerves are still raw and twitchin' from New Year's . . . If a kitten daintily padding across an inch-deep rug-nap sets you groanin' "Pul-lease quit that stompin' around!" . . . Then you're in no fitten shape for such rackety-rax aural calisthenics as I'm prescribing today. For I've got a rugged workout for ya, man, and no softies or kids are gonna stand the gaff.
>
> But if you've got tough ears and constitutions, I can promise you an adventure in new sound you'll never forget. . . .
>
> You'll be feeling no pane either when Stan Kenton gets through with Bob Graettinger's *City of Glass*—probably the most exciting, maybe one of the most vital, and certainly the noisiest symphonic experiment yet achieved by a jazz composer and conductor.
>
> Actually, there's no jazz in it (except for an echo or two in the *Dance Before A Mirror* third movement) but it sure is as "modern" as you can get. It's out of Schoenbergian and Bartokian blood-lines, perhaps, as far as the music itself goes, but all dolled up with the very latest in Graettinger and Kenton-style innovations where the frenzied but dazzling interplay of sonorities is concerned.
>
> It's almost intolerably harsh and shrill in stretches. Some of the stunts are beaten to exhaustion, a few are thrown away before they really get going, and oftentimes the use of too many effects at once tends to cancel out much of their impact. I wish Graettinger were as clever a dramatic psychologist as he is a sound-pattern weaver, for his work needs more astute editing and organization. Yet, for all that, he's got something here that's brashly alive and at its best tremendously exciting.
>
> . . . Graettinger is a genuine pioneer. . . .

143

Equal time to critic Barry McRae:

> The sheer pomposity of arrangements provided by Graettinger
> marked a nadir in the band's life. Even his scores for 32-bar
> popular songs were uncomfortably formal and, in spite of his
> brilliant use of dissonance, they tended to become flaccid
> performances. There was a certain air of detachment about
> much of his work, and *City of Glass* confirmed that his true
> talent lay outside the field of jazz.

Nobody has ever claimed to understand *City of Glass*.
It was as difficult to play as it was to listen to. Bill Russo
remembers, "A lot of those chords hurt your teeth. Especially
your fillings!" Shelly Manne, attempting to describe what Bob
Graettinger's music was all about, says, "He tried to write
electronically, with conventional instruments. His whole concept of writing was tension and release—to create terrible
tension in a person's ear through dissonance, and then release
it." But the music reflected the man; and always, the tension
exceeded the release.

Graettinger was amused by the pretensions of the critics,
who in turn called his music pretentious. He claimed to use
Downbeat for toilet paper. His music, he said, was a diary
of his life, his emotional autobiography. Unable to relate to
people, he sought relief in the mountains, at the seashore, at
the zoo. And, when all else failed, from a bottle.

To listen to *City of Glass* and its sequel, *This Modern
World*, is to experience the isolation, the exposed nerve ends,
the exquisite anguish of Bob Graettinger. His music defies
time, space and value judgments. But for Stan Kenton, it
might never have been heard.

Stanley with Beulah and Irma Mae.

Gus Arnheim and his Orchestra, 1937. Stanley is at the piano, Jack Ordean in far left saxophone chair, "Pee Wee" George standing at rear. Rice Hotel, Houston.

Stanley and Violet in the early days of their marriage.

The first "Artistry in Rhythm" band—at Frank Dailey's Meadowbrook, in 1942. Trumpets: Chico Alvarez, Frank Beach, Earl Collier. Trombones: Loren Aaron, Dick Cole, Harry Forbes. Saxophones: Bob Gioga, Jack Ordean, Ted Romersa (behind Ordean), Bill Leahy, Red Dorris. Bass: Howard Rumsey. Guitar: Al Costi. Drummer: "Pee Wee" George. Vocalist (behind Stan) is Eve Knight.

Howard Rumsey.

Stanley's first official publicity picture. 1942.

This ad ran nationally in 1942.

Stan with his first arrangers: Gene Howard, Gene Roland and Boots Mussuli. Photo by Gene Howard.

Vocalists Gene Howard and Anita O'Day. Photo by Buddy Childers.

With Stella and Floyd, at the Hollywood Palladium.

Top row: Vido Musso, John Anderson, Milt Kabak, Shelly Manne, Pete Rugulo, Ray Wetzel. Bottom row: Ken Hanna, Gene Howard, Buddy Childers, Eddie Safranski. 1946.

Shelly Manne, June Christy, Bart Varsallona, Chico Alvarez, circa 1947.

With Violet and Leslie, in 1947. Violet commissioned the portrait as a Father's Day gift for Stan, who never liked it . . . Photo by Gene Howard.

. . . but displayed it in his dressing room, nevertheless. Here with Pete Rugulo. Photo by Buddy Childers.

Buddy Childers' twenty-first birthday party, 1947. Behind Buddy's mother (left foreground) are Pete and Jan Rugulo, Carlos and Joan Gastel, Patti Andrews (in fur coat), Bob Cooper, Bob and Dorothy Gioga. Behind Buddy are Mel Tormé, Eddie Safranski (with hand on Tormé's arm), Stan and Shelly.

When the bus broke down on a country road in Iowa, the band marched into town. The three brass players behind leader Ray Wetzel are Milt Bernhart, Buddy Childers, Bart Varsallona.

The Progressive Jazz band at the Commodore Hotel, New York, 1948. Shelly Manne, drums; Eddie Safranski, bass; Jack Costanza, bongos; Laurindo Almeida, guitar. Trumpets: Al Porcino, Buddy Childers, Ray Wetzel, Ken Hanna, Chico Alvarez. Trombones: Eddie Bert, Harry Forbes, Harry Betts, Milt Bernhart, Bart Varsallona. Saxophones: Bob Cooper, Art Pepper, George Weidler, Warner Weidler, Bob Gioga. (The preceding night they had all worn boutonnieres with their new uniforms; only Pepper salvaged his for a second night.)

Shelly Manne, 1948.

Stan and Maynard, 1949.

During the first Innovations tour, Bud Shank and his new bride were serenaded by this quartet from the string section. Photo by Buddy Childers.

DATE	PLACE OF ENGAGEMENT	CITY AND STATE
9/14	Palais Royale	South Bend, Indiana
9/15	Records Universal Studios	Chicago, Illinois
9/16	Lake Side Park	Dayton, Ohio
9/17	Westview Park	Pittsburgh, Pa.
9/18	Onendaga War Mem. (Rehearsals)	Syracuse, N.Y.
9/19	Onendaga War Memorial Aud.	Syracuse, New York
9/20	Maple Leaf Gardens	Toronto, Canada
9/21	The Forum	Montreal, Canada
9/22	Memorial Auditorium	Guelph, Canada
9/23	London Arena	London, Ontario, Can.
9/24	Memorial Hall	Columbus, Ohio
9/25	Auditorium	Atlanta, Georgia
9/26	Bell Memorial Aud.	Augusta, Georgia
9/27	Ft. Hesterly Armory	Tampa, Florida
9/28	Miami Beach Aud. (4 P.M)	Miami Beach, Fla.
9/28	Dinner Key Aud. (8:30 P.M.)	Miami, Florida
9/29	Gater Bowl Stadium	Jacksonville, Fla.
9/30	County Hall	Charleston, S. C.
10/1	Columbia Township Aud.	Columbia, S. C.
10/2	Auditorium	Raleigh, North Carolina
10/3	Memorial Aud.	Norfolk, Virginia
10/4	Mosque Theatre	Richmond, Va.
10/5	National Guard Armory	Washington, D. C.
10/6	The Coliseum	Baltimore, Maryland
10/7	Mosque	Newark, New Jersey
10/8	Westchester County Centre	White Plains, N. Y.
10/9	Bashnell Memorial Aud.	Hartford, Conn.
10/10	Arena	Philadelphia, Pa.
10/11	Carnegie Hall	New York City
10/12	Rhode Island Aud.	Providence, R. I.
10/13	Boston Gardens	Boston, Mass.
10/14	Auditorium	Worcester, Mass.
10/15	R.P.I. Field House	Troy, New York
10/16	Open	
10/17	Arena	Cleveland, Ohio
10/18	Cincinnati Gardens	Cincinnati, Ohio
10/19	Civic Opera House	Chicago, Illinois
10/20	Open	
10/21	Allen County Memorial Coliseum	Fort Wayne, Indiana
10/22	Auditorium	Charleston, W. Va.
10/23	Stambough Aud.	Youngstown, Ohio
10/24	The Gardens	Pittsburgh, Pa.
10/25	Arena	Toledo, Ohio
10/26	I.N.A. Auditorium	Flint, Michigan
10/27	Michigan State College	E. Lansing, Mich.
10/28	Municipal Auditorium	Grand Rapids, Mich.
10/29	Indiana Theatre	Indianapolis, Ind.
10/30	Gym University Illinois	Urbana, Illinois
10/31	Open	
11/1	Kiel Aud. Opera House	St. Louis, Mo.
11/2	Auditorium	Kansas City, Mo.
11/3	The Shrine Aud.	Springfield, Mo.
11/4	The Forum	Witchita, Kansas
11/5	The Coliseum, Univ. of Nebr.	Lincoln, Nebraska
11/6	Open	
11/7	Field House Univ. of Wisconsin	Madison, Wisconsin
11/8	Auditorium	Milwaukee, Wisconsin
11/9	Open	
11/10	WRNT Radio Theatre	Des Moines, Iowa

This Route subject to change, cancellation and additions.

A typical eight-week itinerary.

1952. George Roberts (seated), Conti Candoli, Buddy Childers. Photo by Gene Howard.

The young Bob Graettinger—in high school.

Stan and Graettinger at a rehearsal.
Photo by Buddy Childers.

Art Pepper.

June and Stan arriving in Amsterdam, 1953. Photo by Gene Howard.

Band and entourage about to conquer Europe. From left: Bill Russo, Don Smith, Buddy Childers (with camera), Tony Farina, Harry Forbes, Lee Konitz, George Morte (on ground). Standing, center, are Frank Rosolino, Zoot Sims, Bill Smiley. Stan and June are at far right. Photo by Gene Howard.

Bill and Joce Holman in Europe, 1953. Photo by Buddy Childers.

Some sidemen during the 1953 European tour. Photo by Buddy Childers.

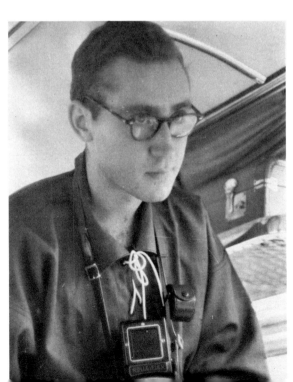

Lee Konitz, 1953. Photo by Buddy Childers.

Zoot Sims on the bus during the 1953 European tour.
Photo by Buddy Childers.

Ann Richards, at eighteen, posed for her first publicity picture. At this time she had not met Stan. Photo by Lance Rock.

Father of the bride (Leslie). Photo by Gene Howard.

With Ann and Lance, 1959. Photo by Gene Howard.

Lance, Jo Ann, Stan and Dana, after the wedding.

The Redlands clinic, 1970. Photo by Clifford Munkacsy.

11 More Changes

"Everybody was there because it was a hot band. It was like being with The Beatles!"

STAN LEVEY, *drummer*

THE 1950 Innovations tour officially opened in Seattle in February. Reviewer Ted Hallock strained for words adequate to his rapture:

> What happened at this city's auditorium last night should happen to the country at large, and will be happening during the coming three months. At 8:30 P.M. Thursday, lanky Stan Kenton raised the curtain on a musical aggregation bound to shock, thrill and puzzle young and old for years to come.
>
> With the first, beautifully-shaded notes of Kenton's theme, *Artistry In Rhythm*, Stan's orchestra revealed an intellectual intent unparalleled in the history of modern American music . . . and I do not qualify that statement with the use of such restrictive categorization as "dance," "jazz," "swing," "be-bop," or any other *one* type of playing. Kenton's music is the first produced in this country since the immortal Duke Ellington's real heyday (1940-45) which cannot be typed, compared to, contrasted with, or placed neatly in this "school" or that.
>
> Stan Kenton's 40 serious young gentlemen, schooled

145

musicians all, blew, pounded, scraped, and plucked the most significant collections of sounds (and Kenton delights in toying with that word) these ears, those of the audience (3000) and probably those of the musicians themselves had ever heard . . . sounds quite apart from the at-times blatant blowing of Stan's last all-brass band.

Sectional phrasing, intonation, attack, and "emotional projection" was beyond belief. If this sounds a bit thick, it is meant to be just that, a commendation in words much too inadequate to convey any idea of what *did* happen on the Seattle stage.

Specifically, bop addicts were satisfied with the individual instrumental efforts of altoist Art Pepper, drummer Shelly Manne, trumpeter Shorty Rogers, and such bop-spiced compositions as Rogers' *An Expression From Rogers* and *Blues In Riff*.

Tone color in all its true vital majesty was manifest as always in the gutty, brilliant scores of longtime Kenton arranger Pete Rugulo—such compositions as *Mirage* and *Conflict*.

The technical virtuosity of Brazilian guitarist Laurindo Almeida and conga drummer Carlos Vidal was spectacularly showcased in *Amazonia* and *Cuban Episode*. But then we've already said that critical language just can't cope with this man and his music.

I would suggest that you be present Saturday evening, February 11, at The Auditorium, Portland, to see and hear for yourself what Stan Kenton's "Innovations in Modern Music for 1950" is all about.

From Seattle, they swung east to Chicago, Canada and Carnegie Hall, then circled south through New Orleans, Memphis and Texas. The tour ended at the Hollywood Bowl on June 3. By then, Innovations in Modern Music had cost Stan $125,000.

He let the "fiddle players" go, but kept the nucleus of a dance band intact and recouped some of his loss playing weekends, Fridays through Sundays, back at Balboa's Rendezvous. The hysterical fans of '41 had aged and mellowed somewhat, and many had been alienated by the Innovations.

But business was adequate, if not sensational, and after the rigors of the road, it was a pleasant summer, especially for Easterners like Buddy Childers. "Balboa was a ball. The band was good. When you're only playin' three nights a week, it's somethin' to look forward to. You don't play the things to death; you don't get a chance to get sick of 'em. There was a good feeling down there in that ballroom."

(Can it have been the same ballroom, and the same summer, of which Art Pepper says, "It was like one of those Bette Davis movies, one of the new ones—like trying to revive something that was dead. It was very depressing."?)

When the summer season ended, the band took to the road again, playing one-nighters, but only in clubs—no dances. This meant longer jumps between jobs, and longer, costlier layovers. They played the Oasis in Hollywood, the Blue Note in Chicago, the Steel Pier at Atlantic City, "The Ed Sullivan Show." Under Carlos's management, the advance work—publicity, newspaper, radio and TV interviews, record store and other personal appearances—had operated like a well-oiled, precision machine. Now the machine took on a Rube Goldberg aspect. The business manager was in Los Angeles. The road manager was Dorothy Gioga, Bob's wife; her main duties were to clock the gate, thwarting any unscrupulous club owners who might try to diddle them out of their rightful percentage, and to handle the receipts and payroll. If a musician needed a "draw," he went to Dorothy, whose job was complicated by Stan's insistence that she keep no written record of these advances. He felt it would be "demeaning" to the musicians.

Bob Allison, Stan's titular manager after Carlos, was more drinking partner, ego stroker and worshiper than administrator. Unlike Carlos, Allison had to be told what to do; even then, he was often ineffectual. So the bulk of the advance work fell to Stan, driving all night in his white Buick, blazing

147

a trail for his bus full of migrant workers. Which was exactly how he wanted it.

When the band was in the East, Stella occasionally brought her granddaughter Leslie to visit her father. During the Innovations rehearsals, Violet had obtained her divorce. Stan admits to feeling only relief, as though something a long time dead was finally being decently buried:

"I remember how calm and collected I was. I said, 'Well, I'll be at the rehearsal if you need me.' She was gone for three or four hours, and she came back, and I said, 'How did everything go?'

" 'Fine.'

"You didn't need me?

" 'Oh, no.'

"She waited till the rehearsal was over, and we went and had dinner. And that was it! I never suffered any kind of things from that separation."

Separation, not divorce, was the operative word. In late September of 1951, Violet and Jimmy Foster were married and living with Leslie and their new baby daughter Christy in Visalia, California. They invited Stan up one weekend for a family party.

"He came up and, of course, he'd been drinking. He said, 'I came to take you home—you and Christy and Leslie—where you belong.' And he was serious!

"Then he decided that he wasn't going to stay for the weekend, after all. He drove to Tulare, a small town just south of Visalia, and he kept drivin' around tryin' to find a gas station. A policeman stopped him and asked if he'd been drinking. Well, he *was* drunk. And he was honest, and said, 'Yeah.' So they booked him!"

He pleaded guilty and was sentenced to six months' probation and a $250 fine. Ten days later, on October 5, the second Innovations orchestra debuted at Chicago's Civic Opera

House. If anyone even remembered the Tulare incident, it was only as "a bum rap."

The 1951 Innovations orchestra had substantially the same personnel as the first. Guitarist Ralph Blaze replaced Laurindo Almeida, whose career as a soloist had taken off. Trombonists Dick Kenney and George Roberts replaced Bernhart and Varsalona. The main change was in the trumpet section, where Maynard Ferguson was the only holdover. Alvarez, Childers, Paladino and Rogers were gone, replaced by Conte Candoli, John Coppola, John Howell and Stu Williamson.

The keystone of the trumpet section is not the jazz soloist, who gets all the glory, but the first trumpet, or lead player. He sits in the center of the section and *leads*. In any Kenton orchestra, his responsibility is exceeded only by that of the drummer. But where there is only one drummer, there are five trumpet players, and jealousy proliferates accordingly.

Buddy Childers had taken over the lead chair at a tender age, for the wrong reasons. "Stan had warned the trumpet players about showing off on the high notes, instead of just playing their parts. One night, they got into a kind of high-note contest. Stan was furious. He pointed at each of them—'You, you, you—you're fired!' And that's how I got to be first trumpet. But although he handed me the first trumpet book, he took all the first parts and gave 'em to somebody else! I guess he just didn't feel I could handle it. But it undermined my confidence. It'd been better if he'd come to me and said, 'I was mad the other night, I think you're not ready. You play well enough but you haven't had enough experience, and I'm gonna let this guy do it.' Maybe he just wanted the best band he could possibly get, and maybe he felt that if he kept enough competition going between the guys in the section, they'd really outdo each other. But I don't think that's the way a good section is made."

149

Each time Stan had reorganized his band, Buddy had returned—but not always to play lead. "I went out on the road with Stan for the summer, just before that second Innovations tour. And he stuck me in the fourth trumpet chair. It was an unfortunate position. . . . He had a guy on first trumpet who really wasn't capable of playin' the parts, and he'd say, 'Hey, will you play that note for me?' or, 'I can't make that bar, will you take it?' Instead of saying, 'Screw you, play it yourself,' I said, 'Sure.' Finally, I realized I had been grossly underpaid for a long time. I went to Stan and asked him for not a ridiculous amount of money—I think $225 a week. He was finally beginning to realize that if the section was going to be together, I was gonna have to do it. So he said okay.

"I had been talkin' to my roommate about leavin' the band, and he knew I was goin' down to talk to Stan. So he says, afterwards, 'Buddy, you leavin'?'

"I said, 'Well, we've come to an agreement.' And that's all I said. But my roommate musta said somethin' to somebody else, 'cause some other guys started hittin' Stan up for more money. 'You gave *him* a raise, *I* want a raise!'

"I guess he thought I'd gone around sayin', 'Hey, guys, I got a raise!' We were in New York; I was at Bart Varsalona's house, havin' dinner, and I got a phone call from Stan. It was one of the few times I ever knew him to really splutter and lose control of himself. He was really hollerin'! I don't think I said three words! He said words to the effect that, 'Forget it, there is not only no raise, you're fired!'

"I said okay—but I was talkin' to an empty phone. He had hung up. I was dumbfounded!"

No one could fault Buddy Childers as long as he kept his horn in his mouth. All his problems came about when he took it out and started talking. Even though he had joined the band at fifteen and never really had an opportunity to grow up, Jan Rugulo found his immaturity infuriating.

"Buddy took his wife along on the road a lot. Buddy and his wife had *scads* of children—five or six. Buddy made a *fantastic* salary—during the war, he was one of the highest-paid guys in that band. And he *never* had any money! Like, he bought a *plane*, which I think he had two days, and broke it up in the mountains. He could get *anything* out of Stan—Stan was always financing him. Then he went nuts over *camera* equipment! And they kept having *children*! Like, she must have known there was a contraceptive of *some* kind! And Buddy just never matured! I never saw any *change*! He knew that certain things would be needed for running a household, for the children, but he was just liable to go out and blow everything! He was just an unintelligent consumer!"

Shorty Rogers left the trumpet section because he wanted to direct his creative energy toward writing and arranging. His arrangements—"Jolly Rogers" was a favorite—were the most swinging the band had ever had, and they loved to play them. The "Maynard Ferguson" piece was one of a series Rogers dedicated to and entitled for individual soloists. The series included "Coop's Solo" and "Art Pepper." These inspired Stan to do likewise. His "June Christy" had June using her voice like an instrument, without lyrics; "Shelly Manne" showcased the drummer's virtuosity; and he wrote the romantic "Theme for Sunday" for himself. But he was curiously ambivalent about his own music.

BUDDY CHILDERS: "Stan wrote a couple of things for the 1950 Innovations orchestra that were magnificent! One was a tone poem, ballad type, lush and *gorgeous*, trombones and fiddles ('Theme for Sunday')—oh, my God, the string writing he did was just *beautiful*! He said it was a bunch of shit—trash, he called it. Shelly Manne's feature thing—I think he

151

had tried to hand that off to a couple of other writers and nobody could come up with anything, so he just went home and like scratched out a *magnificent* thing. Just great! But that isn't what he wants to write! He considers that trash!"

The logistics and economics of transporting a forty-piece orchestra require a tireless commander-in-chief with unlimited resources. Merely unloading the equipment and setting up for a performance was a formidable, two-hour chore; and all the dates were one-nighters. Attendance was spotty, for the same reason that few art lovers would flock to an exhibit that combined the work of Andy Warhol and Norman Rockwell. The two Innovations tours wound up costing Stan a quarter of a million dollars. Still, in his eyes, the venture was a success. He had presented, by God, the music he had determined to present, on his terms. *The New York Times* had even hailed the orchestra as exactly what Stan had intended: "The first successful attempt to bridge the gap between classical and jazz music." And he had proved to his satisfaction the exclusivity of his music—something he perversely relished, in spite of the enormous cost. Financial disaster was proof that his music was too good, too complicated, too specialized for the masses. To Stan, every financial loss has been an award of merit.

In the spring of 1952, he surrendered briefly to economic necessity and organized New Concepts in Artistry in Rhythm—a nineteen-piece band that would play dances as well as concerts. The band underwent its most drastic turnover in personnel since its inception. After the excitement and challenge of the Innovations, many of the musicians balked at the prospect of returning to the old grind of uninspired one-nighters. When the Innovations tour ended in Southern California, the New Yorkers were enthralled with the relaxed lifestyle, the lower cost of living, the security offered by studio work and, most of all, the space. They loved the idea of back yards, where they could practice their horns in peace. Shelly, Shorty, Coop, Art Pepper, Bud Shank, Milt Bernhart and even, for a while, Bob Graettinger, stayed in Los Angeles.

Stan considers every musician expendable, but the loss of Shelly Manne was a blow.

"Stan thought I left the band because I wanted more money. But I left the band because I wanted to stay here with my wife! I'd had it—I didn't want to go out anymore. But I don't think Stan ever quite believed me. Because one morning, Flip and I were having breakfast in our little house that we'd built, and there came a knock on the door. I opened the door, and there's Stan Kenton! We talked and kibbitzed, and finally he said, 'I'm having trouble getting a drummer; the drummer I was supposed to get can't join the band right away. So would you join the band until he can make it?' And he offered me a much higher price than I had been getting, maybe fifty dollars a week more. I said, 'Yeah, Stan, I'll come back—but not unless you pay me my old salary.' We talked a little more, and he left. 'Cause he knew then that I meant it, that I wasn't tryin' to hold him up for more money. I wanted him to know I would be doing it just to really help him, if he was stuck, but I had no intention of staying. If I had gone back at more money, he would have thought I had gotten my raise and I'd stay. So I never did work for Stan again."

Buddy Childers did return, to lead a trumpet section made up of Conte Candoli, Don Dennis, Ruben McFall and, re-placing Maynard as high-note man, Ernie Royal.

More and more, Stan was playing Psychiatrist. It jazzed him to feel he was guiding other people's lives, and he had become quite skilled at manipulating his unsuspecting musi-cians. In 1952, he decided it was time Maynard started a band of his own. As a favor to Maynard and to music (he said), he fired him. And, obediently, Maynard started a band.

George Roberts, Bob Fitzpatrick and Bill Russo returned

153

to the trombone section, which was rounded out by Bob "Butter" Burgess and soloist Frank Rosolino. Of the charter members of the band, only Bob Gioga remained. With him in the saxophone section were Vinnie Dean, Bill Holman, Richie Kamuca and alto soloist Lee Konitz.

MILT BERNHART: "Lee and I were kids together in Chicago; we both lived on the North Side. We had a close rapport; music was all that mattered. If I picked up a record, I'd call him up and make him listen to it on the phone, and vice-versa. When I got out of the army, he had started taking coaching lessons from Lennie Tristano. Lennie was a Svengali to his students; and that was strange, because he's blind. But he had this hypnotic quality, and he demanded total dedication. Lee tried to talk me into studying with Lennie, but I got this call from Kenton. And I remember Lee saying, 'This is ridiculous! Why would you go with a band like that? That's foolishness, that bunch of noisemakers!' When he turned up with the band at the Palladium, I gave him a little of the same thing."

LEE KONITZ: "It was actually kind of a thrill for Stan to call me. I secretly used to have a crush on Stan, as a kid, when I saw him in the theaters. He told me he was interested in starting a 'jazz band,' in quotes, and he was hiring jazz people. There were some good writers—Bill Holman, Gerry Mulligan. Gerry had a player's feeling for writing, especially for saxophone players, and in that band, it was welcome. You could finally feel your own weight as a saxophone player. It was very difficult for a saxophone player to play in that band, with ten brass."

BILL RUSSO: "Lee was difficult. Stan was intimidated by him. He represented that whole intellectual, jazzistically authentic idiom of Lennie's that was so foreign to Stan, but that Stan hoped to use. And Lee has this death wish; he would lay out for eight bars during solos. . . ."

HANK LEVY, *trombone*: "Stan was so impressed by Lee's ability to *wait* sixteen bars to begin a solo—the way a great orator holds his audience. He'd just stand there, and finally blow just a 'bop.' Then a few more bars, and a couple more bops. And then a whole *stream* of music!"

STAN KENTON: "Lee was an important influence . . . the first alto saxophone player in the band who started creating the concept of discipline. Before that, it was kind of a wild, helter-skelter sort of thing. Lee knew the value of restraint. But we fought like hell."

BOBBY BURGESS: "Konitz was like Stan. He only cared about music."

With Don Bagley on bass, Sal Salvador on guitar and Stan Levey on drums, the band cut some records for Capitol and then, in April, hit the road. Their undiminished drawing power skewed a falling curve; in terms of big bands, the road was a lot less crowded in 1952 than it had been in the forties. Most of the two hundred amusement parks that had booked bands ten years earlier were gone. Colleges began booking local groups for two or three hundred dollars, as opposed to fourteen hundred dollars for a big name. As profits dwindled and prospects darkened, Stan became a popular scapegoat. He was accused by Charlie Barnet and others of having killed the dance-band business by refusing to play music people could dance to. But Stan maintained that he had never intended or pretended to have a dance band—that his efforts to be booked and billed as a concert orchestra had been repeatedly thwarted by greedy agencies and ballroom operators who refused to consider the compatibility of their audience with his band's style. But he was the blind man describing the elephant. The economics of the day, combined with the growing domination of television, delivered the coup de grace to the long-suffering patient. The only band whose drawing power actually increased in the fifties was Lawrence Welk's.

155

In June, Bob Wogan, a long-time fan who happened to be Eastern Program Manager for NBC Radio, sold the network the idea of broadcasting "remote" weekly Kenton concerts from wherever the band was playing. NBC publicists touted "Concerts in Miniature" as "The first merging of Progressive Jazz with network radio." Stan announced that the object of the series was to allow him to *explain* his music to the public. He was credited as Producer-Writer, and delivered his own commentary.

The first broadcast emanated from a concert hall in Kitchener, Ontario. "Between ditties," said *Billboard*'s reviewer, "Kenton continued his pleasant line of chatter. He did not really explain much about his music, but his continuity was so enjoyable that this really didn't matter."

What he said was, "This is an orchestra. A group of musicians gathered together because of a belief in a particular music. Like all orchestras, this orchestra is unique. In that the artistic ideal is more important than personal differences. These musicians, for this instance, came from all corners of America. The character of the music to follow is the result of their understanding and adjustment to each other. Some of this music is written. Some is improvised. There are times when a musician will express his individuality, and other moments when he will melt with the rest to create an organized sound. This is a cross-section view of this orchestra."

On other broadcasts he was more relaxed, more fun. "We are rehearsing applause here," he announced in Vancouver. "Let's take it on the downbeat—watch it, everybody! A clean cutoff, please! Some of you aren't watching! Once in three-quarters, please. . . . There were a few bebop sounds there! Let's clean it up!" The audiences ate it up.

Stan frequently would introduce trombonist-arranger Bill Russo, the band's resident intellectual, who would in turn introduce his moody composition, "Ennui." "I think I might take a second," Russo would begin, very straight, "to delve into the cosmological and metaphysical aspects of this composition. I think we can say quite simply that the transcendental character of the composition is based on two very definitely Freudian concepts, the first of which has to do with what we might call the continuant. The whole relationship between the first portion of this composition and the French horns as used in the second portion finds its roots in the philosophy of certain early Greek composers. The dichotomy between the Russians and the Ukrainians is a clear example of the lugubrious tendency of early Greek art. The whole relationship between this concept and certain basic concepts, say, of James Joyce, is the fact that motorcycle riders find salted popcorn extremely good under those conditions."

In 1952, Bill Russo was a composer in search of direction. He had first heard the band in 1948, sitting in the front row of the Aragon Ballroom, in Chicago. "The band wore puffy ties, morticians' outfits. I sat there with my mouth open, listening to those fantastic nine- and ten-note chords!"

Russo studied for a while in Lennie Tristano's "cell," from which he emerged with rather snobbish musical taste. But when Pete Rugulo invited him to play in and write for the 1950 Innovations, he was thrilled. During the next four years, Russo contributed a wide range of solid, craftsmanlike work, from the semiclassical "Solitaire" to the lighter, jazzier things like "Bill's Blues." He shared Stan's fondness for exotic titles; "23°N, 82°W," for example, was a Latin chart named for the coordinates of Havana. But in the eyes of the puristic, jazz-oriented players like Konitz, Pepper, Rogers, Candoli, Kamuca and, later, Zoot Sims, Russo was guilty of the cardinal sin. His music didn't swing.

Swinging is one of those elusive and indefinable terms. Like soul, you know it when you hear it. Swinging implies looseness, freedom, spontaneity and instinctively flawless rhythm.

157

It has probably been associated with Count Basie as much as with any big bandleader. And Stan has always had a horror of his band's sounding like Basie's—or Duke's, or Woody's, or any other bandleader's. Once he established his own sound, it was straight ahead, let the critics fall where they may. More than a principle was at stake; to Stan, it was a matter of identity.

But while swinging turns Stan off, jazz players turn him on. And therein lies Stan's (to use Bill Russo's word) dichotomy. He covets their lack of restraint, even while shying away from it. He hires them out of respect for their talents, and lets them wail their hearts out in their solo work. But the arrangements he favors do not swing. And to a jazz player, there is simply no substitute for swinging! So the musicians bitch, and exert varying degrees of pressure in all sorts of subtle, and sometimes not-so-subtle, ways. And Stan has made compromises.

His most notable compromise took place in 1952, when he began buying charts from Gerry Mulligan and Bill Holman—two uncommonly talented, uncompromisingly swinging writers.

No band, no rehearsal hall, no concert stage was ever large enough to contain the combined egos of Stan Kenton and Gerry Mulligan. Perhaps because of his drug habit, which he has since overcome, Mulligan was arrogant, rude, abrasive and rebellious. He frequently made it clear to anybody within earshot that he didn't give a shit about Stan Kenton's music, that he had more musical expertise in his little finger . . . and so on, ad nauseam. He insisted on overrehearsing the band, as though his charts were their sole concern. Stan loved the way he wrote—"Swing House" was one of the band's most popular numbers—but, "If I had let the orchestra play Mulligan's music exactly the way he wanted it played, it wouldn't have had a Kenton sound at all." For his part, Mulligan remembers that

Kenton would "tell his drums to play so loud they sounded like they were part of a whole separate band!"

Tall, handsome Bill Holman was just as complex a personality as Mulligan, but he was as personable as Mulligan was obnoxious. He joined the saxophone section with the understanding that he would also do some writing. "But after I joined the band and started playing his music, I really had no idea what to write. I'd done some things at Westlake and some charts for local bands, but that was my first This Is It kind of experience. I really didn't think that his music was The Answer, but here I was, going through my learning process, playing his music every night. I think he knew that my idea about music and his weren't that close together; yet he kept encouraging me.

"I felt that his music had been predicated on exaggeration. I think music should be a little more homey, a little more human, a little warmer than his had been. I felt that the band should swing. Which would normally put me more in the Woody Herman end of it, or Count Basie. But I was in Stan's band! And I kind of felt a personal need to make his band swing. There's always been a lot of weight there, and if you can get that amount of weight to approach swinging, you've got a formidable product. But because of that weight, it's that much harder to get to that point. That was our main difference. He used to say that was all in the past. And it was, because we were kind of acting out our exposure to Basie and all those people in the thirties and forties who had bands that swung. The harmony wasn't very sophisticated, and the melodies weren't all that hot—they just had a kind of raw, rhythmic energy.

"When I was trying to push swing music at him, he was already into the Afro-Cuban things. There's a rhythmic element in those that's like a lot of the rock music going on now;

so in that way, you could say he was fifteen years ahead of his time. But to me, if he was going to have a jazz band, he wasn't fifteen years ahead of his time—he was just plain Wrong!

"The band was so unwieldy, I used to try to write things that would make it sound smaller. I did one thing called 'Boop Boobie Doop.' Stan could never bring himself to introduce it; he would make me do it, even on the radio. He always wanted titles like 'Artistry in Cosmic Radiation.' 'September Song' was kind of humorous, but not intentionally so. It was torture sitting in a supposedly hip club like Birdland, and Basie's band is wailing away fifty feet away, and there we are doing 'September Song.' But everyone wants to hear the hits. Woody Herman's still doing 'Woodchopper's Ball.'

"But Stan *contributed.* He made it possible for a lot of guys to be heard. He lives through his band, and his band needs music that is relevant to enough people to support it. He assembles the people that can create it and presents them and holds them together and makes them able to function. And in return for that, they give him a certain part of their music for a certain period of time. It's not a religious experience; it's just an agreement that works out. But in the end, he's the guy that makes it happen. The dreamer that has the impossible dreams. And when they haven't happened, he's never tried to blame anybody else. Okay, on to the next thing. Whether or not he would have become another Stravinksy had he decided to stay at home in his garret and write, we'll never know. But he had that vision at the time when it counted."

The "Concerts in Miniature" series ran on NBC for over a year without picking up a single sponsor. Kenton was not considered commercial.

In mid-September, the band joined forces with Nat Cole and Sarah Vaughn for an eight-week tour of the East and Midwest. With such a powerful bill, bookings were prestigious and crowds tumultuous. In December, NBC aired four consecutive weekly broadcasts called "My Voice Is Music," another Wogan brainchild, intended to portray the behind-the-scenes life of an orchestra. As narrator, Stan was disarmingly candid:

"What a baffling thing, the music business! It's based upon public affection. We all are working for their favor, and without their favor, we cannot exist. You know, insecurity in this field is something worse than a green-eyed monster. You can have seven successful records, and the eighth one will miss. Already you become afraid. Like on the road. You have three months of successful one-nighters. All of a sudden, it says STAN KENTON AND HIS ORCHESTRA, and no one comes. Panic—immediately. What happened? What did we do last year when we played here? Did they like it? Is this the first time? Are the records heard around here? Maybe this reign of popularity that we've enjoyed has exhausted itself. And this panic will prevail until another successful date comes along to start bolstering this thing that we call ego again. What a wonderful business—the music business."

12 Conquering Europe

"In 1953, we crossed the Swiss border more times than a smuggler."

BUDDY CHILDERS

As an experiment in economy, Stan abandoned the bus and chartered a fleet of automobiles for the musicians, who rode four to a car. The jumps were long, and the driving tiring. Bill Holman was one of the drivers:

"We left some place in Idaho—Konitz and Bill Russo and Richie Kamuca and me—in the middle of winter. We'd driven through these *impossible* mountain passes—really spooky, with snow piled up along the edge of the road, and it was like a mile down to the bottom of these canyons. We got through that slowly and safely, we got down out of the mountains and speeded up, and we came through a patch of ice on a curve, going fifty or sixty."

LEE KONITZ: "The car teetered for a minute on the edge of a six-foot embankment. During that teeter, I could've gotten out—but I couldn't. I had to go down with these cats, 'cause I loved all of these cats! The car landed upside-down, and there was a hush for a moment. We all looked at each other and realized simultaneously that no one was hurt. And we just crawled out the windows and laughed hysterically for five minutes."

That night, in the pitch blackness of Idaho's flatlands, Stan misjudged a curve and drove *his* car off the road. Angela Levey was in the back seat, with Bobby Burgess. "Burgess was sitting next to the door, with a can of beer in his hand, and the *second* we went off the road, he opened the door and stepped out! Nobody was hurt, but Stan was *very* embarrassed. The car wouldn't move. We spent the night in Shoshone, Idaho, and Stan got up at the crack of dawn and got it fixed.

"When we got to Seattle—oh, God, we traveled!—the minute we walked into the hotel, they were paging Stan. Somebody told him about the other accident, over the phone. He was screaming at the top of his lungs, in this *enormous* lobby, 'WHERE'S THAT GOD DAMN PERSON THAT PUT US ON THIS GOD DAMN TOUR?'"

For a while, Holman rode in Stan's "Command Car." "We were in these dark mountains of New Mexico, in a terrible snowstorm, and the gas was running low. There were no towns in sight or on the map. We saw some lights up ahead, and it turned out to be a State Highway Department substation, with garages for their trucks. They were all out fighting the snowstorm and clearing the roads, and we were in dire need of gas. And they had a gas pump. We knocked at the house, but nobody answered. So we just pulled up, filled the tank with gas and split.

"We got down the road an hour or so, and here comes this truck after us, with some kind of a light winking, and sounding their horn. It's these guys from the Highway Department—and they're carrying shovels, and one had a pitchfork! They thought we were really crooks!

"Stan got out and tried to explain what had happened. They told him to check in with the sheriff at the next town,

163

down out of the mountains. So we got to this town in the morning, Stan got us checked in at the motel, and he went down to the sheriff's thing. We didn't hear anything the rest of the day, and that night we asked him about it. He said, 'Yeah, I got down there and I said, I'm the guy that stole the gas.' And they had no *idea* who he was! Those other guys hadn't called—it was just their way of getting even. I guess Stan thought they'd put the cuffs on him!"

What the cars saved Stan in cash, they cost him in headaches. Somebody was always late, or lost, usually Buddy Childers, who frequently drove ninety miles an hour—the wrong way. No matter how early Buddy left one town, he was invariably the last to arrive at the next. He liked to "buzz" the other cars, zapping Ping Pong balls through their windows with a toy cannon, shouting, "This is Sky King! We are approaching target! Bomb bay doors open!"

What had been a tight ship threatened to become a leaky tub. The musicians were bored and tired. Seven sidemen, including Bob Gioga, Ernie Royal, Richie Kamuca and George Roberts, quit. Bill Holman would have been the eighth, but when he heard that Zoot Sims was replacing Kamuca on tenor, he decided to stick around. Sims had been his idol for years.

In 1953, Zoot Sims was known as a musicians' musician—with a drug habit (since overcome). But the jazz scene was so riddled with dope at that time, and Zoot was such a beautiful player, Stan decided to take a chance on him.

"I was working a club in New York when Stan called and asked if I'd join his band. He said, 'Understand that we can't stand any scandals in this band!' I said, 'Stan, don't worry about it. I'm cool.' So I flew to Chicago and took a train to where they make all that beer—Milwaukee. I joined the band there. Then we went to Europe. That was the worst tour I ever made—the hardest gig I ever had in my life."

Stan's was the first big American band to tour Europe

after the war. He was so thrilled by the prospect that, in an impulsive moment, he invited the musicians' wives to accompany them. Eleven of them accepted with alacrity and promises to remember that the men were there to work, and that they were to keep out of their hair and out of trouble.

Flying Tigers flew them to Shannon, Ireland, on August 22, 1953. From there, they flew to Amsterdam in a converted amphibian they dubbed *The Ruptured Duck*. During takeoff from Shannon Airport, they realized it was raining—inside the plane. Stan Levey, an inveterate gum chewer, plugged up the leaks with Wrigley's Spearmint, solving what turned out to be only the first of a series of crises.

JOCE HOLMAN: "Zoot Sims and Lee Konitz put their saxophones on those little racks over our heads. I was panicking! I said, 'We can't fly that way!' I started to cry, and Willis [Bill Holman] almost hit me; he said, 'Shut up and sit down and strap yourself in!' "

GENE HOWARD: "Bob Allison and I met the band in Amsterdam. I was handling publicity for the tour. It had been a long, hard trip for the band, and they got off the plane absolutely stoned out of their minds. And here are all the guys from the press, waiting! You have never seen such a terrible-looking bunch of people! They looked like the worst bunch of bums you've ever seen!

"From Amsterdam, we flew to Copenhagen, where I had arranged for a bigger press conference. The plane looked like it was held together with rubber bands; it was overloaded by like five thousand pounds, and the pilot was terribly concerned. The takeoff seemed like an absolute eternity. We really never thought we'd get off the ground. I remember grabbing my wife's hand and saying, 'Honey, this is it.'

"The Capitol Records representative in Amsterdam had met the band and had given everybody a little souvenir wooden shoe. And in the shoe was a little bottle of Bols gin—not that they weren't stoned already. So on the plane, everybody went into the wooden shoe. When we finally got to Copenhagen, it was a complete and utter fiasco. I can remember walking guys around, giving them black coffee, trying to sober 'em up, because just about every writer of importance in that whole territory was there at this press conference, and the band was absolutely stupid. It got into the press, too—the condition they were in. That was probably my most embarrassing moment."

By concert time that night, the band had straightened up sufficiently to incite ten thousand screaming, stomping fans to the brink of riot. Midway through the performance, Stan was called backstage to take a transatlantic phone call.

"It was my mother. They hadn't perfected transatlantic phone calls yet; it was all distorted. I said, 'Pop died.' She said, 'Yes.' I completed the concert and another concert that night, and after that I went to a club with some people. I had one drink and I went all to pieces. It was a delayed shock."

During the last ten years of his life, Floyd Kenton had lived on a little farm in California, remote as ever from his son. "I gave him money, bought him a truck. We tried living together in the house on Hollyridge, but it didn't work out. He lived a rather lonely existence. . . . Finally, he got leukemia." Floyd had married again, but it was short-lived. When he died, it was Stella who made and paid for the funeral arrangements.

Copenhagen was the first of twenty-seven cities, in ten countries, in which the band appeared in thirty-two days. Some of the dates were *double* one-nighters—two concerts in one night, in two towns. They used *The Ruptured Duck* only for long hops; mostly, they traveled in a thoroughly uncomfortable sightseeing bus. June Christy, who had been working as a single, had rejoined the band for the tour. "The bus was literally a backbreaker. There was no way you could sleep on it. There were no headrests—just these iron things behind you, and the seats didn't recline. It was astounding the positions people would get into to try to get to sleep. They'd try with their feet up on the seats, or their feet on the back of the person sitting in front of them. The bus had a governor; it could only go thirty-five miles an hour, so we had many rest stops. I never did get used to the ones in the woods.

"There were never any food stops. The German promoter, Herr Hofmeister, provided cold sandwiches and warm beer on the bus. This promoter was making so much money he could have retired after the first week and been a millionaire!"

A lot of people made a lot of money from that tour. Wherever they went, the people went wild.

BILL HOLMAN: "The *adulation* of people who'd been hearing Stan's records all those years and finally got a chance to see him in person was actually frightening at times. The people would stampede! They'd have rows of cops out there, and people'd just bust through the lines."

STAN LEVEY: "They never counted the money, they made so much. They used to just shove it into bags."

BOBBY BURGESS: "It was amazing! Ticker tape parades! The mayors'd be there, and we would be so juiced—they'd give us magnums of everything. Stan would get so loplegged, him and June . . . Every place we played, there was never less than ten, fifteen thousand people. They went mad! A couple of times, it got scary! They'd want autographs, and we'd have to get to another concert, and there'd be thousands of people ringing the bus, rocking it, trying to get us out to sign autographs."

LEE KONITZ: "Stan was usually presented with a liter or some extraordinary-sized cognac bottle—they'd put a spigot on the end of it and bring it on the bus, and everybody'd be going for broke until we got to the next town. And as soon as we got to the next city, the mayor or some dignitary would be there to meet us—and perfect gentlemen walked off the bus and greeted everybody! I saw this in complete amazement! I couldn't believe everybody was straight!"

STAN KENTON: "People were going crazy. I didn't dare be seen on the street; people would rip my clothes off! It was just terrible. And I used to *run* from crowds. I'd just run as fast as I could to get away from these people, and look for doorways to duck into."

ANGELA LEVEY: "The receptions were incredible. The flowers, and the bands, and going through towns in Volkswagens with the tops off. Signs all over: WELCOME STAN KENTON. They met us at the airport with bands, and flowers, and wine, and cars. We couldn't get over the contrast with this country, where we'd go around in the bus and nobody knew if we were dead or alive until we got to the job. But over there, we were always finding ourselves at a banquet somewhere, with people who were very appreciative of the music and treated us just royally!"

The partying never stopped. In many cities, only their luggage saw the inside of their hotel rooms. On the first of their eleven days in Germany, they were handed little blue brochures with itineraries and this greeting:

> Dear Mr. Kenton. Dear Mrs. Christy. Dear Kenton Crew. Welcome to you in Hamburg, the first German town you will see. These informations contain the run of the tour in Germany, Netherlands and Belgium. You will be accompanied by my representative, Mr. Bauss, who will care for you. My best wishes for this tour and touch wood, toi-toi-toi—a great success as you and me want. With kind regards, Hanz Hofmeister, Konzert und Gastspieldirektion.

Although their schedule allowed no time for sightseeing, the musicians found ways of getting acquainted with the culture.

ZOOT SIMS: "When we got to that sin city in Germany, a seaport, I hadn't slept in four days. We went to this joint, this bar, where they had little flags on the table with numbers on them, for the girls at the bar. I went home with this girl and we made love and everything; she was a whore, and she was great—young, and she spoke English. She told me about what happened to her parents during the war. When I woke up, I had missed the plane. We had to be in Berlin for a big parade. The girl had tried to wake me up, and I was so tired I just couldn't make it. She cooked breakfast for me. She played records. She told me how to get to Berlin, and then I couldn't pay her, 'cause it was gonna take all my money to get to Berlin on my own. I missed the parade, but not the show."

That show took place at the Sportpalast, where Hitler had made his "Guns Before Butter" speech and where Goebbels had denounced the "decadent" American jazz. Fifteen thousand West and East Germans crowded into the two concerts.

BILL HOLMAN: "We looked out the window of the dressing room, and the street below was just alive with people. Like one of those old Hitler movies—that mass of humanity down there, all yelling and cheering!"

BILL RUSSO: "The audience applauded by stomping their feet. You had the feeling you were in Nazi Germany, striking a blow for democracy!"

Paris was considered the climax of the tour, and Stan was apprehensive. Parisian audiences were notorious for their rudeness and had been known to express their displeasure with "progressive" music by booing, reading newspapers during performances, even throwing fruit at the musicians. Dedicated groups of French Dixieland fans made a practice of invading and disrupting "modernist" concerts. But when the curtain rose at the Alhambra on the evening of September 18, the band was greeted by warm applause. Every number was well re-

169

ceived, and Zoot Sims's rendition of Bill Holman's "Zoot" brought him a standing, shouting ovation. When the program concluded, the crowd called, "*Bis! Bis!*" demanding more and more encores, until Stan stepped forward and thanked them. "You have been very wonderful," he said, adding, with relief, "I was most concerned."

Jazz trombone soloist Frank Rosolino had staked out Italy as his territory. Rosolino was Stan's kind of Italian—warm, friendly and ingenuous (as opposed to brooding Mafioso types like Russo and Boots Mussuli). Rosolino was quite capable of throwing a lighted firecracker under the piano during one of Stan's solos and getting away with it; he had done just that, in Detroit. His scatting on "I've Got a Right To Sing the Blues" and his comic yodeling on "Pennies from Heaven" were popular with audiences everywhere.

When Rosolino had learned that Milan was on the itinerary, he had implored Stan not to bother finding an interpreter. "I speak the language," he explained, "and I'll take care of everything. You won't have any problems at all."

When they arrived at Milan Airport, Stan said, "Okay, Frank. You can interpret for us." Frank furiously fired directions at the baggage handlers, who pointedly ignored him. Then he asked one of the customs officials, in Sicilian, "Where's the bathroom?" The official, unfamiliar with Frank's dialect, thought Frank had ordered him to go to the toilet. A fist fight was narrowly averted.

Because of a disagreement between the American (Petrillo's) and the British musicians union, the band could not perform in England. Undaunted, hundreds of British fans, many of them musicians, had chartered planes and caught the show in Brussels. Another *three thousand* fans traveled for *thirty-six hours* by train (*The Jazz Express*), boat and train again, to see one or both of the Dublin concerts, the last of the tour. *Melody Maker* (*Downbeat*'s British counterpart) headlined:

DUBLIN GOES KENTON CRAZY AS 7,000 FANS STORM CONCERTS

September 20, 1953, will go down in jazz history as the day Dublin went Kenton Crazy. For fifteen hours the city was mad. All through the streets fans roamed in clusters, waving their patriotic green programmes, and hunting for Stan Kenton or members of his band.

Kenton sidemen were jumped on in isolated streets for autographs, and in no time a crowd gathered. Kenton himself had to be smuggled out of back doors, ushered under close guard into cars.

Crowds besieged the Gresham Hotel, where Kenton was staying, and Stan had to battle his way back to the theatre to make the second concert.

"I shall never forget this," said Stan. "It is something for which I can never show my appreciation."

After the last concert, Kenton was almost in a state of collapse. His friends pleaded with him to return to his hotel. But he insisted on travelling to the distant Bar B Ranchhouse Ballroom to hear the Jack Parnell Band.

The Kenton band's ambition to visit London was fulfilled. But what a visit! They spent two hours in Town on Saturday while *en route* from Paris to Scunthorpe; but there was an administrative slip-up. They had no money.

Administrative slip-ups were par for the course.

STAN KENTON: "There was tremendous confusion. The language hassle was great. And the promoters were very greedy. We'd do two concerts a day in different cities, one about six in the evening and another one, seventy-five or one hundred miles away, at midnight. After a few weeks of that, it was terrible. An army on a push. The musicians damn near died, and so did I."

BILL HOLMAN: "There were certain things that hadn't been ironed out. Once the promoters got us over there, the trans-

171

portation was foul; they worked our heads off. We were really kind of guinea pigs. The next trip by a big band over there, I guess it was Woody Herman's, things had improved some."

BILL RUSSO: "It was agony!"

When Russo had learned that Bill Holman was taking his wife to Europe, he asked, "Why are you taking your sandwich to the picnic?" On this picnic, the wives made themselves about as welcome as ants. Most were young, unsophisticated and incapable of entertaining themselves for a moment. They wanted to sight-see. They wanted to shop. They wanted to *vacation* with their husbands, who had been out on the road all year while they had stayed home with the kids. But the tour was to a vacation what Ex-Lax is to candy, and the wives took out their disappointment in a hundred counterproductive ways. They bitched and whined and nagged and pleaded and cried and harangued, and embarrassed Stan by wearing slacks in public; and when the time came to fly from London to Milan, Stan left them in London.

Despite the wear and tear of the tour, Stan was pleased. He was surprised and flattered to learn that European dance companies—modern and ballet, including Sadler's Wells—were choreographing the Innovations music. In France and Italy, he saw experimental art films that had been created around his music. The fans' enthusiasm and the critics' respect—such a welcome contrast to the condescension of many American reviewers—encouraged him to seek new worlds to conquer. As soon as he returned to the U.S., he threw himself into a brand-new venture.

A Festival of Modern American Jazz was a blockbuster of a concert package. Top billing went to saxophonist Charlie Parker; featured were Billie Holiday, Dizzy Gillespie, June Christy, Candido and the Stan Kenton Orchestra. The company traveled in two buses, caravan-style.

The bus driver is more crucial to a band than any soloist;

getting there always has top priority. A good bus driver has the sense of direction of a salmon, the stamina of an athlete, the concentration of a brain surgeon, the nerves of a hippopotamus, the judgment of King Solomon. It is his responsibility to calculate the time, the route and the risks, such as what floods, snowstorms and other acts of God are passable. The company that chartered the buses provided the drivers; this created some hairy situations. During Eddie Safranski's time with the band, the driver used to juice right along with the musicians until he'd pass out, whereupon Safranski would don his uniform and take the wheel. The Progressive Jazz band had a driver who, one dark night, for reasons never explained, parked the bus so close to a train track that the musicians awoke, terrified, to flashing lights, clanging bells and the crash of the train knocking the side mirror off the bus.

The band had gone through enough bus drivers by the time they acquired "Eric" Erickson that they appreciated what a find he was. Eric was the ideal bus driver—with one minor eccentricity. He had a habit of dozing off while driving—but with his eyes open. He was quite capable of driving in this condition, but newcomers to the band were frequently unnerved by his snoring. All things considered, Eric was a superior driver. But Eric could drive only one bus at a time; and Festival of Modern American Jazz had two.

After a concert in Newark, New Jersey, on November 20, the two buses pulled onto the Pennsylvania Turnpike en route to Pittsburgh. Eric's bus, with Stan aboard, was in the second position. Most of the musicians were asleep. George Morte, who had succeeded Bob Allison as road manager, was sitting in the front seat of the first bus.

"I had my adding machine, briefcase, typewriter and everything on the seat next to me, and I was sittin' with my feet over the guard rail. The bus driver was going at a pretty good clip. There was a tractor-trailer rig that was either stopped or very slow in the right-hand lane, and the bus just went right into the rear of it, with a great smash! I went right through the windshield, hit the truck and came down right on the Pennsylvania Turnpike. Stan thought I was dead. When I came to, I was in the Carlisle Hospital. I looked like a mummy—bandages all over, all I could see was my eyes. I had glass infested [sic] all over my face, and I had a larcerated [sic] jaw."

Three other members of the band were seriously injured, and ten more were given emergency treatment for minor cuts and abrasions. The most serious injury was to everyone's nerves and morale.

BOBBY BURGESS: "Conte Candoli's wife was pregnant, and she got a broken back. Everybody on that bus got cut up. My tongue got cut in half, my chin all chewed up. I really got scared! I was afraid to get back on that bus! I had two new babies, and I said, oh, man, as much as I loved Stan, the idea of getting back on that bus. . . . I'd been with him three years straight; we had done ninety-six straight one-nighters, with no days off, when that wreck happened! I left the band. It took me a year and a half to get back on another bus!"

ZOOT SIMS: "After the accident, Stan did the only thing I ever disagreed with. Our saxophone players were intact, but a lot of the brass players had to leave, they got their mouths hurt. We had to get replacements for the whole trombone section.

"That next day, Stan called rehearsal for the whole band! My thoughts were that the saxophones didn't need to rehearse. It's his band, I realize that. I was just tired, like everybody else, and somebody said something about how he didn't need the saxophones to rehearse. Stan said, 'Well, if anyone don't like it, just say so.' And I said, 'Okay, I'm leaving.' And that's how I left. But I was ready to leave, anyway."

BILL HOLMAN: "The last night that Zoot played with us, I realized that all these reservations I had had about being on the road with that band at that time were all gonna come back now that my old friend wasn't gonna be there. So I put in *my* notice then, too. I had a wife and a new baby boy and a new house, and all of a sudden the road was not so hot anymore. It just wasn't Out There for me."

A cycle was ending for other key men in the band. Bill Russo left "because I felt the instrument wasn't that good. Not enough time to rehearse. And players in that band were unsympathetic to what I was doing. After two or three years of that, you get tired of it. I left with a certain amount of revulsion."

Lee Konitz had left before the accident. "One day I just said, 'Fifteen months of this is enough!' And I quit!"

Stan wound up replacing nearly half the band. The Four Freshmen, whom Stan had literally discovered singing in an obscure club in Dayton, Ohio, in 1950, joined the tour. Freshman Ross Barbour recalls that "They had Gene Howard and Buddy Childers and the Freshmen and Stan and everybody singing, adding unison voices, so it would, as Stan said, give it more character. One night when the band was about as low emotionally as I've ever seen it, they told Conte Candoli that his mother had died. It was just that kind of a night. I think that's the lowest I ever saw Stan."

Progressive Jazz, Innovations, the European tour—these were golden times, for Stan and for everyone involved with his music. The music was moving—although nobody seemed sure in what direction—and the musicians had a sense of potency and promise that sustained them in the low periods and sent them soaring through the highs. Bill Russo still marvels at "how little sense we had of being in The Big Time. That innocence that characterized the band. It enabled us to play *fearlessly*. And we all had this fantasy that being famous would open doors of all kinds for us." For many of them, it did. But in 1954, when Capitol released an expensive, four-record album called *The Kenton Era*, at least one Kenton era had ended.

13 Intermission Riff

"I never remember anything he says, because it's all I can do to withstand his Presence!"

BILL HOLMAN

In 1953, Edward R. Murrow asked Stan to contribute to his "This I Believe" series.

"I sat down one night and said, 'What the hell do I believe?' So I wrote it out. I had to go to a recording studio to say it in my own voice, so it would be in the album. Then it was put into the book. And I was very happy with what I found out that I believed!"

The result is vintage Kenton rhetoric. Stan's voice, even in casual conversation, has a quality that conveys the urgency of God speaking to Moses. In cold type, his words are more sophomoric than profound; still, reading them, one cannot help but react to his sincerity—even while reaching for the Excedrin.

I am at present forty-one years of age. It is difficult to even imagine what will come about within me in the rest of my life that lies ahead. My values and the justification of my theories concerning the existence of mankind are the results of my education and experiences as I have lived to this day. My only and real concern is the development of humanity in all phases. Humanity is a vast, all-encompassing term applying to the peoples of not only my own country but of the entire world. Because the essence of the laws of nature is growth and development, change is a positive thing and always for a better state of being. It is necessary for every effort and endeavor in every phase of achievement to be thrown into one gigantic storehouse to be used as humanity's needs are made evident. Man is most complex. There are three parts of him that must grow evenly and steadily. Some things contribute to his spiritual development and others to his intellectual self, and necessary also are his needs for emotional growth. No one part of our culture can lead over the others for very long without having to be detained to wait for the development of the rest that must be a part of the overall growth for everyone. My work pertains to the arts. To be more specific, I am a part of the modern world of music. I have found that as I became more appreciative of the arts, I developed sensitivities that broadened my awareness of others' needs. Music is food for the emotions and growth demands our being made aware of it constantly because we are reaching deeper into our inner selves. As time moves on, the emotional hunger can only be satisfied by music that constantly says more. I want to be a part of this creative need in satisfying the desire for fresh music. The most reassuring thought to me personally is that in creating and performing in my own field, I am actually helping to condition people to accept growth in other phases of their development. And by the same function of others in this tremendously involved mechanism of humanity, I gain and grow to another level along with the rest of mankind. To attempt to list in itemized form all of the varied contributions made to all people by individual effort would be totally futile. It is consolation enough to know that every moment is being used to help make the world better in his own way and all effort somehow is a part of the total gain for all. All I have and enjoy today was given me by those that came before. My music would not be such without the music created in the past. My strong obligation is to those with whom

I live and to those who come after me. I must help through my music to make life more rich in emotional awareness. In my field of endeavor I am attempting to replace the conventional type of hackneyed material with a more contemporary form of music that will more nearly satisfy the needs of today. In considering the vastness of mankind since the beginning of time, no one can possibly believe that this generation or his personal self is more important than any other period or person since the beginning of humanity's existence. No one person or group of people can live happily without the help of others. Regardless of the differences of individual purpose, we are dependent upon each other. What I have stated so far is the philosophy that propels me, and without these things I can see no reason for tomorrow.

This I believe.

14 Ann

"I really think now that he wanted a brood mare. He wanted a new life again, with children and all that. And I was young, and I wanted children. So I sorta lit that spark for him. A rebirth kinda thing. And really, it worked that way for a while.

ANN RICHARDS

BY 1954, most hotels had replaced road-band attractions with house bands, and nightclubs were booking singles almost exclusively. Ballrooms—those that hadn't been converted to bowling alleys—operated only on weekends. Theaters had discontinued stage shows, and the radio networks gradually dropped their remote pickups. The one-nighter circuit had shrunk to the Midwest and South, and two facts of life in the music business had become inescapable: a big road band was no longer economically feasible; and the criterion for success was a hit record. Stan warmed to the challenge. He would become, he decided, an entrepreneur.

He worked out an arrangement with Glenn Wallichs whereby, under the sponsorship of Capitol Records, he would produce a series of albums called *Kenton Presents*. He signed a solid stable of good jazz players—Bill Holman, Frank Rosolino, Boots Mussuli, Bob Cooper, Hampton Hawes, The Four Freshmen—and featured them, with their own backup groups, on the series. The records had quality and integrity. None made money, and the project died.

Stan's prestige was undiminished. That year he became the third musician * elected, by a poll of its readers, to *Downbeat's* "Music Hall of Fame," an honor established for those who "had contributed the most to modern American music in the Twentieth Century." That summer, he presided over the initial concerts of the first Newport Jazz Festival. By September, there seemed only one logical direction in which to proceed: straight ahead. Instead of retrenching, he reorganized.

The Second American Festival of Modern Jazz featured Shorty Rogers and his Giants, Art Tatum's Trio, Johnny Smith, Candido and the Stan Kenton Orchestra. Stan's personnel was mostly new and somewhat unstable. In November, two songwriter friends played him a demonstration record by an eighteen-year-old girl vocalist who seemed to show a lot of promise. He told them to send her around to his office.

ANN RICHARDS: "He asked me one question: What do you want to do with your career? I said, 'Mr. Kenton, if I had a choice of singing with Guy Lombardo and making lots of money or making sixty bucks a week singing jazz, I'd rather spend the rest of my life singing jazz.' He said, 'Okay, you're hired.'"

A handful of vocalists had worked with the band since Christy, but none had her unique combination of popularity and loyalty. If they did well with the band, they soon moved on to concentrate on their careers as singles. In 1952 and '53, Jay Johnson, Kay Brown, Jeri Winters and Chris Connor came and went.

Jeri Winters was very young, very green, very much a product of Cayuga, Indiana. When Stan hired her, her main

---

* Louis Armstrong and Glenn Miller preceded him.

claim to fame was having won the Illinois Harvest Moon Festival.

"I was just scared to death. I'd never been out in the world before, and everything was just more than I could begin to comprehend. I didn't know what was expected of me, and I was too shy to ask. All I knew was just to get out there and sing.

"Stan gave me money for some outfits to wear with the band. I came back with this huge, enormous bouffant net, layers and layers of it, a great big wide-waisted thing with *reams* of this coarse net in powder blues and pinks—like Mary, you know, who had a little lamb. Stan just fell prostrate right on the floor; it was more than his eyes ever thought they would see. I took it back, and I ended up buying a gray suit which was absolutely perfect, but on top of that, for some reason I bought a gray straw hat. Now, what am I gonna do with a gray straw hat on the road? And it sat flat like a pancake, but there was a *roll* all around it. And sitting on top of that was a red rose, and sticking up out of the middle of the red rose was a green stem with a red rosebud on it!

"Being from Indiana, Holy Cow was one of my expressions. After we had done a few radio interviews, Stan suggested to me in a very polite, kind way that it would be best if I'd drop the expression.

"It was a lonely existence, because I didn't have anybody to communicate with. Bill Russo got a kick out of when I wouldn't know what he was talking about, with his fifteen-foot-long words. Or when I'd look out the bus window and make some remark about how the beautiful trees really make you believe in God, don't they? And Bill would crack up, being, so he said, an out-and-out atheist.

"I remember playing afternoon sessions for wealthy people who had large homes and large lawns, and we played for their guests. It was tiring, and extremely boring. The boys were always ready for a party, but I wasn't. But I had no choice! Sometimes we'd already have checked out of the hotel, so we wouldn't have to pay another day. And when you live on the road, the money is never enough. The guys were able to double up on hotel rooms, but I wasn't!

"One night in Chicago, Stan asked me to sing for him. I did. Then he said, 'Jeri, how do you really feel about singing?' I was too shy to tell him how bored I was with doing the same material over and over; it became so painful, I didn't even care about the tune! But because I hadn't worked it out inside me yet, I gave him an answer that was not very deep. And I think he felt disappointed, because Stan likes to psych people out.

"I thought I was very much in love with Stan. If you were in an elevator with him, or in a studio, or even walking down a street, even if people didn't speak to him first, he'd speak to them. If they would just *look* at him, he had a way of making anybody feel, 'Wow, I was just acknowledged!' Everybody set up a thing that he was like a God. He had a great truth about him. I think he was about as near to what he thought he was as anybody could be."

Ann Richards had led a less sheltered life than Jeri, but she was every bit as susceptible to the Kenton charisma.

"He was my idol, of course. From when I was in high school. I had his picture over my bed. I had all his albums, and I'd listen to them all the time when my mother and step-father would go out."

Ann was young, impressionable, sexy, and in search of a father figure. Stan was lonely, in the throes of passing forty, and filled with guilt about his only child, whose mushrooming problems, Violet kept telling him, were all his fault. Maybe, he thought, he could make a new start, have a new family, make up for the past. Besides, Ann turned him on.

It would be hard to judge whose expectations were more unreal. Just before the two met, Ann had seen *A Star Is Born.*

"That film really got to me. I had a girlfriend that I was living with in an apartment in Hollywood; I slept on the couch and gave 'em my unemployment and did the housework for them. I went to see that film and I came home and said, 'Y'know something, if I can just stay in this town, I know the same thing's gonna happen to me!' Delusions of grandeur. But within four months, I was working for my idol. And he was a drinker! But he hasn't waded out in the ocean yet, and I haven't become a star!"

After their meeting, her romanticism escalated. Stan took her to a showing of a television pilot the band had made for a series called "Music, '55." "It was at Glen Wallichs's house on Alta Drive, in Beverly Hills. This was one of the first social things I ever did with Stanley, and it was just like being in the presence of God. I got so excited I went home and told my girlfriend, 'I really think that if I had a husband like Stan Kenton, if I lived in a house like that, wow, could I be happy! I could even give up my singing!'" A little over a year later, they were married and living in that house—and she had given up her singing.

But for most of that next year, during a parody of a courtship, they were on the road. For a woman, the rigors of the road are compounded by the necessity to maintain the public's image of glamour.

"A girl singer always had to look good, like she just came out of a shower. And that wasn't always easy to do. Sometimes we'd drive into a town and we wouldn't have time to check in, we'd go right to the job. I'd have my blue jeans on, and my hair in curlers. I'd have to get my gown that was squished between the funky, smelly band suits, and grab my shoes and my overnight case and go in the ladies room; the guys used the dressing room, if there was one. I'd put my makeup on, take my hair down, change clothes, while the girls were coming in in their prom dresses and corsages. I'd be standing there putting my garter belt on—they used to really stare at me! It was embarrassing! I'd try to get in a john and close the door, but these were like armories and high schools, and some places didn't even have doors on the johns.

"Then later they'd come up and say, 'Y'know, you sound just like June Christy!' and that used to kill me. I'd say, very quietly, 'Gee, thank you,' and I'd smile and walk off. I really didn't dig Christy's singing that much; she always sang kind of flat, and she wasn't too creative a singer.

"Stanley was my knight in shining armor. He could do no wrong. The romance started right after we went on the road. I didn't want anybody to know. He had hired me as a singer, on my talent; I had never been the kind of singer to get involved with bandleaders, like some singers do. I had a great sense of pride. Ethics. Then bit by bit we started traveling in the car, and everybody kinda caught on, 'cause we were staying together in motels and everything.

"We used to *laugh* a lot. I used to do Ethel Merman impersonations, the morning after. He'd wake up and I'd do my bits, and it used to break him up. Stanley has such a great laugh. I used to feel very good when I made him laugh.

"*He* was very clever on the road. I used to say to him before he'd go on, 'C'mon, Stanley, be funny tonight!' He could do just darling things with an audience. He clowned around; he'd even walk silly, kind of prance around. He'd kid with the audience, and he'd get the guys to sing this funny thing in unison. There was a looseness and warmth that he projected, along with the serious side. I remember once he saved me because I was so embarrassed at the Hollywood Bowl. I came in on the wrong note, and he turned around to the saxaphone players and made it look like it was their fault.

"Stanley was very fearful of marriage. I was so in love

with him that I wanted to give up my career and raise a family. Five kids. He said, 'I'll do anything to help you in your career.' And I said, 'I don't want my career anymore. I want to get married! I love you, and I'll make you a happy home!' I guess I had delusions of having him home with me.

"I was attracted to the man's misery, partly. He used to wake up in the middle of the night sometimes before we were married, crying and thrashing out—'Oh, God, how much longer do I have to go on? I'm tired, I'm tired.' Talking in his sleep. And I used to hold him to my bosom and try to comfort him, and wake him up and say, 'Stanley, it's all right.' And I really thought that if he had a home and a family and somebody to love him, he'd be happy."

They were married in the Milwaukee courthouse on October 18, 1955. "Our wedding night wasn't very romantic. I was tired and had a sore throat; I was so sick I couldn't sing that night. He brought all the guys in the band up to the room for a toast. He hadn't told me they were coming. I was in my little wedding nightgown, waiting for him, after the job, and everybody comes piling in.

"We had a fight that night. He played June Christy's new album, so I got a little pissed off. I had some records by Wayne Dunstan, an old friend of mine, and I said, 'Okay, you played Christy for an hour, now let me play Wayne Dunstan.' So he listened to one record and he said, 'Yeah, that's very good. I'm going to go down to the White Tower and get you a hamburger. You want anything else?' And I said, 'NO!' and I threw the records out the window and I screamed. He was gone about an hour, and I slept in the bathtub that night. In fact, we fought so loud that the manager called up and said people had complained. And I cried. It was a very bad wedding night."

Ann was a romantic, but not an innocent. Her reputation as a swinger, while greatly exaggerated, was based on fact.

When Stan announced his marriage to the musicians, there was a long, shocked silence. Trumpeter Al Porcino finally drawled, with heavy sarcasm, "Well, good luck, Stan." Like kids with a new stepmother, they were jealous.

MEL LEWIS, *drummer*: "Nobody was happy about it. Ann was the downfall of the band. From then on, things really changed. How could he relax? How could he be like he was? None of us liked her. She wasn't classy at all. She was climbing. She just wanted to be Mrs. Stan Kenton; she didn't really want to be a wife to him. The minute she married him, she quit singing."

The tour ran almost until Christmas. The band was hot.

AL PORCINO: "Nineteen fifty-five was the closest we came to having a really great swing band. Bill Holman wrote a fantastic library for the band; it was heaven to play his music. But right from the first rehearsal, I could see where there was gonna be dead wood on the band. At least two players in each section. We did make one great album, *Contemporary Concepts,* all Bill Holman arrangements except one Gerry Mulligan. But I think Stan feels when the band really starts swinging and the guys are having a ball, he's not in control. What's ironical is that he's come so close on so many occasions to *having* great swing bands! But all he's ever wanted to do is make history! Try and do some kind of different music, so he can say, 'This is Stan Kenton, and Stan Kenton alone!' "

When Porcino took over the lead trumpet chair, Sammy Noto quit in disgust. "I split without notice. I had been playing half the lead parts; then Porcino came on, and I had *no* lead parts. Three times I gave notice, and Stan said, 'You can't quit.' Finally, one night in New York, I said, 'I'm leaving tonight.' He said, 'You giving me that shit again?' The next night, they were shy a trumpet player."

Mel Lewis was never the most popular player in the band, but he was one of the strongest. His playing was looser than

Shelly's, and funkier. He had more insight into Stan's position than he had into Ann's.

"There's always dead weight in every band, and the reason for that, usually, is salaries. Stan can't pay everybody a top salary; no leader can. What he paid me in those days was reasonable for the times. I think I was worth more. I think he'd like to have paid me more. My top salary in his band was around $245, gross. I was twenty-six years old, married; I had a kid. I had to send my wife money every week, and I had to live like a human being on the road—get my uniform cleaned, keep myself neat, eat decently. The electric bill, the car payment, the food bill at home, they go on whether you're there or not. So it's rough.

"Stan hired certain key men, and they sorta ran that band. They worked hard and set the pace, and if they got along good with each other, they became a clique. They hated the guys that were sitting there sucking on their horns, not contributing. And they'd want to get rid of them. Those guys would feel that pressure, so *they'd* form a clique, and they'd hate the *other* guys! So you could always tell who went to eat with who, who sat at what table, who hung out with each other . . . because the hot guys, the jazz players, the outstanding players, they'd stick together. And the weaker guys would stick together, to protect themselves and keep their jobs. Sometimes the strong clique would have a way of working on the leader, trying to make the weaker guys quit or get fired, so they could get some other strong guys in—which didn't always pay off. Sometimes some of the so-called strong guys turned out to have other bad things going, even though they played good."

CBS bought "Music, '55" on a sustaining basis, and throughout the summer Stan would fly to New York every Tuesday to do the show with the CBS house band, which Johnny Richards had rehearsed during the week. It was an imaginative and expensive show; it had exciting music, dramatic production numbers with guest stars like Gloria de Haven and Lena Horne, and competent writing by jazz critic Leonard Feather. Reviews were favorable. Ratings were not. No sponsor was forthcoming, and the network dropped the show.

In December, after seven months of one-nighters, Stan took Ann home to Hollyridge for Christmas.

"I had never been in that house before, and when we'd been there just five days, *Violet* came to stay, with Leslie and Jimmy and Christy, their daughter! And I was like the outsider, 'cause she had lived there with him, in that house. It had never been touched or changed since she left. And I just accepted it! Of *course* he wanted his ex-wife to come and visit! I went along with everything; I was very cooperative!"

In January, the band played Zardi's and some other Los Angeles engagements. In March, they embarked upon another whirlwind tour of Europe, this time including England where, as the first American band to play there in twenty years, they were received with the same wild adulation that had so overwhelmed them on the 1953 tour. Mel Lewis remembers, "I never signed so many autographs in my life! They were treating me like I was Buddy Rich or somebody really famous, and I wasn't! We all got stormed—they treated us all so fabulously —the press, the writeups, the receptions we got were somethin' else. And Stan mixed and mingled with everybody; he never stopped. He always did the right thing."

The schedule was a killer. In addition to the performances, most of which were SRO, Stan had to meet with Capitol's representatives, be available for radio, newspaper and television interviews, attend receptions given by local dignitaries, meet with union officials, music critics, recording-company executives, fan clubs and record dealers and make personal appearances in record stores. At one Portsmouth record shop, a huge sign read PERSONAL APPEARANCE OF THE FAMOUS

ANN

AMERICAN BANDLEADER AND CAPITOL RECORDING ARTISTE, STAN
KENTON. MEET HIM IN PERSON. GET YOUR SOUVENIR RECORD
AUTOGRAPHED. COME AND GIVE HIM A REAL WELCOME! Barricades
had to be hastily erected to protect the windows from the
mob. In Nottingham, the crowds stopped traffic and the police
had to send for reinforcements.

All seven performances at London's 7,500-seat Albert Hall
were jammed with fans who paid five pounds (fourteen
dollars) per ticket. Most of the critics were ecstatic; but, as
always, there were dissenters. Gerald Lascelles wrote in his
book *Just Jazz*, "It was unfortunate that the first band to play
the English jazz circuit was Stan Kenton's—a startlingly loud
and uninspiring conglomeration of musicians whose remaining
vestiges of individuality were overwhelmed by the pens of an
army of arrangers."

There were the inevitable mishaps, not all of them minor.
The bus they traveled in had a disproportionate number of
flat tires, causing them to arrive for some concerts literally at
the last minute. Three weeks into the tour, two of the musicians had to be replaced. One sideman had gotten himself
into serious trouble with the angry parents of a young girl;
and Ed Leddy, the lead trumpet player, developed pneumonia.
This was an unmitigated disaster for everyone except Sammy
Noto, who had rejoined the band just before the tour (Al
Porcino having left), and who took over Leddy's lead parts.

As on the previous tour, the wives promised to behave
themselves—and did, until the plane took off from New York.
Stan took them along primarily to justify taking his own wife.
But Ann was suffering from the discomforts of pregnancy and
from a growing disenchantment.

"I saw so little of him in Europe. I couldn't travel to every
concert—the roads were bad, and the bus was jerky. So I
would wait in the hotel all day long, and look forward to just
spending some time with him after work. But after he'd been

189

traveling for an hour or two on the bus, and he always drank after the jobs, he'd come in and he'd be drunk! I was just miserable. I was so alone, and so disillusioned. I had read that when a woman is unhappy and under a strain, I could lose the baby. So I decided to come home."

Stan felt his young wife might benefit from therapy, and his sister Beulah recommended a Mrs. Williams. "When I told her how I felt, and about the problems in the marriage, she said, 'You have to realize he's an alcoholic!' And I got so mad I walked out of the place and I never went back. I wouldn't accept that.

"After that, I just stayed home a lot. I lived up on the hill; I didn't even drive. I was all alone most of the time, for about two months."

Meanwhile, Stan was blithely writing letters that told of buying steel knives and forks in Denmark, "the very nicest I could find. And a set for Stella, too. In Sweden, I went crazy buying glass." In Finland, it was crystal. "I have been so alone and by myself," he said in one letter. "Just music and I. Now I have you. Everything is complete."

Stan had wanted a son to carry on the Kenton name, but when Dana Lynn was born in August of 1956, he adored her—as, indeed, he had adored Leslie. He bought Glenn Wallichs's impressive big home in Beverly Hills, and moved his family in: Ann, Dana, and Leslie.

"Leslie had somehow figured out that it was her mother's fault, the divorce. And she decided she would try to make it up to me. It was a mess. You know it's happening, but you're helpless! It never was a real father-daughter relationship. It was more like a man and a woman."

When Stan had called his daughter at boarding school to tell her she had a stepmother, she threw a tantrum and locked herself in a closet. When she learned that Ann was only four years her senior, catastrophe became inevitable.

Leslie had never been easy to live with. To Gene Howard, "She was the first experience I had with anyone trying to raise an uninhibited child. Whatever she did or said was 'an honest release of emotion.' She could walk up to someone she'd never met before and kick 'em in the shins and say, 'I don't like you!' and Violet and Stan would say, 'Isn't that nice, she's expressing an honest emotion!' She used to write on Stan's Steinway with her crayons!"

Jan Rugulo freely admits that "Leslie I would like to've *drowned*! She really was a little monster. But her problems were brought on by *their* problems! They experimented too much with this child! They were so Freudian bent! Everything was sex! They were watching her for all of her little sexual things she had goin' on when she was a child! And they thought it was all right to *discuss* it! She was like a guinea pig! No *wonder* she was mixed up! *They* were so mixed up! There was far too much permissiveness. She should've been kicked in the teeth *many* times!"

By the time Leslie reached adolescence, she was unmanageable at home and at school. It was with some relief that Violet acceded to her request to live with her father. Ann was not consulted.

"I should have seen the writing on the wall. She was a very, very strong, highly neurotic girl, and I wanted so badly to be friendly to her! I was always reaching out to her, and she just hated me. I took her father away from her. I always wanted a sister, and I really wanted her to be like a younger sister to me. But she didn't want anything to do with me. She used to say terrible things about me in front of him—'She's dumb! She's stupid!'—and he never defended me. Every dinner with Stanley and me, *she* monopolized and controlled the whole evening's mood, by *her* moods. There was always such tension. I felt as though I was living with a *tarantula* in the house!

"At fifteen, she'd come home at two in the morning some-times from her drama class, and say that the car had a flat tire or ran out of gas or something. I'd say to Stanley, 'Don't you think that's a little late for her to come home?' And he'd say, 'No, I trust her.' He *never* would take a stand with her.

"When Dana was about three months old, I started going to a marriage counselor, a psychologist. I said to her, 'If I had to live another year like this, I think I would go crazy.' I had the man I thought I wanted, I had a beautiful child, I had a home, security—and I was miserable. And she said, 'Well, we'll work on that.' So I went for four years, and whenever Stanley was home, he and I went together. He told her that he didn't have any problem—*I* did!

"It didn't help us."

15 Back to Balboa

"It really was a fiasco. It was an excellent band—that wasn't the problem. The people were dancing The Balboa!"

BUD BRISBOIS, *trumpet*

In the fall of 1956, Stan took a nucleus of key men on a brief tour of Australia, augmenting the band with local musicians. It was part of a package that featured Lionel Hampton, Kathy Carr and some leftover vaudeville acts. After the tour, Stan resumed his studies with Dr. Paul Held.

"I felt that I wanted to study seriously in 1955—advanced counterpoint—and I didn't dig the teachers that a lot of guys around town were studying with. I felt they were exploiters. I'd always admired Victor Young so much, and I'd never known him. So one time I got on an airplane, and there was Young! *He* recognized *me*! I said, 'Do you feel like you'd like to talk?' He said, 'Yeah, let's talk!' So it was about ten and a half hours from New York to Los Angeles, and we talked the whole way. And I confided in him. I told him I wanted to start studying; who should I study with? He said, 'There's an old gentleman that just moved to L.A., a guy I studied with in

Chicago. You gotta find him. He knows more about music than anybody I know in the world.'

"Dr. Held was an old Austrian, about eighty-two years old, who grew up in Germany. I called him and told him that Victor Young had recommended him to me as a teacher. He said, 'Well, I've got to interview you first.' And I said, 'Certainly.' I think he was gonna charge me ten dollars for the interview. So I walked through the door and sat down, and he said, 'You want to study music? You're too old!'

"I said, 'Now, wait! Slow down!' So he visited with me a little bit, and then he said, 'Sit down at the piano and show me what you know. Don't play me a lot of nonsense, just play me some triads.' I didn't understand what kind of triads he wanted, but I played for about half a minute and he said, 'You don't know anything! If you want to study with me, you'll have to go clear back to the beginning.' I said, 'That's the idea.'

"I started studying with him, and we had a wonderful relationship for about four months. Then all of a sudden I went for a lesson and he was very upset. He said, 'I've gotta talk to you before we start studying today. I can't say that you lied to me, because I never asked you, but you're a very famous musician!' And I said, 'Oh, you found out.'

"He said, 'Are you trying to study with me to make more money, or are you trying to learn about music?' I said, 'I don't need any money! I want to learn about music!' He said, 'Okay.' I studied with him until 1957; then I wandered away, went on the road. In 1963, I studied with him again for a couple of years. He died about 1967."

On a hot afternoon in the early spring of 1957, while Stan was waiting for Ann and Dana at the pediatrician's office, he called Bob Allison about some business. It was Allison who told him, "Graettinger's dead."

Graettinger had undergone surgery for lung cancer the

previous Thanksgiving, and it was diagnosed then as terminal; still, he had clung to a faint hope that he might recover. He was desperately anxious to finish the septet he was working on, and confided to a musician friend, Forrest Westbrook, that he felt that for the first time he was really getting things down the way he wanted them. The septet was written for three woodwinds, a French horn, violin, viola and cello; it was contemporary classical music.

Graettinger worked as though possessed those last few months, writing for eight-hour stretches, resting only when weakness forced him to bed. He completed three movements; the fourth and last movement was sketched out in graph form, but some bars were missing, and there were no nuance markings (i.e., *pianissimo, andante, forte*).

Graettinger's last years were the most solitary of his life. Stan occasionally took him out to eat. "Sometimes Bob would get juiced and he'd say, 'What time is it?' I'd say, 'It's three A.M.' He'd say, 'Do we have time to go down and look at the ocean?' I'd drive him down to Santa Monica, and he'd sit there and look at the ocean for a while. And then I'd take him home."

After Graettinger's death, Forrest Westbrook worked on the septet for a year, trying to complete it. The work cannot be played without the last movement; and Westbrook isn't sure whether the last movement is performable.

The funeral was the kind of conventional religious service Bob would have despised. Stan and Pete Rugulo were among the handful of musicians who attended. Afterward, Stan went with Graettinger's brother to Bob's tiny apartment and gathered up all the scores, graphs and worksheets scattered about, in no apparent order. Stored in a back room of the Kenton office, they await analysis by some dedicated musicologist. The whereabouts of the original *City of Glass* score are unknown—except for one graph that hangs, framed, in Graettinger's

195

mother's living room. She says it makes a wonderful conversation piece.

Stan's midfifties band—the one many of the musicians still refer to as "the Bill Holman band"—recorded *Contemporary Concepts* (arrangements by Bill Holman), *Kenton Showcase* (Holman and Russo) and *Kenton in Hi-Fi*, an updated version of some of the early Kenton-Rugulo hits. Keeping the band intact was a continuing problem, and Stan, much to his dismay, was discovering that he had recreated for himself the dilemma of Road versus Family. In the fall of 1957, he thought he had solved it at last.

"Lawrence Welk had made a big success of the Aragon Ballroom at Santa Monica, and I thought, why the hell can't *we* establish a home for the band? And I said, there's no place to do it other than the Rendezvous Ballroom at Balboa. I figured what with Disneyland and all the other development down there in Orange County, it would be healthy enough to support us. So I leased it with an option to buy.

"The old joint was really beat, and we refurbished it completely—bought new furniture, new p.a. systems, everything. We had a big ballyhoo, and we opened it up just before Christmas. For the first time in my life, I asked some of my friends to come down and appear at a gigantic opening. Nat Cole came down—for nothing! The Four Freshmen came down, and June Christy.

"I should've known that opening night it was the kiss of death. Because when we used to play one-nighters down at the Rendezvous, we'd have anywhere from three thousand to four thousand people. And that night, with all that powerful box office attraction, we had twenty-four hundred people."

GEORGE MORTE: "Maybe Stan felt that word-of-mouth would get the word out—but he should have got a bigger campaign going that the band was coming there. I remember one night when I went down there, Ann Richards spotted us at the door and she said, 'Oh, come on in!' I took a peek inside and saw so few people, I says, 'Uh-uh, I'm gonna pay!' It really hurt me to see that. It was a great band, too. But the business just wasn't coming."

Stan arranged for a local television station to televise the proceedings. "I don't think television is ready for jazz," he told the press. "We're going to try for a show with mass appeal—nothing arty. Jazz scares some people. If a guy takes off, I'll just say he's doing an improvised solo." *The Los Angeles Times* reported that he wanted the show "to concentrate on the enormous creative activity of the Southern California coast, from Santa Barbara to the Border." There would be ceramics on the show, paintings, various art works. And local college talent would be showcased.

BUDDY CHILDERS: "It was one of the most self-destructive things I ever saw him do! Stan paid for a remote crew to come down and produce this hour-long show for thirteen weeks—all production and everything out of his pocket. There was no prerecording, none of the things they do to make it sound good. It was *live.* And they stuck it in the spot opposite the Disney show!"

One of the few pleasant surprises of that brief season was a "reunion," instigated by Howard Rumsey, of the band that had opened at the Rendezvous in 1941. When Stan returned to the bandstand one night after an intermission, there, like a lineup of phantoms, sat Rumsey, Jack Ordean, Frank Beach, Bill Leahy, Ted Romersa, Earl Collier, Harry Forbes and Al Costi. Rumsey made a little speech and presented Stan with a plaque inscribed "To the greatest influence on American music since George Gershwin."

On January 15, 1958, Ann gave birth to a son, Lance.

"Stanley went ape. He was so happy, he picked up the doctor and swung him around in a circle. And I felt like I'd really done my duty."

A month later, they were celebrating Stan's forty-fifth birthday at the ballroom. Ann left early in her car, to go home (they were renting a place on the peninsula) to nurse the baby. Stan stayed until quite late, drinking, with Bob Allison and some other cronies. Driving home, he smashed into a parked car on Balboa Boulevard, with sufficient force to overturn his sports car.

ANN RICHARDS: "He passed out, is what he did. He could've been killed, but he was lucky; he only gashed his forehead. The police didn't arrest him. They felt grateful for what he was trying to do for their town. But it scared him. He said to me, 'You've always been telling me about my drinking, and I'm beginning to believe that I've got a problem. I'm going to stop drinking.'

"At that time, I had had it with him. I was emotionally closed off from him, very hostile. But when I didn't see him drunk for two months, he rekindled something in me. I used to ride my little bicycle down to the ballroom and meet him for lunch or a hot dog, and he'd be writing at the piano, and I began to feel a little of the old romance coming back. At times he would get very fidgety, because he actually was going through a physical thing. 'Isn't it cold in here?' he'd say, or 'Isn't it hot in here?' And he'd say, 'I'm famished!' or 'I don't feel well.' He was going through all these ups and downs."

He hung on by his fingernails while the Rendezvous venture crumbled around him. The band had opened at Christmastime with the expectation that by Easter vacation, when the college kids came swarming to town, all the wrinkles would be ironed out. But that year, the kids decided to spend their spring vacation in Palm Springs.

SAMMY NOTO: "I had moved my family out there, and I

wound up working one night a week, playing first trumpet for thirty-five dollars a week. I saw the handwriting on the wall, and I left."

ARCHIE LE COQUE, *trombone*: "It just didn't make it; another one of his experiments. I was out of work for three months. Stood in line at the employment office in Santa Ana to pick oranges."

STAN KENTON: "I kept borrowing money, month after month, to keep it going. We lasted a little over three months, and by that time I was in over one hundred thousand dollars, so I just junked it. That's when I realized that Lawrence Welk could do it because his music appealed to the masses."

In July, he went back on the road—and off the wagon.

16 The Beat Goes On

"He was gone one time for eleven months. I felt like a war bride."

ANN RICHARDS

In August, Stan flew back to Beverly Hills for a hastily arranged wedding: Leslie's. Stan's grandson Branton Dau was born the following January, on Lance's second birthday. Leslie was seventeen.

With Leslie out of the house, Ann still had Stella to contend with. "When we were newlyweds, we'd just got back from the road. We'd sleep in late, 'cause we were used to the night life. We'd hear somebody downstairs, from about nine on! He'd say, 'Oh, that's my mother. Go back to sleep.' She had a key to let herself in! She'd walk around downstairs, make herself a cup of coffee and read the newspaper and wait for him to get up! I finally said, 'Stanley, don't you think she should call and *ask* if she could come over?' 'Well,' he says, 'I can't do that to her.'

"I got back into singing and went back on the road myself, to get away from the marriage. And I did get this tremendous, burning desire to sing again, because my ego had gotten to be about the size of a pinhead. I used to wonder, why did he ever marry me? He didn't want me to change, or grow. He always treated me like a little girl. I kept blaming myself for everything. His drinking was *my* problem, not his, because he told me all his friends drank more than *he* did. And I *missed* my singing; that was where my identity was sort of wrapped up. We had a maid and everything; the children didn't need me. I loved the children and I really enjoyed being a mother, but it *wasn't enough for me.*

"I'd only go out for three weeks at a time, spasmodically. It was a lonely existence, but at least I had my freedom. In a town where I was singing, at least there was a little glamour involved, and I could go out and be with people, and even date and screw around if I wanted to. I was escaping, just like he was."

When Ann played a two-week engagement at the Sands in Las Vegas, Stan sent a series of affectionate but oddly impersonal wires:

September 10, from Camden, New Jersey: DEAR ANN: BE SURE AND DO A GREAT JOB. I AM THINKING ABOUT YOU AND LOVE YOU WITH ALL MY MIGHT. YOUR LONESOME HUSBAND.

September 20, from New York: DEAR ANN: WOULD YOU PLEASE TELL MY WIFE I MISS HER AND LOVE HER VERY MUCH. REGARDS. STAN KENTON.

September 21: DEAR ANN: THERE IS A GUY HERE IN NEW YORK THAT LOVES YOU VERY MUCH. HE IS THE BANDLEADER AT BIRDLAND. REGARDS. STAN KENTON.

September 24: YOUR HUSBAND WISHES TO THANK YOU FOR YOUR WONDERFUL LETTER. AS EVER. STAN KENTON.

There were times when Stan found himself in the unfamiliar position of staying at home with the kids while their mother was on the road.

Ann sent the kids cards to be filled out and returned to her.

For Lance. Dear Mommie.

1. HARRY IS GETTING FAT   YES___   NO_X_
2. CRAIG AND I ARE PLAYING
    VERY WELL TOGETHER   YES_X_   NO___
3. WE SAW UNCLE BENNY LATELY   YES___   NO_X_
4. I HAVEN'T BEEN TEASING DANA   YES___   NO_X_
5. I WENT ICE SKATING WITH
    DANA   YES___   NO_X_
6. I HAVE BEEN TELLING TRUE
    FACTS ALMOST ALWAYS AND
    NOT MADE UP ANYTHING   YES_X_   NO___   I THINK SO___
7. I'M A VERY GOOD AND
    DELICIOUS HAMBURGER   YES_X_   NO___

For Dana.

1. IT'S BEEN VERY NICE WEATHER
    LATELY   YES_X_   NO___
2. I HAD A GOOD LESSON WITH
    JANE AT DANCE   YES_X_   NO___
3. I HAVE BEEN VERY CRANKY
    LATELY   sort of_X_   YES___   NO___
4. I DIDN'T FALL DOWN ONCE AT
    ICE SKATING   YES_X_   NO___
5. CARMEL SET MY HAIR FOR ME   YES___   NO_X_
6. I AM THE SWEETEST LOVELIEST
    GIRL MOST OF THE TIME   YES___   NO___   I TRY_X_
7. I CAN RIDE MY BYCICLE [sic]
    40 MILES AN HOUR   YES_X_   NO___
8. I'M A PUMPKIN PIE   YES_X_   NO___

In the late fifties, the road was rockier, rougher, less hospitable to big bands than ever; only a handful remained. It was *cold* out there.

ARCHIE LE COQUE: "In 1958, there was a recession. It wasn't like the old road-band days. This was a scuffle. We worked as a background band for singers, anything we could get, just to keep going. None of us had any money. It was a bad time.

We played anyplace—ballrooms with three hundred people, that could hold four thousand."

June Christy and The Four Freshmen joined the tour for a month, forming a package called Road Show.

ROSS BARBOUR: "It was hard. There were a lotta miles between jobs. The guys would get sullen. They'd get quiet. They'd get grumbly. Everybody tries to make paper airplanes or talk silly or have a few funny things goin', but they'd all worn out. You can tell the morale of the troops if they bitch a lot. This bunch wasn't even bitchin'.

"We'd sing some country-pickin' songs on the bus every three or four days, when things'd get dull or sullen. June had a song that started B-I-B-L-E spells Bible, J-E-S-U-S spells Jesus, that's our little old song for today. And the whole band would join in, 'For today. For today. That's our little old song for today.' Everybody'd lean on that. 'Cause it gets to be like an iron lung when you're trapped inside that bus."

BUD BRISBOIS: "I was just twenty-one when I went with Stan. I was a very green trumpet player that could hit high notes. Being stuck on a bus for that long can break you, mentally. I saw it take its toll on people who left the band not playing as well as they did when they started. Others would find the means and devices to get through it—drinking, pot, poker. Some guys would drink cough syrup."

By the time he quit the band in 1961, Brisbois had taken over the lead trumpet chair; but his name never became the household word that Maynard's had. This was not so much a reflection on Brisbois as it was a reflection of the fact that, as jazz had specialized itself into a corner, the Age of Rock had descended upon the land.

DALTON SMITH, *trumpet*: "We used to ask Stan, 'How does it feel having us here after Maynard and Conte and all those superstars?' He'd say, 'You have to remember that when those guys first joined the band, they were just like you. Every band I've had is my very best band.' And he means it!"

In December of 1961, Stan won the Best Big Band *Playboy* Jazz Poll Award for the fourth consecutive year. Awards were prestigious, but they did nothing for business. Not since the early days of the war had Stan struggled so hard for survival. The bus broke down along with morale. Every night, Eric would set out at least a dozen tin cans to catch the oil leaks. Sometimes everyone had to get out and push.

The back of the bus was trumpeter Jack Sheldon's domain. He slept on the floor, surrounded by empty Cocinal cough syrup bottles. Dalton Smith and trombonist Bobby Knight, from Mississippi and Louisiana respectively, were the Dixie members of the band. When they reached the deep South, Dalton would interpret. Dalton was famous for his comment on an avalanche that just missed the bus early one morning. "I do believe," he announced to the startled musicians, "that vol-ca-no done co-*rupted!*"

Saxophonists Charlie Mariano and Bill Perkins were key players. Mariano's style was loose, sensitive, soulful. So was Perkins's, but he lacked Mariano's light touch. He kept a graph on his bandbook that indicated his mood each day, ranging from Elated to Depressed; people were supposed to check the graph before speaking to him. The day came when the line hit the bottom of the page and disappeared, and nobody talked to Bill Perkins at all that day.

In the middle of the hot, humid summer of 1960, the band traveled across Mexico, doing fourteen concerts in four cities: Tampico, Guadalajara, Monterrey and Mexico City. The musicians remember flashes of washboard roads, dysentery and sweltering in their new gray flannel uniforms.

When Archie LeCoque went home for Christmas after three years with the band, his son asked, "Are you really my

Daddy?" and he decided to get off the road. For Stan, the answer was less clear-cut. From Salt Lake City, he wired: FOR ALL MY VALENTINES AT HOME. I LOVE YOU ALL, ESPECIALLY THE ONE NAMED ANN. DADDY.

From Providence, Rhode Island, he wrote: "This is for Dana. It is a picture of the bus we ride on when I am away from home. I love you Dana. Daddy."

From Anniston, Alabama: "It's incredible the number of times I find myself staring at the pictures of the kids with a comb or razor in my hand, seeming to forget what I'm doing for the moment."

After four years of therapy Ann decided, "If I couldn't save the marriage, at least I could save myself. I finally said, 'Stanley, I no longer am in love with you. I just can't go on like this.' He asked if I wanted a divorce, and I said yes, I did. And the first line out of his mouth was, 'Of course, I'll take the kids.'

"I said, 'What do you mean, you'll take the kids?' And he said, 'Well, I think I'm better for the children than you. You're younger, and you're all mixed up right now. I'd make a better home for them.'

"His mother told me I should give the children up to him. She asked me why I was getting divorced, and I told her Stanley's drinking was a big part of it. She said, 'Well, you take a drink yourself, don't you?' I said, 'Oh, yes, Stella, I drink, but I don't drink like Stanley does!' She said, 'Well, I've never seen him drunk!' He used to get drunk every time she'd leave. Every time she'd come over and visit, she'd have a list of things that she'd saved all week to discuss with him. As soon as she'd go out, I knew I couldn't talk to him anymore, 'cause he'd get the sauce and start!

"Leslie called me and told me I should give the children up to him. I began to think, well, maybe they're right! I *am* pretty screwy; I'm not gonna be too good an influence on the kids right now, messed up. And I didn't want to impose a neurotic mother on them, like *I* had had.

"I didn't want to live in that house anymore. I hated it. It was all bad memories and unhappiness to me. And I felt it wouldn't be fair for me to pull the kids out of it. They were used to that home. They had the yard, and the maid, and everything. So finally I said, 'I'll tell you what, Stanley. You and I will have mutual custody. And I'll let them stay in the house.' And I got a little apartment about five minutes away, so I could be close to the children."

She filed suit for divorce in August, 1961. "I took no alimony, not even a dollar. And *no* community property. I took nothing but my car and my clothes.

"I had told my lawyer, 'I don't want *anything!* I will make my own money, I know I will!' And he said, 'Well, you're entitled to *something* after six and a half years.' I said, 'What do you think is fair?' And he said, 'Let the judge decide.'

"Then Stanley put a detective on me, trying to prove me an unfit mother, and I got angry. Then he told his lawyer that he would pay me thirty-five thousand dollars and not a penny more. Then I *really* got mad! So we settled on fifty thousand dollars."

The kids stayed in Beverly Hills with the housekeeper while their father toured. To Dana, "It was as though he was on another planet."

In October, 1961, Stan gave a New York *Herald Tribune* reporter an extraordinary interview. "'I'm sick and tired,'" he announced, "'of those sugary jazzmen, those effeminate players with their watered-down sounds. And you know what's causing it? Mothers. More and more they're dominating their sons so that virility is missing in so many young men. How did this ever get started in jazz, anyway?'

"Kenton, who some years ago was about ready to chuck

jazz and become a psychiatrist, said, 'This lack of masculinity among jazzmen has to do with the fear of becoming an individual. When they were kids they hid behind their mothers. Now, instead of creating boldly, they hide behind the music of others and just imitate. But any experienced musician can detect an imitator so fast, and, of course, he has no respect for one.

" 'What the jazz world needs to know more about,' continued Stan, 'is real men like Coleman Hawkins and Sam Donahue.' Donahue's aggressive tenor sax style sparked the new Kenton band that swung so strongly during its recent Basin Street East engagement."

Stan had christened this "new" band, with typical Kenton hyperbole, A New Era in Modern American Music. The library, again a combination of concert and dance arrangements, was largely the work of two gifted and disparate writers: Johnny Richards and Gene Roland. Roland had literally set the tone of this band by selling Stan on the idea of a new instrument: the mellophonium.

In his endless experimentation, Stan had tried to give his brass sound different shadings by expanding the saxophone section, using a soprano saxophone lead. He had tried adding trumpets, finally an entire second section of them, pitched at alto range; but they sounded too much like the trombones. French horns responded too slowly, too sluggishly for a jazz band. Finally, Roland suggested the mellophonium—a bastard instrument that combined elements of the trumpet, trombone and French horn. Stan liked the brilliance of its sound.

Roland organized, rehearsed, wrote for and played in the four-man section. "It was hard, because there aren't any mellophonium players! The section was made up of one French horn guy and the other three of us were all trumpet players. It's a deceptively easy instrument to play. It has a wide range, but it gets away from you. It gets sharp in the high register and flat in the lower register if you don't watch it. We did a lot of woodshedding; we worked very hard to make the section sound good."

The new section triggered a colossal battle of egos in the band. The trombone section resented the mellophoniums' intrusion on *its* sound. The trumpet section (never known for its humility) felt a double threat. Not only did the mellophonium sound detract from the trumpets; they knew that each of the young, eager trumpet players in the new section was only biding his time until an opening appeared in the trumpet section, and they reacted predictably.

BUD BRISBOIS: "To my ear, the mellophoniums were no good at all! They have disastrously bad intonation. Nobody could play them in tune. It's a very loud instrument that's uncontrollable! And *four* of them—that was just too much!"

JOHN WORSTER: "When the mellophonium trip started, those guys got treated like third-class citizens. They didn't even have seats! They had to sit in the aisle, or on their horns—or back by the head, with the clothes. They wanted to play trumpet with the band—that's the only reason they agreed to play those bastard instruments. We would sleep in, and they would rehearse. And after a while, they were playing the hell out of those things!"

Time Magazine's report, in July of 1962, that the band was "riding the crest of a post-rock 'n' roll revival of interest in bands" was greatly exaggerated. Their drawing power never approached that of Elvis or Darin or Dylan—still, their bookings and crowds had improved steadily since the nadir in 1958. In an article to which Stan took exception ("They made the band sound like all it is is a poker game!"), *Time* described the mellophonium as a kind of straightened French horn developed to fill in an unexploited range of sound somewhere between the trumpet and trombone. "Whipped by the rhythm section's artfully lagging beat, the buttery mellophonium sound

THE BEAT GOES ON

satisfies the taste of as many as 5,000 a night. As a result, the Kenton band is this summer's briskest moneymaker."

The Mellophonium band, as it came to be known, was on the road for nine months of 1961, '62 and '63, traveling up to one hundred thousand miles each year. During that time, they managed to record eleven albums.

Among Capitol's executives, Kenton's advocates were as loyal as ever. But as Capitol had grown into one of the giants of the recording industry, Stan's position in the hierarchy of their artists had shifted accordingly. Lee Gillette had begun producing Stan's albums in 1951.

"In the sixties we tried to get Stan into a commercial field on albums. The jazz things and progressive things were not selling too much, whereas things like 'September Song' and 'Laura' *were* selling. So I talked Stan into doing two or three albums of standard material. We used the piano a lot more on ballads, like *The Ballad Style of Stan Kenton,* those things, which were very successful. Then I talked him into a couple of Broadway albums, which were extremely successful. Stan went along with it, but these were not his favorite types of music.

"It involved sitting down with him and saying, 'Look, Stan, we've gotta sell some records! We've gotta get some air play— we're not gettin' any air play!' And he admitted it. He said, 'You think this is the answer, that we'll get air play with these things?' And I said, 'Well, we stand a better chance of gettin' it that way than with some of these far-out things we're making.' So he went along with it, and we did get air play. And it reflected in his business on the road, on one-nighters."

Stan's concessions to practicality included one happy synthesis of artistic *and* commercial quality: *West Side Story,* arranged by Johnny Richards. Richards had assisted in the design of the mellophonium, and wrote brilliantly for that difficult instrument. Pete Rugulo was noted for his themes, Bill

Holman for his swinging, Bob Graettinger for his experimentation; Johnny Richards's music was *substantial*—"steel and concrete," Stan called it. "Johnny was probably the best schooled, musically, of all of us put together."

At fifteen, Richards had been house arranger for a Philadelphia theater. He studied composition and orchestration with some of the finest teachers in the world, including Schoenberg, and at twenty-five, as Victor Young's assistant at Paramount, he was considered by many musicians to be this country's most promising composer.

When Stan first met Richards, "I was seventeen and John was sixteen. He was a very debonair, romantic-European-type guy. He used to click his heels together and bow, all that kinda stuff. Johnny was a tenor saxophone player, and we worked together with bands once in a while. But we never got very close. I never liked Johnny because he was kinda, I thought, phony, with his European approach.

"Years went by, and John, he had his band going before I had mine going. In fact, I recall one night his band was playing at Balboa and I was standing outside, wishing I could be on that bandstand instead of John. I don't know what happened, but he petered out somehow and we got the job.

"By the time the Innovations orchestra started, Johnny had been through the whole gamut of a composer. He'd worked for Paramount, he'd gone to Paris and scored motion pictures. I asked him, 'Why don't you write some music for this thing?' And he got interested, and he did.

"In 1952, I heard that Johnny was in trouble, and I said, 'John, whyn't you come with us?' And so John did. We were extremely close. He was a real genuine human being, but he still had these affectations. But later I learned to live with 'em. That was just John. When he'd conduct our band, he'd walk on a stage and he always had that gracious European thing where he'd lift out his arms. . . . Like when he'd meet somebody, he wouldn't do like an American does, stick out your hand—John would always give you this two-hand thing."

JOEL KAYE, *saxophone*: "In most bands, the first part in a section is the loudest, the second part almost as loud, the third part not quite as loud and the fourth part a little softer. You hear the lead voices, and the rest of the ensemble is softer. But Stan and Johnny always wanted to hear all those parts equally loud. They were always telling the trumpet players to blow their parts out—because they're harder to play loud, and they're not used to it.

"When you play ballads, guys count 1 . . . 2 . . . 3 . . . and they get kinda sloppy on the notes in between. Johnny and Stan were always talking about 'Count double-time! 1 and 2 and 3! Count that in your head all the time!' Subdividing the beat. It works! I remember playing a job in Chicago, and a bunch of musicians I knew came out and listened and said, 'My God, it sounds like the band's counting double-time all the time!' And I said, 'Well, it is! We were told to do that!' Stan says, 'Do it, it's gonna make the ballads sound right!' You play the eighth notes better; that's the technical explanation.

"Some of those things may have originated with John's concept of orchestra music. The size of the ensemble kept getting bigger. John always wanted to use a bass saxophone and a tuba, and finally, when they had the band with the mellophoniums, they had a full-time chair which was baritone and bass saxophone which I played, and a guy that played tuba, he doubled bass trombone. John always wanted the bottom of the band in what he wrote!"

Kenton's *Cuban Fire* album, recorded in 1958, was one of Richards's outstanding works. *Adventures in Time*, recorded in 1963 (and winner of a Grammy award), was another. The "adventure" was into unusual time signatures—5/4, 7/4, 6/8— the kind of music that later became Don Ellis's trademark. But

211

at that time, it had never been attempted by a large orchestra. The music was so different and difficult that it required nine sessions to record, as opposed to the usual three. Stan's attitude was, expense be damned! This is important music! "This band belongs to John," he often remarked, "as much as it belongs to me!"

The same year, he recorded an album with Tex Ritter, thus creating, at one stroke, the most bizarre team in show business and one of the biggest duds Capitol ever released. He did it to illustrate a characteristically Kentonian theory:

"I used to think about how phony people were about their taste in music—how much bigotry there was. I always loved Red Foley. He was supposed to be a country-and-Western singer. But every time I'd hear Red sing, I'd say, God damn it, that's jazz. Because he had such emotion. He was a hell of a singer!

"Red was always with Decca, and I was with Capitol, so we couldn't get together. All of a sudden one day I said, 'My God, I've got the greatest in the world right here at Capitol! Tex Ritter!' Tex and I had been friends for a long time. We used to have dinner together with Gillette, and we had a lot of fun together. So I told Gillette, 'You've gotta get Tex conditioned to making an album with us, 'cause I want to disprove some of this bigotry in music!'

"It took five years to get Tex to do it, but he finally did it. And it's a wonderful album, it really is. If you listen to music sincerely, and forget the fact that Tex is a country-'n-Western guy and I'm a jazz guy. Because the jazz fans can't conceive of any jazz musician ever hangin' around with a cowboy—and vice versa. So the album was made, and it was a big flop. People come up to Tex and say, 'How come you did it?' And Tex'll say, 'Stan made me.' "

By means of his special psychological alchemy, Stan had

once again transformed a defeat into a vindication. Every year, the cocoon of rationalizations he spun round himself had grown thicker, stronger, safer. Until 1963, when reality broke through with a vengeance.

17 Devils

"After that second tour of England, I just went into some kind of seclusion. It was probably the lowest, the most depressing period of my whole life."

THE Mellophonium band that went to England for a sixteen-day tour in November of 1963 was a tired but solidly professional ensemble. While they did not expect to be received like The Beatles, they were hardly prepared to be almost totally ignored.

"Before we went to Great Britain, I kept checking with the International people at Capitol and they'd say, 'Everything's fine, it's all set over there.' And when I got over there, I found out they'd lied to me and deceited me and everything, and business was bad. They hadn't released any of our records in Great Britain for five years!

"Some of the times we were supposed to play two concerts a night, they were canceled out and put into one. It was a terrible thing."

JOEL KAYE: "One of the fanatical Kenton fans from the States, he musta had a lotta money, went over there and traveled around with us. He was a Goldwater conservative, and he was

plastering Goldwater stickers all over England. We were playing a concert in Birmingham, and the curtain came down for
intermission. And Eric, our bus driver, came out on stage with
this Goldwater fanatic, and they told us that the President was
shot.

"I said, 'Come on, you're putting us on!' Then I saw Eric
crying, and I got chills. I said, 'Oh my God, no!' We were
stunned! We went on with the second half of the concert, and
everybody didn't know what to think! We didn't know if a
Civil War was going on over here! For days we weren't sure
if it wasn't some kind of foreign plot, or what. It was really
frightening to be away."

The assassination destroyed any last vestige of esprit de
corps among the troops; for the remainder of the tour, they
grumbled incessantly about the food, the weather, the transportation. When at last it ended, the band was demoralized,
dispirited—and dissolved. Some of the musicians stayed in
England, some vacationed in Europe and others came home
to the States. As for Stan, his old nightmare had finally come to
pass. The signs had said STAN KENTON AND HIS OR-
CHESTRA, and no one had come.

"After I'd been home about a month, Lee Gillette called
and said, 'I'd like to talk to you about making some records.'
And I said, 'No, Lee, no more records for Capitol. I'm finished.
You guys have bullshitted me enough and I don't want any
more of it.' So he hung up, and I just remained in seclusion.
I wouldn't answer the phone. I wouldn't look at my mail. I
wouldn't do anything."

A formidable accumulation of devils had pursued him
across years and continents. In Beverly Hills, they caught up
with him. During the time he had studied with Dr. Held, he
had once written Ann, "I am so enthused about working on
solfeggio that the 'death fears' are diminishing." After England,
they returned in force, along with other long-suppressed fears

215

and uncertainties. The most persistent devils of all were "the guilts." He felt rejected as a husband, inadequate as a father— and he had lost his professional nerve. His band and his music had *defined* him. Without them, his identity blurred.

For nearly a year, he stayed inside the Beverly Hills house with his housekeeper, his children and his demons. Alcohol alleviated the guilts at night, but exacerbated them with remorse the next morning.

DANA LYNN KENTON: "The first incident I can remember in my life was when I was about six years old. My Dad had a drinking problem. And when I was a little kid, I didn't know what it was. I used to think, God, Dad's goin' crazy! He talked weird, and I felt really weird with him. So I was gonna run away from home. I put on my slip, and I was about ready to leave, but I was scared. So I called up my Mom. I said, 'Dad's goin' crazy! He's droppin' dishes now!' That's about the first thing I can remember."

ANN RICHARDS: "My daughter called me, and she was hysterical. She said, 'Daddy's acting funny!' and she wanted me to come over. So I did, and he was just in a stupor, with that glaze, I used to call it The Lizard Look. He was sitting at the table, kinda reading his paper and smoking a cigarette. Lance was so young nothing upset him at that time. So I said, 'Stanley, I'm going to take Dana home with me tonight!'

"So we were driving home. It was a warm summer night. I had my top down. And she said, 'Mother, I think Dad's crazy sometimes.' And she went through a whole thing, 'He drops things, and he fumbles, and he hits his head.' I had always tried to cover for him—'Your Dad's tired,' you know. And I thought it was time I leveled with her.

"I said, 'Honey, how does Daddy act when he has a few martinis?' And she said, 'But he didn't have a drink at all!' And I said, 'Have you ever thought that maybe he drank the drink when you weren't there? That maybe you were in the other room when he had his drink?' I said, 'I think that's probably it, honey—that he just had a few drinks and you didn't see him drink 'em. It's not that he's crazy.' And she was so relieved."

Gradually, steadily, inexorably, the "drinking problem" had progressed from incipient to manageable to chronic.

RED DORRIS: "When the band first started, Stan would go for months until he couldn't go anymore. Then he'd ask somebody, usually me, to get him a jug. He'd get stoned, and the next day he'd be hung over and ready to go back to work."

MILT BERNHART: "When I first joined the band, in the forties, he would have a fifth of Scotch in the bus, after the job, and he'd drink some of it. Later, it got to be all of it."

MEL LEWIS: "He'd drink too fast; he'd get drunk quick, for the trip. It's hard to sleep on the bus unless you can help it along a little bit. He'd get loaded, and next thing you know he'd be up and down the aisles, hugging and kissing and being very emotional with everybody, just letting everybody know how much he appreciated them. He was showing affection, but when he'd grab you—he's a big man—he'd be tearing your head off your shoulders, or bending your glasses. Sometimes we used to say, 'Uh-oh, here he comes,' and you'd put your light out."

Popular mythology to the contrary, not all jazz musicians are dopers or drunks. Some don't drink at all, or even smoke. Still, jazz is traditionally a drinking man's game.

MILT BERNHART: "There was so much time spent in traveling that it made for a very boring life. On rare occasions we'd have a day off in a town, but so what? There are movies. . . . The temptation to drink, just to pass the time away, was strong, so that it wrecked a lot of people, a lot of players who unquestionably, if they'd been in one place, would have spent their time constructively and not fallen into the easy trap of, 'Come on, boy, let's all go get out of our heads' school."

ART PEPPER: "We used to have contests to see who could drink the most. I remember one time we left Hollywood, and we all started drinking. And the last two people that were awake was me and June. We drank everybody else out. That's what I think about when I think about the bus."

ROSS BARBOUR: "I learned to drink Scotch with Stan, in a hotel room at the Croydon. Out of a warm bottle, passed from one to the other. A sacramental kind of thing. Like an Indian peace pipe."

ANITA O'DAY: "The show's over, and nothing's happening! You try to make it continue. The curtain goes down, you go home to a hotel room. There's nothing there! I used to drink to forget . . . and I did!"

MEL LEWIS: "Most of us consider ourselves artists. And we hate to have to play shit all the time. We want to be accepted playing what we want to play. And we can't. So some people are able to accept it and say, 'I'll get in as much time as I can for myself' and do the rest of the job the way it has to be done. But there are other guys who just cannot do that, and they're so bitter over it, and so resentful, that they'll drink themselves out, or become junkies."

It was Stan's long-time rule never, but *never*, to drink before a job. The rule supported his contention that his drinking was under control. But in 1964, there was no job. No music. And no audience.

The curse of charisma is that it requires an audience. On the bandstand, Stan was the conductor not only of his orchestra but of powerful currents of energy; after twenty-five years, that nightly charge had become a necessity. In addition, he had acquired—as does every performer—a considerable Applause Habit. Even offstage, there had always been a handy quorum of sycophants, willing jockstraps for the old ego.

VIOLET FOSTER: "He had a knack for bringing home the God damnedest phonies! He was consistent about it. And he got to believe all those Yes-men. He has such poor taste in people!"

ANN RICHARDS: "Stanley had a lotta cuckoo clocks around. One Christmas morning, the doorbell rings. I've got my bathrobe on. We'd gotten up early with the presents and all that. And this guy is standing there, and he says, 'I'm Don. Is Stan in?' Christmas morning! I'd never seen him before! I said, 'Well, he's kinda busy right now.' He says, 'Can I see him please?' And Stanley says, 'WHO IS IT?'

"I said, 'Don somebody.' He says, 'Oh, come on in, Don!' So now I'm in the kitchen trying to clean up the dishes, and Don says, 'Hi, Stanley! My mother's out in the car, may I go get her?' 'Sure!' They stayed for four hours! On Christmas morning! And they were such bores, both of 'em! But he dug that! He wouldn't say, 'Gee, Don, I'm sorry, but I've got a family.' I resented it terribly.

"Another fanatic Kenton fan, Don Mupo, had a bar up in Oakland, The Golden Nugget. He had all the Kenton pictures up in there, like a shrine. There were all Kenton records on the jukebox, and he used to play the theme song at two o'clock every morning. He knew everything Stanley was doing, and when he was doing it. He'd close up his bar and go and join the band on the road for a week or two. He lives, thinks, dreams and sleeps Stan Kenton. He lost a wife over it!

"So many people were always around *flattering* Stanley, telling him what he wanted to hear. I guess when you love somebody, you really don't like people like that. You can see through them. But Stanley has always gone for that sort of thing. He buys it, hook, line and sinker."

The initial attraction was always the music. But the continuing attraction, the one that kept a constant complement of fans, fawners and flatterers stuck to Stan like barnacles, was the call of the old charisma. Once exposed to the pull of that magnetic field, they would follow him through ballrooms, nightclubs, stage doors, coffee shops, restaurants, elevators, lobbies, hotel rooms; the more intrepid would snuggle up beside him on the piano bench while he played. Encouraged by his unfailing courtesy and his phenomenal memory for names, many scheduled their vacations around the band's itinerary, following it from state to state, like middle-aged pilgrims. Zombie people living zombie lives vied for position, competing for each glance, each smile, each word; in Stan's presence, they felt alive. Total strangers dumped their most personal problems on him. Requests to visit a dying relative were not unusual.

Morning, noon and nighttime, they chanted his name like a mantra. "Drove all the way from Dubuque to hear you tonight, Stan!" "The wife and I used to go down t'hear you at Balboa, Stan!" " 'Peanut Vendor' sounds better than ever, Stan!" "Aren't you going to play 'Eager Beaver' tonight, Stan?" "Stan, I'd like you to meet my wife/son/daughter-in-law/mother/uncle/neighbor." "Stan, would you mind autographing this record/menu/napkin/postcard/matchbook?" "How's about a drink, Stan?" "Stan, the band sounds just great!" "Band sounds great, Stan!" "Great, Stan!" "Stan . . . Stan . . . Stan . . . !"

On the bus, he made rounds. Bill Russo used to say the bus was a hospital, and all its passengers patients. Stan was The Great Physician—All-knowing, All-seeing, All-powerful, a catalyst for feelings ranging from borderline homosexual to no-bones-about-it-filial. As a father to his own children he was, by his own admission, a washout. But on the bus, he played the role to perfection. "I can always tell what kind of relationship a musician has had with his father," he says, "by the way he treats me."

MEL LEWIS: "I could tell him my troubles. *Anything!* He's a bright man—he went to college! [sic] I'm a street man, I never went that far. He studied some medicine and everything; he went to school! He treated everybody like a son."

BUDDY CHILDERS: "I've always wished I could be close to him, and I never will be. As many scuffles as I had with the guy . . . I guess I love him. It all boils down to that. I made him a father image, even though I had no right to do it."

ARCHIE LECOQUE: "My own father died when I was younger, so Stan was more or less my father. He's a guide. I always looked up to him."

BILL HOLMAN: "Guys who were impressionable, whatever the reason, their age or their musical status or whatever, they would stake their lives on Stanley. Some guys, even after they left the band, would work in the office. They'd wake up every morning with, 'What are Stan and I gonna do today?'

"When I first joined the band and he used to look at me with those eyes, I'd think he was really peering into the center of my soul—that I was laying there, bare.

"When he gets spinning these rhetorical webs, if you really listen to what he's saying, if you try to pin him down . . . but not many people do! That's the answer! His presence! He sweats and pants a little bit, and makes it really seem real! He plays on our states; *we're* the ones that read meaning into those big long speeches he gives."

Unlike other bandleaders who travel by plane or chauffeured limousine, Stan has always been on the bus whenever possible, like a solicitous coach before a championship game. The unanimous refrain among Kenton alumnae is, "Stan treats you more like a person, an individual, than any other leader!" —and the younger, less secure musicians have always responded with a degree of loyalty never accorded a Buddy Rich or a Woody Herman. But the more experienced and professional members of the band resented Stan's psychological games and manipulations. They contended that Buddy's and

Woody's bands were musically superior precisely because the men were treated as a group, an ensemble, rather than as individuals. They also objected to Stan's sometimes whimsical (meaning nonmusical) reasons for hiring and firing players.

In the hospital, the intensive-care unit was reserved for the junkies. Stan never knowingly hired a practicing junkie and rarely hesitated to fire one, once discovered. He considered the entire drug scene senseless and idiotic; after all, a booze stop was so much simpler to make than a drug stop! He had done some youthful experimenting with grass, but its effects were too powerful, too unpredictable: "I can handle the juice, but that stuff sent me outa my nut!" If his patience with the hard-drug users was minimal, with the potheads it was zilch.

JUNE CHRISTY: "He got us together at rehearsal one day. When I think back, it was rather childlike. He said, 'All right, any of you guys who have been smoking pot, I want you to raise your hand.' Naturally, no one raised their hand. So he fired about half the band! It was like, 'You, get your horn and get out! You, get your horn . . . !' We were down to just a small nucleus of the band when he got through! But then he rehired most everyone. It was just a stern warning."

He considered the heroin addicts to be sick as well as stupid, and made some abortive attempts to psych them out of their habits.

ART PEPPER: "He gave us talks, but he had no understanding about dope. He just raved at you. He told us that if anyone got busted, it woulda really been bad for the image of the band, and we would be fired without any notice—which woulda really been bad for us as far as the union goes. So we tried to cool it."

The Jazz Man As Junkie syndrome (and the mythology that distorted and glamorized it) reached its height in the late forties.

BILL HOLMAN: "It was fashionable then to be a junkie—

to be stealing to support your habit, pouring forth your mis'ry in your music. Of course, jazz supposedly was born out of mis'ry; there seems to be this idea that a person who's like tortured all day goes home at night to his cabin and pulls out his battered old trumpet and then he *lives* for a few hours, pouring out all his mis'ry that he's suffered all through the day into these few choruses on his battered old horn. That thing just seems to have propagated itself, and people would listen to a Billie Holiday or a Charlie Parker and think they had to suffer that same way to be as great!"

Some musicians have claimed, in defense of drugs, that in an art form that demands instantaneous response, dope slows down time and heightens awareness. On a good night, a jazz player can experience an intensity of emotion comparable to an arrested orgasm. Some drugs prolong that feeling of ecstasy; others cool it down. And in a twisted but perfectly understandable way, addiction has given some players who feel unacceptable in society at large a feeling of belonging to a group—even if the group is a bunch of tormented, self-destructive junkies.

A creative jazz player's awareness is as wide open as a child's. So is his vulnerability. Dope is a tempting defense. The problem has been explored and exploited in a glut of movies, novels, pseudoanalytical papers, theses and texts. None has the simple eloquence of Art Pepper's story of Parky Groat.

"We played Detroit one time and we had lost a trombone player, so some local guys auditioned. Parky Groat was a real small, slender little kid, he was around twenty, and he came in the band. And I'd never heard anybody play as beautiful as him. We had a thing, 'They Didn't Believe Me'—June Christy sang it, and after she sang the first chorus, then the trombone section played a solo, and Parky Groat played lead. And after he played lead for a certain portion of the tune, then the rest of the trombones just went into like a chord background, just sustained chords behind him, and he went into a solo part. Even to this day, I've never heard anything more beautiful than that. He would play, and I would just get chills up and down my spine. And everybody in the band, when he would finish they would look at him and just shake their heads. Every time he did it.

"Then he started using heroin. We were at the Clique Club in Philadelphia, and it's one of those stands that revolves. And when the stand starts to revolve, you have to be sitting on the back, 'cause once it revolves, there's no way to get on it, 'cause it's like above the bar. During an intermission, Parky and I went to score, and we didn't get back in time. I remember running into the place, and we just missed the rotating of the stand. So they had to play a whole set without Parky Groat, who played the trombone jazz solos, and myself, who played all the alto solos. And Stan just flipped out at us, he just really wigged out.

"I had been with the band for a long time, so he gave me a break. Parky Groat was the newest guy, so he fired him. And Parky went back to Detroit. I understand that he got a job in a factory and he got half of his hand cut off. It's just one of those really awful things that happen. I've never heard anything more about him. But I've never heard anybody play more beautiful than Parky Groat."

18 Neophonic

"It was like a lot of my ventures—a little bit of artistic recognition, accompanied by financial chaos. But you can't create music unless you take chances—wild chances! Sometimes you wind up in the toilet, you get slapped down —but you took a chance, at least!"

LEE Gillette finally hit upon an idea unorthodox enough to lure Stan back to the recording studio: Wagner. Wagner themes, all that bombast and fury, arranged by Kenton and Johnny Richards and recorded with studio musicians. At the same time, they recorded an improbable album of Christmas music, arranged by Ralph Carmichael. Neither album seemed destined to break any sales records.

Enter Sid Garis and George Grief, a team of high-powered Hollywood promoters who were also jazz buffs and long-time Kenton fans. Garis and Grief proposed to form a nonprofit corporation that would present an annual series of four concerts in the most dazzling, most prestigious concert hall west of the Rockies: the Pavilion of Los Angeles's brand-new Music Center, said to be an acoustical miracle. The music would be contemporary—*neophonic*, from the Greek "new sounds"—and created by the profusion of jazz-oriented talents languishing in motion picture, television and recording studios. The composers would have absolute freedom. They could write for the Kenton sound if they wished to use that voicing or for any other sound that could be produced by a top-drawer twenty-six-piece symphony orchestra. The conductor, and president of the corporation, would be Stan Kenton.

Stan would have done it for nothing. (Ultimately, he did it for less than that.) It would be a once-in-a-lifetime opportunity to write, commission music and conduct a symphonic orchestra, on his own terms. And it would enable him to live in Beverly Hills with his children. Some hushed-up drunk-driving charges and a frightening collision with a divider on the Hollywood Freeway one night had prompted Ann to threaten to sue for full custody of the kids. Stan felt that if he went on the road again, she might repossess them.

Some of Hollywood's brightest composing talents, long frustrated by the restrictions of the mass media, vied for a chance to stretch their creative limits. Pete Rugulo, Lalo Schifrin, Johnny Richards, Marty Paich, Hugo Montenegro, Morty Stevens, Bill Holman, Bobby Troup, Dee Barton, Ralph Carmichael, Carl Fischer, Shorty Rogers, Nelson Riddle, Dizzy Gillespie, Oliver Nelson and George Shearing were among those who contributed original music to the Neophonic. The sidemen, many of them Kenton alumnae, were so enthused that they passed up studio calls to attend, gratis, extra rehearsals held in each other's homes. To all concerned, the Neophonic seemed too good to be true.

At the premiere concert on January 4, 1965, in the dramatic, plush setting of the Pavilion, all crystal chandeliers and velvet and beautiful people, the orchestra, in tuxedos, could not have looked more impressive. Claude Williamson was pianist, leaving Stan free to conduct; his presence was so commanding, he might have descended from Olympus solely for the performance. The music was the logical step beyond

Innovations—a blending of jazz and the classics that music critics had labeled Third Stream. Because every note was new and experimental, there were some ragged moments. But the second concert, a month later, went more smoothly. The L.A. *Times* said, "Kenton band hits stride," and praised it as a "big, eager, masculine orchestra that for the most part eschews third rate imitations of modern classical music for the best its own jazz idiom has to offer. An inspired group . . . with the precision and assurance of a winning racehorse."

Stan promoted the project with all the vigor of his early road days, appearing before student bodies, civic groups, fraternal organizations, service clubs, urging anyone who would listen to support the orchestra. While everyone commended him for his noble efforts, the Neophonic slid steadily into the red to the tune of fifteen thousand dollars a year.

There had never been any question of anyone profiting from the Neophonic. The most its backers had hoped for was to break even. So during its three-year tenure, Stan explored other potential sources of income.

With a pickup band, he toured in the summers, cut some albums, did some TV guest shots, played some one-nighters and a few longer engagements in local theaters like Melodyland and jazz clubs. Coincidentally, the most solidly established of these were in one case owned, in the other operated, by former Kenton rhythm men. In 1949, Howard Rumsey had persuaded the owner of a foundering bar in Hermosa Beach to institute Sunday afternoon jam sessions, featuring a group Rumsey called The Lighthouse All Stars. The club, and the group, became an institution, where the finest jazz artists in the country alternated sets with the All Stars. The group also served as a sort of decompression chamber for Kenton dropouts, easing the transition from the road to the comparative tranquillity—and sterility—of studio work. Shelly Manne, Shorty

227

Rogers, Maynard Ferguson, Bud Shank, Frank Rosolino, Milt Bernhart, Art Pepper and Bob Cooper all played in the All Stars for varying lengths of time.

In 1960, Shelly opened the Manne Hole in Hollywood, with his own swinging house band and a policy similar to that of the Lighthouse. Whenever possible, Shelly booked his onetime boss, Stan Kenton.

In an even more ironic reversal of roles, Stan found himself working for television producer Jimmy Komack. In 1941, Komack, then a teen-ager in Washington Heights, New York, had been president of the first Stan Kenton Fan Club.

James Komack is a shrewd, successful executive; *Hennessey, Mr. Roberts* and *The Courtship of Eddie's Father* were his productions. But when Komack relates the details of his relationship with Stan, all sophistication drops away. The faraway look, the hushed tones, the total recall are those of a man describing his first love—or automobile. The phenomenon is peculiar to Kenton fans, many of whom are—and this is a source of pride to Stan—"professional people." During these fans' most impressionable years, Stan's music touched their lives in an intimate, ineradicable way; it introduced them to passion. Little wonder then that encounters Stan could only regard as casual were, to fans like Komack, focal points of their adolescence.

"We charged twenty-five cents to join the Stan Kenton Fan Club; the membership cards were blue and yellow. We would mail the members newsletters, and photographs signed by Stan: 'With appreciation for your belief in us.' We used to put KKK on all our letters: Keep Kenton Kicking.

"Stan got to like me. He would take me to coffee breaks, dinner—once when they played a theater in the Bronx, he let me backstage. I watched six shows that day, and a rehearsal.

"Dolly Mitchell was vocalist with the band then. I used to try to meet her at drugstores; she never showed up. One time I waited three hours. It never occurred to me that she would stand me up!"

When the band went west, Stan kept in touch. "He wrote on gray stationery, in brown ink. The postman would fall down. Nobody had believed I went to dinner with him; then they saw the letters! I could prove it! They were groovy letters from a friend to a friend, not from a star to a child.

"After the war, I got into show business. I was working in a funky little club in D.C. I went to see Stan, very proud, to tell him, 'I'm in show business too!' I met him after the show, at a restaurant, for coffee. By now he was divorced from Violet, and that had been such a blow to me. How could she divorce Stan Kenton, my idol? He was with a girl, and it didn't register for him to be on that kind of trip. I told him my big news and he said, 'Oh, great,' and that was it. A period of my life was over with. I knew he was a human being."

Komack went to California and got into television. When he went to Warner's as producer of *Mr. Roberts*, it was his job to assign the music. He wanted "a World War II sound."

"George Grief was a friend, and he was managing Stan. I asked George to suggest someone who could write that kind of music, and he said, 'Why not Stan? He's available.' I couldn't believe it! I suddenly realized, 'I'm gonna hire Stan Kenton!'

"He shows up in my office. He's no longer as I remember him—he seems more cold. But maybe as a child I couldn't see it. He had never scored before, so I had to explain what we needed. I'm singing his arrangements to him! . . . All I really wanted was his inventiveness . . . and a theme song.

"Everyone at Warner's was nervous. They said I was out of my mind. Finally, they made me call him. I said, 'You've gotta play me the theme song! I've gotta hear something!' So he comes down to Warner's, they get him a piano, and he says, 'I can't play piano that well, but I'll give you an idea how it

goes.' It was a very nervous time for him. Everyone recognized
he was nervous. I was so anxious to relieve the tension, after
he played about two notes I was saying, 'Terrific!' Anything
to get through that moment!

"We put his music into the pilot, and junked it. It was
too strong. It wasn't Stan's fault. He wrote beautiful cues, a
beautiful theme. It was just too soon, in 1965, to lay down
Stan Kenton music with a half-hour TV series. It was just
before Lalo Schifrin and Quincy Jones, "Mission Impossible."
In today's TV series, it would be great!

"I had to tell him. He came to my office, and I had to
say, 'Stan, I'm not going to use the music in the show.'

"He seemed relieved. He was a perfect gentleman. And
I recognized, still, that coldness. I had imagined his life should
be all groovy, because he had done so many groovy things.
But in this moment of rejection, I saw hundreds of other re-
jections. But he was first class. First cabin."

Fantasies die hard. For the first time in thirty years, the
thought strikes Komack that "I guess I never really had anything in common with him except our love for the music. I
never drank with him or balled with him or worked with
him. . . . I had to go to school. I was just a kid. But . . . his
music never left me. I still can listen to it all day long."

The final performance of the bankrupt Neophonic was
presented in the spring of 1967. The wonder is not that the
Neophonic went broke but that it survived three seasons
against insurmountable odds. The costs, to begin with, were
prohibitive. Even though the composers and arrangers *donated*
their services and the musicians worked for scale, scale for
twenty-six men (including just enough rehearsal time to play
the music through one time—really insufficient) adds up. Each
concert featured a guest star—George Shearing, Miles Davis,
Dizzie Gillespie, Gerry Mulligan, The Modern Jazz Quartet—
and most of them charged healthy prices, donating nothing.

Clinton Romer's copying bill, not unreasonable, ran up to two thousand dollars for each concert—for music that was performed only once! "But where we really got killed," Romer claims, "was the God damn Music Center itself. The rental on that building is tremendous—something like twenty-five hundred dollars a night. *Plus* rental for dress rehearsal time. Then if the ballet had been in the night before, the shell was struck and you had to pay something like a thousand bucks to erect that set! It was probably cursed from the beginning. But when Stanley wants to do something, he doesn't sit down with a piece of graph paper and a pencil and see whether he can do it or not. He says, 'I'm gonna do it!' And he goes straight ahead!"

The exorbitant costs would have been justified, had there been a sizable audience for the music. All the publicity scrupulously avoided the four-letter word *jazz*, in the hope of attracting some of the Philharmonic faithful. But anyone who recognized the name Kenton automatically associated it with Progressive Jazz, and that eliminated most of the regular symphony concertgoers. The people who did come—an average of 2,200 in the 3,250-seat house—were batted and baffled by two- and three-hour barrages of demanding music, most of it in exotic time signatures, with no repetition to put them at ease with it. Even Stan admits, "It takes practically a person that's addicted on music to be able to absorb that much new music. The audience would just be tired out. But it seemed like we caught ourselves in a trap. We had boasted that the music was fresh, new music—so when once or twice we did resort to some things that were kind of known, like when Jimmy Smith was a guest artist and played 'Slaughter on Tenth Avenue,' the Neophonic people were offended, they would just flip! 'What're you doin' that for? can hear that crap on television, I don't want to hear it at the Music Center!' "

Any chance the Neophonic ever had of weathering its

financial and artistic storms was torpedoed by Stan's intransigence on the matter of subsidy. Despite the fact that not one symphony orchestra in the country is totally self-supporting, Stan was adamant: if the public wouldn't support it, they didn't deserve it. To him, subsidy meant begging, and there was no dissuading him from that conviction—not even for the sinking Neophonic.

There was talk of a New York Neophonic, a Chicago Neophonic, an International Neophonic. None ever came together. A double album, grudgingly recorded by Capitol, is the only tangible legacy of that magnificent venture. But an intangible legacy, elusive as a Muse, remains with everyone who played or heard those concerts. It defies definition, but seems somehow to relate to a surprisingly direct, even profound, statement Stan made in 1966. "Music," he told an L.A. *Times* reporter, "can give people things they can't get from any other source except religious faith."

19 Jo Ann

"I just couldn't be married to somebody and have them come first. And every God damn one of 'em knew that at the outset, before we got married; but after they get married, they change."

In 1965, Stan moved to Palos Verdes, leaving a large chunk of his past in Beverly Hills. "I had tons of awards and trophies in the garage. One night, when I was getting ready to move to Palos Verdes, I fixed myself a Scotch and soda. Then another Scotch and soda. Then I went out to the garage and filled three fifty-gallon barrels with that stuff, and set 'em out in the alley. Then I lived in horror that the rubbish men would return it to me!"

The house in Palos Verdes, an exclusive coastal suburb of Los Angeles, was relatively modest, but comfortable, and only five minutes away from the retirement community that housed Stella. But Stan's true home was the road. And he was homesick.

The drawback, of course, was the kids. Since their infancy, there had been a succession of housekeepers who either stole or drank or neglected them or spoiled them rotten. One spent Stan's money on steak for herself and hamburger for the kids.

233

Another terrified them by threatening to put them in the cellar "where the rats will eat you up!" In Palos Verdes, they had Carmel Blake, a good-hearted, superstitious Irishwoman who was as lenient with them as their father.

Except for a few rare, uncontrolled outbursts, Stan had never been able to discipline Leslie, Dana or Lance. The guilts precluded it. Spiritually abandoned by his own father, he surely sensed, though he never acknowledged, his children's feelings when he left on a tour. He expressed his discomfort by teasing them.

LANCE: "He'd say, 'I'm goin' to the airport and I'm never comin' back,' and we used to believe it, 'cause he wouldn't come back for such a long time."

DANA: "When he left, I used to hate it. I'd go 'Bye,' and I remember just sitting there in front of the door while he'd get in the taxi. It'd be terrible, 'cause he'd be gone *nine months!* It seemed like forever! And we'd be stuck with these house-keepers all the time, and that would be icky. But when he'd come back, we would always have fun. The family would come over, and the guys in the band would come over and get drunk."

LANCE: "Sometimes he took us on the road with him. On the bus, all the guys used to play around with us kids. And at nighttime, when he was at work, we used to have fun 'cause we'd be in the hotel all by ourselves. We used to sneak out and play in the elevators, and climb around on the roofs."

Lance was too young to remember the time before his parents divorced, but Dana frequently cried out in her sleep for her mother. Ann had used some of her settlement to buy a house in the Hollywood Hills, and Dana pleaded to live there with her. For a year-and-a-half, she did. But her mother was a firm disciplinarian, and Dana, accustomed to having a maid all her life, resented the chores Ann assigned her. She also resented her mother's singing, feeling—naturally enough for an eight-year-old—that it stole time and attention that rightfully belonged to her. Eventually, she moved back to the permissiveness of her father's house.

The children's naked need for a resident mother-figure aggravated the guilts, but there seemed no way out. The subject of remarriage was anathema. Stan was vice-president of NAGMA, the ultimate fraternal organization; the initials stood for Never Again Get Married. Bob Flanagan of The Four Freshmen had founded the club in the early sixties, and a sizable portion of the band carried membership cards stating the organization's basic rule: If you met a chick you got hung up on, you looked up another member, who would get drunk with you and talk you out of it. Over the years, the organization turned out to be singularly ineffective. Under the onslaught of Jo Ann Hill, it collapsed completely.

At thirty-seven, Jo Ann was a devout believer in astrology, numerology, ESP and the proposition that if you wanted something badly enough, you could get it. She had been an airline stewardess, a neophyte actress and a singer—and, since the age of twelve, a dedicated Kenton fan. Stan was her idol. She pursued him with the tenacity of Israeli manhunters tracking a Nazi war criminal.

Stan was relaxing in his dressing room at ABC-TV one day after taping a Christmas special when a tall ash blonde with the look of a former homecoming queen walked in and introduced herself. Searching for a topic of mutual interest, she mentioned a tenuous connection with Pete Rugulo and his wife. "I don't see them very much," Stan blurted, panicked. "I live in Palos Verdes and I have two children and when I'm not working, I'm with my children. And I don't have time to date!"

"That's all right," Jo Ann reassured him. "I just wanted to tell you how much I admire your work. I'm a big fan!" She told him she was a production assistant for a psychology show at ABC, and that piqued his interest. But after a few minutes he said nervously, "I've gotta go, gotta get home to the kids," and left.

Jo Ann enlisted the aid of Jimmy Baker, a producer at ABC and a friend of Stan's. Baker enjoyed playing matchmaker, and bugged Stan for weeks: "Why don't you call that girl, take her out?" Finally, Stan relented and took her to dinner; but between his awkwardness and her awe, the evening was painfully strained. Stan has no knack for small talk—his intense manner and narrow interests make it impossible—and each of Jo Ann's attempts at conversation quickly aborted. Finally she tried to draw him out about music. "Don't you think Burt Bacharach's music is great?" she asked brightly.

"Who's Burt Bacharach?"

On their second date, Jo Ann assured him that she shared his political and philosophical views, and that gave them something to talk about. On their third date, he introduced her to Stella.

"First I met the mother, who glared through me, and then I went over to the house to meet the kids and Carmel, the housekeeper, who thought she was going to marry Stan. She just sent darts through me.

"We went to the PTA dance at the grammar school in Palos Verdes. Stan was trying to do his best for the sake of his kids. We sat at the head table—he was like the royal honored guest—and he's trying so hard to be *proper*, and he's so un*com*fortable. He smoked one cigarette after another. The gym teacher is the leader of this corny little high school band, and he's scared to death to play in front of Stan. Stan's telling him, 'Wonderful! Who does your arranging?' He's just *quivering* when we're dancing—he does the box step: One, two! One, two!—and saying, 'My God, when can we get out of here?' He needed a drink!"

After that, she didn't hear from him for twelve days. "I

couldn't figure it out! I hadn't slept with him, so I didn't think I'd lost him that way! I thought, what did I do wrong? I was dying!"

On the twelfth day he called; would she meet him after a rehearsal? Would she! They went to a bar. "I guess you're wondering why you haven't heard from me," he said, obviously distraught.

"No," said Jo coolly. "It doesn't make any difference."

"Well," said Stan miserably, "I have fallen in love with you—and I don't ever want to get married again. I've had two marriages and they both were disasters. I have two children to raise, and I don't know what to do about it. I'm going on the road, and I'll be gone three months."

On the bus heading east, he told Dalton Smith, "I really dig this chick—but if I try to marry her, I want you to kill me." But Dalton was married, a nonmember of NAGMA, and by now the odds against Stan's staying single were astronomical.

The band had barely reached Arizona when Stan got a phone call from Jo Ann: Carmel, she reported, had been calling her, drunk, making wild accusations about Stan, his drinking, what a horrible man he was. Shaken, Stan flew home, fired Carmel, realized belatedly that no immediate replacement was available, apologized to Carmel, rehired her and flew back to Arizona, having resolved nothing.

He wrestled with his misgivings all the way to Kansas City, then called Jo and asked her to fly back. Dalton felt that traveling with the band would be a good test. "When you put a true pearl in vinegar, it doesn't dissolve," was how he put it.

Bearing Stan's imprimatur, Jo Ann thoroughly ingratiated herself with the musicians. She was charming, poised and pretty; she said all the right things and seemed a good sport about the road. By the time they got to Iowa, Stan was undone. Trembling and weeping with trepidation, he proposed.

Engaged, they completed the tour and returned to Los

Angeles in May, 1967, to accustom the children to the idea of a stepmother.

LANCE: "She used to come down every weekend, and go places with him. Then she started comin' down every night, and cooking dinner. And then she started comin' down every day! And going wherever we went, and cleaning the house, and doing things for him. And then they got married."

DANA: "They just came up to us one day and said, 'We're gettin' married. We're gonna elope to Las Vegas tomorrow, only we're gonna bring the kids with us.'

"We went to this little Christian Science chapel. The priest had cowboy boots on, and a black robe. There was nobody in the church except Dad, Jo Ann, Jim Amlotte [trombone player and road manager for the band] and his wife. Jim was best man, and I was maid of honor.

"At the end of the wedding, the photographer took pictures of us. And then Dad and Jo Ann got a taxi and went off, and we went, 'What about us?' And Jim Amlotte and Flo took us back to the hotel.

"That night we all went to all these different hotels—the Flamingo, Caesar's Palace, the Riviera—and saw the shows. We just had fun. It was kinda like a vacation. And we went home the next day. And that was the end of the wedding."

As a new bride, Jo Ann was initiated into the family with a visit to Violet and Jimmy Foster. A week later, Leslie brought *her* three children for a week-long stay in Palos Verdes. Leslie was now living unhappily with her second husband in London. She was fascinated to learn that Jo Ann had undergone LSD therapy and eager to hear the details. Meanwhile, Carmel, the housekeeper, had walked out—after telling Dana, in tears, "I have to leave you because there's a new lady in the house now." While Jo Ann tried to cope with the household, Stan turned his attention elsewhere.

At the age of fifty-five, he was becoming an elder statesman of the jazz world. Since 1959 he had been an important force in the nationwide development of the music clinic movement; the clinics were so successful that he had begun recruiting sidemen from them. In 1968, Villanova University awarded him an honorary doctorate. In cap and gown, he beamed with pride. The same year, he produced two films on jazz. The first, *Bound To Be Heard*, was quasi-academic; it cost him twenty thousand dollars and received limited distribution in schools. The second, *Crusade for Jazz*, was more ambitious and expensive, and intended as an hour-long television special. It gave a superficial, romanticized glimpse of life on the road ("This phantom bus carries musicians, music, equipment and dreams"). At a time when, to all but the most biased observer, road bands had become a vanishing species of wildlife, Stan's narration was more wishful thinking than fact:

> I've never seen such musicians as I have now. They're graduates of conservatories and universities, and they're capable of playing classical music as well as jazz. They believe an explosion is taking place in the world of big band jazz, and they're a part of bringing it about. . . . It used to be guys would goof off and get stoned and there was a great deal of fooling around. But you don't find that in the younger musicians. These guys are really dedicated to music. . . .
>
> There's so much of this activity happening all over the country that all of us feel something is about to happen. A breakthrough somewhere. The bands are getting better and better. Most of the activity is in college bands. They're playing the most involved, exciting stuff you ever heard in your life, and it's knocking the people out! With this band, we'll play concerts where we'll have two or three standing ovations, and the people are really communicating with it. *We're about to witness the most exciting period jazz has ever known.*

Even though it was made in the late sixties, *Crusade for Jazz* seems a product of the fifties—stilted, anachronistic, dated in concept and execution. Perhaps because it fails to convey the excitement the band creates in a live performance, it never found a market.

In the sixties, Stan also ventured into politics. The man whose name was synonymous with Progressive Jazz was in fact a political conservative as far back as the Innovations days, when he suspected all the left-leaning Jewish string players in the orchestra of being Communists. Bill Russo recalls that "Stan was always expecting a revolution. Once when the bus company was on strike, we had a scab driver. Some guys in the band went to talk to him, in the middle of night. There was no trouble, no threats. But Stan was sure it was those Communist string players!"

In 1964, Stan publicly endorsed Goldwater; in '68, he voted for Wallace, whom he considers "profound—a great human being." Stan believes that these men, along with Vice-President Agnew, stand for rugged individualism.

His most active political involvement was with The National Committee for the Recording Arts, an organization that attempted to provide that royalties from radio, TV and jukebox play of records would be shared by the performers who made them. According to archaic copyright laws, only composers and publishers receive such royalties. NCRA was one of a number of attempts by different segments of the recording industry to remedy this inequity. With mass audiences leading inevitably to fewer jobs for musicians, Stan contended that without this minimal form of security, the very future of the music profession was in jeopardy.

NCRA's strategy was to set up meetings and cocktail parties at which performers with long-familiar names—Freddy Martin, Artur Rubinstein, Bing Crosby, Stan Kenton and dozens of others—would personally plead their case before small groups of legislators. Stan traveled thousands of miles for the cause, speaking before the musicians union in New

JO ANN

York, the American Bar Association Conference in Dallas, congressional subcommittees in Washington. But the lack of cooperation among his friends in the recording industry who, as he saw it, stood only to gain from the proposed legislation—some were actively working for the same ends, but through different channels—was disheartening. So was the lack of responsiveness among legislators, many of whom were up for reelection and hardly about to antagonize the broadcasters, dispensers of free air time.

"What makes this all so frustrating," Stan told a reporter in 1969, "is that today in the United States we are going through a period of nationwide protests and demonstrations. . . . In this atmosphere of chaos, the NCRA has had to pursue its goal. But the recording artists aren't threatening to strike. We're not picketing Congress or the White House. I've made no threats. . . . None of us has considered vandalism against jukebox and background music. We're not even asking for better working conditions. We seek our goals with dignity, but time drags by and here we are, still groping and hoping."

He was groping and hoping at home, as well. "The thing with Jo Ann wasn't even a marriage; it was a crime I committed. I knew the night before we got married that it would be a terrible mistake, and I almost called it off. But I didn't. On paper, it looked great. I really thought it would be somethin'. And she thought it'd be great to be married to me. But Jesus Christ, three months after we were married, it was gettin' so bent outa shape, it was awful! The kids were little snots, I snored too loud, I had b.o. . . . It wound up a terrible fiasco!"

What most musicians want in a wife is a mother. Stan had a mother and then some, but he wanted one for his children, and also to complete the image of himself as the family

241

man his father had never been. With Jo Ann, they looked just like the All-American family in the commercials—with just about as much dimension.

Stan tried in the only ways he knew to give his fantasy substance, but all his efforts went awry.

JO ANN: "The gifts he got me were really a disappointment. For Christmas I got a salt and pepper shaker. And a caftan that would have fit a woman the size of a barn. I asked him, 'How big do you think I am?' He said, 'I don't know, the woman said it would fit any size.' I returned it and got something else.

"I told him once I thought the most beautiful gift a man could give his wife would be a song written for her. One day we were hurrying to a recording session and in the car he showed me 'Theme for Jo.' It's a beautiful song . . . but the tempo was so *draggy*. I said, 'Couldn't you have made me a little livelier?' "

Stella had taught her son all about the difference between Nice Girls and The Other Kind. Jo Ann clearly belonged in the former category, and Stan treated her accordingly. Where his manner with Ann had been a casual slap on the rear and "Hasn't my broad got a good-lookin' ass?" or "How d'ya like the tits on her?" in Jo's presence his language was that of a Boy Scout. But Jo Ann wanted more than respect; she had fantasies of her own to sustain. She had fallen in love with the image, but married the man.

Her extravagance was a bone of contention from the start. She freely admits that she thinks about spending money "all the time," yet she argued against having a child on economic grounds—"My God, with the cost of living, look what it costs to feed and house *this* family!" Stan never stinted on household expenses, but he was careful with his money. Clothes and furnishings and decor *mattered* to Jo Ann; Stan bought everything at Sears. She had anticipated meeting the cream of

Hollywood at parties; he, fearful of another drunk-driving charge or accident, either avoided them or left early.

"He didn't like to entertain. He never said, 'Let's have so-and-so over for dinner,' never called his friends, never did anything to nurture a friendship. Finally, *I* decided to have a dinner party. It was gonna be the highlight of changing my life, having people in."

She invited her sister and her husband, a musician, and Pete and Edie Rugulo, and she cooked a gourmet dinner—ignoring the fact that the guests were drinkers, not gourmands. During dinner, her brother-in-law, suffering from too many cocktails, had to leave. "Then Stan and Pete got into a fight about music, TV scoring. Then *Dana* acted up, and Stan went down the hall and we heard whack, crash, he was going to break down her door. She had locked it on him. Pete and Edie looked at me and I'm thinking, oh, God, what else is going to happen? About ten minutes later, Stan walks out in the living room with his pajamas on! It's about eleven thirty! Pete looked at his watch and said, 'Ohmigosh, I guess we've stayed a little late!' I said, 'No, it's not late, sit down and have another drink!' So we played some records and Stan staggered around in his pajamas, really out of it, and finally they left. That was the last time I entertained."

During their courtship, little squabbles were followed by touching little notes of apology from Stan. Later, the squabbles—and the notes—got longer. His drinking caused the most bitter confrontations. Lance, blessed with a sunny, steady disposition, seemed to take it all in stride. He had attached himself to Jo like a lost puppy, and their relationship was the only positive effect of the marriage. But Dana, at eleven, seethed with internal conflicts as destructive as those around her. Her wild mood swings and temper tantrums prompted Jo to suggest that the child might benefit from therapy, but Stan refused, insisting that he could handle her. At Dana's request, he sent her to a private boarding school in Ojai, seventy-five miles northwest of Palos Verdes.

DANA: "Boarding school was one of the funnest times I ever had, 'cause I used to get into a lot of mischief. I was just all-round incorrigible. I would start up big riots and things, we'd go and rob a place, I'd sneak out of the girls dorm at nighttime and go into the guys dorm. A couple of times I ran away. I didn't *do* anything—it was just for fun. But I was also miserable. I was so frustrated and mad and just crazy, I didn't know what to do. The real topper was a joke I played on my dorm mother, because I didn't want to go to bed one night. I slit the back of my hands, and they were all dripping with blood. The principal called up my father and I went home, with bandages on both my hands, to Palos Verdes."

JO ANN: "One night we got a call at dinner. They said they couldn't handle her, and Stan should come pick her up. He just broke down right at the table and cried, it hurt him so bad."

Jo Ann, who had never liked the Palos Verdes house—"a hellhole," she called it—now argued that Dana might be better off in another environment, with new friends. So the family went househunting. Incredibly, Jo Ann was still attempting to fit the man into the image.

DANA: "Dad liked just plain stuff, nice homey houses—he didn't care if they were real rich-looking or showoff houses. He just wanted a nice house with enough room to live in. But Jo would say, 'This house doesn't look as if Stan Kenton is the person who lives in it!' And he'd agree with her."

In October of 1968, they moved into a $140,000 house in Westwood and enrolled Dana in public school. At Ojai, a boy had taught her to smoke grass. In Westwood, she learned about pills.

Stan got a call from the school one day: his daughter wasn't feeling well, could he pick her up? "When I got to the school, I took one look at her and I could see she was stoned out of her nut!" Frightened and racked with guilt, he gave her a stern lecture and started watching her carefully, even driving her to school every morning. Undeterred by his vigilance, she set off the fire alarm at school one day—the loudest cry for help available to her—and ran away. Days later, the police picked her up and took her to Juvenile Hall.

Dana was no junkie, just a disturbed twelve-and-a-half-year-old child who had experimented with pills. But when Stan told the social worker assigned to Dana that he felt "emotionally incapable of being a father," she placed the child at Synanon in nearby Santa Monica. Synanon had originated as a live-in rehabilitation facility for drug addicts and had been expanded to include nonaddicts who chose to adopt Synanon's controversial philosophy and lifestyle.

Ann was relieved; she was sold on Synanon's honest—sometimes brutally so—program, and felt it was the best place for her daughter at the time. So did Stan, who had a new band and a tour lined up. But what to do with his son presented other problems. By now (spring, '69) Jo Ann had announced her intention to file for divorce. Lance begged tearfully to live with his stepmother, but Stan refused to consider it. Ann urged that he put the boy into Synanon, but even though he staunchly defended the place for his daughter, it was not the environment he wanted for his son. But . . . the alternative was another house, another housekeeper, and the likelihood that Lance would eventually follow his sister to Synanon the hard way. Sobbing and protesting every step of the way, Lance went to Synanon.

20 Keeping the Faith

*"When Stan gets within fifty miles of a date, he's like a dog
that sniffs something in the air—the next place he's gonna
play just pulls him like a magnet! He just can't wait to get
to the next place where he's gonna perform! I remember
one time in Long Beach, we're gonna play at the Civic
Auditorium. I go there early and I'm sittin' in this restaurant,
having coffee and waiting, and I see Stan going across the
street. Violet and Carlos were with him. They're walking
toward the auditorium. And the lift that was on his face, and
he was standing taller than ever—it was as if he just
couldn't wait to get to that building! Just drawn like a
magnet."*

HOWARD RUMSEY

NINETEEN seventy-two was the band's third successive
year on the road, playing one-nighters, mostly, from the
Tillamook, Oregon, Elks Lodge to New York's prestigious
Philharmonic Hall. In July, they played a private party in
New Jersey—sprung for by a forty-one-year-old lawyer who
claims to have attended over two hundred Kenton concerts—
and headed west in a new sixty-thousand-dollar air-conditioned
bus with NOWHERE on the manifest.

Some sidemen grumbled that the money would have been
better spent on long-postponed salary increases. More than half
of the band that played Redlands the previous summer had
left or given notice. Saxophonist Kim Frizell, "Ratso," got a
gig on a cruise ship to the Orient. Baron Von Ohlen split to
accompany a religious group on a pilgrimage to India, then
returned to his home town of Indianapolis and formed his own
band. Saxophonist Chuck Carter had family problems. Trumpeter Gary Pack went back to school. Mike Vax lost his fi-

ancée (Miss Burlington) and his position as lead trumpet player and left, nursing his ego. His successor, Jay Saunders, became a father and took a teaching job. Bassist Gary Todd went looking for work in Europe. Two trombone players were fired and a third, Graham Ellis, simply reached his road threshold and quit.

From New Jersey, the bus snaked through Connecticut, Ohio, Michigan, Illinois, Minnesota, Wisconsin, Iowa, Missouri, Kansas, Colorado and finally, in August, reached California, where the band settled in at Disneyland for their first two-week engagement in a year. The mood and situation were strikingly similar to that pre-Tuscaloosa time when, as Buddy Childers had said it, when they weren't workin', they were workin'. They spent five long afternoons in a Hollywood recording studio, cutting an album that mystified musicians and technicians alike; they exchanged looks that clearly said, "What the hell, he's Stan Kenton! He must know what he's doing!"

The album was inspired by a swinging arrangement—Robert Curnow's—of "God Save the Queen." The band had played it in London, where it was so well received that trumpeter Dennis Noday had casually remarked, "We ought to record some more anthems."

"You're God damn right!" Stan replied. "We should record 'em of the whole world!"

He settled for forty, all they could fit into a double album: Bulgaria, Poland, Israel, Portugal, Germany, Italy, Japan, India, Venezuela and thirty-one more, all arranged by Curnow in the Kenton style.

It is impossible to imagine anyone else in the music business seriously considering such a project, let alone bringing it off. Stan was able to only because in 1970, after twenty-five years and forty-eight albums—forty-eighty albums!—with Capitol, he had formed his own label: The Creative World. With Glenn Wallichs's blessing, Stan raided Capitol's archives for masters of his discontinued albums. He has reissued over forty of these, and released five new ones. Distribution is almost exclusively by mail order. The albums are merchandised through a newsletter that goes to over one hundred thousand of the Kenton faithful. Wherever the band plays, Stan solicits new names for the mailing list.

When Stan indicts the recording companies, distributors, rack jobbers and dealers for failing to promote good music—jazz—in favor of quick-buck rock, he forgets that at the time when they promoted *his* music so zealously, it was also in the name of profit and not good music. In that sense, the business hasn't changed. Only the tastes and the times have.

The people who run the business end of The Creative World have one qualification in common for their respective jobs: each of them would gladly die for Stan Kenton. Chuck Anderson, hired in 1971 to drive the bus, now runs the Creative World office and functions as Stan's manager. Dennis Justice, who drove the bus before Anderson, handles the myriad details of booking the band. Phil Herring, hired as a trombonist out of the Redlands Clinic, now works in the office supervising the music publishing end of the business. Former band boys work in the warehouse. Jennie Ladd, Dick Shearer's "lady," travels with the band and sells records wherever they play.

On the first of September, two days before the band was to depart for the Northwest, Stan suddenly collapsed in his office in West Los Angeles. He had suffered an aneurism; had he been more than minutes away from a hospital, he would rapidly have bled to death. Surgeons spent six hours replacing fourteen inches of ruptured artery with plastic tubing. Postoperatively, he developed pneumonia. A tracheotomy was performed. He appeared moribund. He refused to die.

A stunned band proceeded north without him. Only Dick

Shearer knew the gravity of the Old Man's condition; the sidemen were told he had ruptured a blood vessel and expected him to rejoin them in days. The canceled bookings, recalcitrant club owners and disappointed audiences were a nightmarish reprise of the 1971 experience. The band struggled and straggled along until mid-December, then broke for Christmas. When they reopened in San Francisco on the New Year's weekend, Stan was with them.

On February 15, 1973, in the middle of yet another European tour, he celebrated his sixty-first birthday. His body, so long neglected, had rebelled. His weight and his strength had dropped off dramatically during his illness, and for months his incision refused to heal properly. His doctors warned that to drink or smoke again would be suicidal. He quit smoking.

No yardstick can measure, no musicologist can trace the influence of Stan Kenton on the popular music of the mid-twentieth century. The volume of his music is exceeded only by the volume of his music. As for quality, the critics, who have called him everything from the savior of American music to an empty noise, end in canceling each other out.

The dimensions of his contribution are staggering. Beyond the music created, commissioned and presented by Kenton are thousands of musicians, professional and not, who were weaned on his music, through clinics and the widespread use of his library, the first "professional" scores available to students and band directors. And beyond even that, his band has served as a training ground for a generation of musicians dedicated to keeping the flickering flame of jazz alive in an alien environment. For even while the Old Man contends, with his double-jointed logic, that a renaissance of big bands is imminent, New York and Hollywood are glutted with out-of-work sidemen all singing the same refrain: "There's no places to play!" Stan solicits new jazz compositions through his newsletter, and

249

argues as persuasively as ever for the need to develop leaders, fresh blood for the band business. The blood is there, but the arteries, like Stan's, are debilitated.

Every sideman dreams of someday "getting his shit together," having a band of his own. But musicianship, never enough in itself, is now just a fraction of what a self-supporting band requires. The weekly nut for Stan's band is twelve thousand dollars, and big bandleaders today constitute a shrinking roster of geriatric cases, tilting at time with their batons.

The exceptions prove the rule. Mel Lewis keeps the faith with a swinging band he co-leads with Thad Jones; but they play only weekends, and rarely leave Greenwich Village. Howard Rumsey finally has his own club, Concerts by the Sea, in Redondo Beach, near Los Angeles—but Shelly's Manne Hole is no more, and only one other club in Los Angeles, Donte's, has a full-time policy of "pure" jazz attractions. An astonishingly high percentage of the performers featured there and at other (dwindling) jazz clubs across the country share an incalculable debt to the Old Man. Zoot Sims. Bud Shank. Laurindo Almeida. Frank Rosolino. Kai Winding. Lee Konitz. Anita O'Day. Maynard Ferguson. Chris Connor. Dee Barton. Stan Getz. Gerry Mulligan.

Other Kenton grads have a lucrative corner on studio work: Buddy Childers, Jim Amlotte, Conte Candoli, Milt Bernhart, Bill Perkins, Bud Brisbois, Bob Cooper, Shelly Manne, Jack Sheldon, Eddie Safranski, Dalton Smith and scores of others. Stan says they've sold out—and in his terms, they have. For them, the price was right. But with the failure of NCRA and related efforts, even studio work is in short supply these days.

Chico Alvarez is an official of the musicians union in Las Vegas, another haven for Kenton alumnae including Vido Musso, Sammy Noto, Archie LeCoque (many would agree with LeCoque when he says, "That time with Stan was the high point of my career. I started at the top, and I've been working my way down ever since."). In a shack near the Las Vegas Airport, a much-mellowed Jack Ordean practices his alto and reads Christian Science literature. Of the other members of that first Artistry in Rhythm band, only Harry Forbes and Al Costi still play occasionally. Bob Gioga is comfortably retired. Earl Collier is a golf pro; Bill Leahy, a lithographer; Pee Wee George supervises dredging operations in Balboa Bay. Dick Cole quit music and later committed suicide. Red Dorris is the night clerk at a seedy Hollywood hotel. Ever since the Rendezvous Ballroom burned to the ground in 1966, the site has been a parking lot.

Pete Rugulo and Bill Holman are among Hollywood's most sought-after composer-arrangers; both confess to deep doubts about their creative (as opposed to inventive) talents, after having written to order for so many years. Johnny Richards died, despondent, in 1968 (Stan's reaction was, "If he'd been out with the band, he wouldn't have died! It would've given him the will to live!"). Ray Wetzel is dead as a result of an auto crash; Boots Mussuli and Glenn Wallichs, of cancer; Carlos Gastel, of his excesses.

Violet Foster lives with Jimmy in Carmel, California, where she is studying to become, she will tell you, "a great artist." Ann Richards sings—better than ever, some say—where she can: a Vegas lounge, a San Diego health spa-resort, a Beverly Hills nightclub. Jo Ann Kenton, thirty-four thousand dollars richer since her divorce settlement, sells condominiums in Newport Beach. After nearly four years at Synanon, Lance now considers it home; but Dana, although she credits Synanon with having saved her life, now attends a boarding school in Arizona. Leslie, twice-divorced and mother of three, is studying acupuncture in London and has no contact with her father. Stella, at eighty-three, endures; her Stanley convalesced in her apartment. His furniture is in storage. More than ever, the road is his home.

Stan has taken the necessary legal steps to insure that there will never be a Stan Kenton ghost band—a la Tex Beneke and the Glenn Miller Orchestra. When Stan goes, the band goes—although, as a seventeen-year-old alto player attending the Redlands clinic put it, "It's hard to imagine the world without it." Meanwhile . . . The April itinerary is firm:

  1 Century II Convention Hall; Wichita, Kansas
  2 American Legion Hall; Olathee, Kansas
  3 Coffeyville Community Junior College, Roosevelt Junior High School; Coffeyville, Kansas
  5 Southwestern State College; Weatherford, Oklahoma
  8 Grants Cabin; St. Louis, Missouri
  9 Lancer Steak House; Shaumberg, Illinois
10 Wilmar High School, Wilmar, Minnesota
14 Drury College Fieldhouse; Springfield, Missouri
16 Brat Cellar; Sioux City, Iowa
17 Algona High School; Algona, Iowa
18 Prom Ballroom; St. Paul, Minnesota
22 The Flying "V" Ballroom, Utica, Nebraska
23 Odebott High School; Odebott, Iowa
25 Manitoba Centennial Auditorium; Winnipeg, Manitoba
26 Centennial Auditorium; Saskatoon, Saskatchewan
27 Regina Center for the Arts; Regina, Saskatchewan
28 Jubilee Auditorium; Calgary, Alberta

Straight ahead.